God
is in
the
Radio

God is in the Radio

UNBRIDLED ENTHUSIASMS 1980–2020
BARNEY HOSKYNS

OMNIBUS PRESS
London / New York / Paris / Sydney / Copenhagen / Berlin / Madrid / Tokyo

For M. J. Mott, my mother

And what, finally, he felt, understood, and enjoyed, sitting there with folded hands, looking into the black slats of the jalousies whence it all issued, was the triumphant idealism of the music, of art, of the human spirit; the high and irrefragable power they had of shrouding with a veil of beauty the vulgar horror of actual fact.

Thomas Mann, *The Magic Mountain*

Contents

Two: Long Players

Preface
Speech Of The Heart

Author sketched by Mother, circa 1964

If my memories were stacked in a heap on the back of my life's trailer, music was the rope that held them together and kept it, my life, in position.

Karl Ove Knausgaard, *Dancing In The Dark*

Now I'm so much better
And if my words don't come together
Listen to the melody
'Cause my love is in there hiding…

Leon Russell, 'A Song For You'

AGED FOUR or five – or so my mother tells me – I would stand on chairs to "conduct" the music I heard coming out of the family gramophone. Whether this was because I'd seen conductors on the family television, their thin wands darting in the air, or because I felt in some way compelled to choreograph my response to the music I was hearing, I can't say. Clearly my parents' classical albums *did* something to me, moved me to move in time to the sounds I heard – a miniature maestro in pyjamas waving an imaginary baton.

I never knew if the Beatles' *Twist And Shout* and *All My Loving* EPs were bought solely for my benefit, or because my mother and father were still young enough to realise the group were very different to the vapid fluff that pop had hitherto coughed up. What did it mean to listen repeatedly to those records, the monophonic noise that sprung from the tinny record-player: the guitars I pictured the Beatles playing; the cooing exuberant harmonies; the markedly different personae of John Lennon (on 'Twist And Shout') and Paul McCartney (on 'All My Loving') that made it possible to imagine them as people – Lennon as sardonically sexy; McCartney as a sort of choirboy-next-door. Though I never became a Beatles obsessive – I soon developed a more powerful fixation on the more malevolent Rolling Stones – I still feel a relationship to those two EPs purer than any I've had with other records.

My parents bought other pop discs that sat uneasily alongside their classical albums. These were an odd assortment of singles – Donovan's 'Hurdy Gurdy Man', the Monkees' 'I'm A Believer'/'Last Train To Clarksville', Marlene Dietrich's version of Pete Seeger's 'Where Have All The Flowers Gone?' – and albums: *Sgt. Pepper* and *Bridge Over Troubled Water*, plus a budget release on Pye's Marble Arch label entitled *Sweet And Swingin' Simone*. I recall my mother explaining that the *blumen* Dietrich sang about in her smoky, androgynous contralto weren't flowers at all, but young men killed in battle. She never said how she'd discovered Nina Simone, whose peculiarly masculine timbre haunted me when my parents played certain songs on *Sweet And Swingin'* – above all, Nina's versions of Irving Berlin's 'You Can Have Him' and Jessie Mae Robinson's 'The Other Woman', performances that can still reduce me to heaving tears after 50 years. It wasn't that I no longer responded to their classical albums, but even at ten years old I heard them as museum pieces that had little to do with my young unfolding life.

When my South London primary school moved to larger premises nearby, I befriended the flamboyantly funny Tom Fry, who kept assiduous notes on the line-ups of the day's pop groups in red exercise books I was allowed to peruse. He was my playground mentor, the boy who'd rush up at break-time to ask breathlessly if I'd heard the Stones' new 'Jumpin' Jack Flash'. He knew about soul music, too. When I went to his house for tea, he'd pull out the splintered-mirror sleeve of *Motown Chartbusters, Vol. 3*. More of a shock to my system was an act he later saw live, at the tender age of 12: Captain Beefheart & the Magic Band, a picture of whom he extracted one afternoon from his satchel.

Pop came truly alive for me in 1971. At long last I had my own transistor radio, a contraption barely the size of a large Bryant & May matchbox. I still remember the frosty morning on the walk to school when T. Rex's 'Hot Love' came on Radio 1 and, for the first time, I heard the fey tones of Marc Bolan. Soon I was staring at posters of this elfin androgyne and falling into some kind of confusing love that fully exploded when I watched him lip-synch to 'Get It On' on *Top Of The Pops*. Was I any different to the teenage girls who squealed their love for Marc at Wembley's Empire Pool? Only in this regard: that I was obsessed in a geeky male way by the attendant details, the records themselves, the labels and the names on them.

Even now, 50 years later, the singles I bought then seem more magical to me than the albums: the one track on each side, the one spiralling disc delivering the one perfect sonic rush. I still own the first I ever bought: the Stones' 'Brown Sugar', purchased for ten shillings at the baldly named Record Shop in Sudbury, Suffolk. Owning it meant the world to me. I put it on the crappy turntable, and in an instant – as Keith Richards let loose his louche riff (which turned out, years later, to have been Mick Jagger's) – rock'n'roll began. I watched the disc spin, the lolling-tongue logo revolving demonically as the sound rose up to me. It was as if the group was *inside the contraption*, in some notional dark space with their amplifiers and retinue of hangers-on. (My very first gig – appropriately enough, given the first piece in the 'Long Players' section of this book – was a Beach Boys concert at London's Royal Albert Hall in December 1970… but it was a birthday party outing for a family friend, and I was too young to understand how great they were.)

When did I begin to *read* about pop? I'm not sure I can legitimately count the copies of *Sounds* I bought in 1972/3, since I was really only buying them for the double-spread colour posters (of T. Rex, Slade, Roxy Music *et al.*) that were featured in the centre of the paper. The true moment of discovery came with the purchase – in the local WH Smith, on a sudden whim – of the April 1974 issue of *Let It Rock* magazine. This was my portal to a new understanding that pop already had a rich history, and that you could write with insight and gravitas about "girl groups", country music, even heavy metal. From there it wasn't a giant leap to such early rock books as Nik Cohn's *A WopBopaLooBop ALopBamBoom*, Charlie Gillett's *Sound Of The City*, Greil Marcus' *Mystery Train* and Guy Peelleart's revelatory *Rock Dreams*.

By the time I was at public school, sharing a room with my future *NME* and *MOJO* colleague Mat Snow, a bunch of us were reading "the *NME*" and devouring epic pieces by Nick Kent, Mick Farren, Ian MacDonald and

Charles Shaar Murray. On Wednesday afternoons I bought second-hand albums at Soho's Cheapo Cheapo Records; on Sundays I took the Northern Line up to Chalk Farm to watch cult Californians and pedestrian pub rockers play at the Roundhouse. Mat, it must be said, latched on to punk before I did: I'm pretty sure he was talking about the Sex Pistols in 1975, a year in which I shoplifted an import copy of the MC5's protopunk classic *Back In The USA* from a shop on the Charing Cross Road. But I'm sure we listened to the Ramones' debut album together the following spring, when I saw the Stones for the first time during their week-long occupation of Earls Court.

I'd always wanted to be a writer. English was the only thing I'd ever been any good at, and it got me into Oxford in 1977. But I didn't think in any serious way of becoming a rock critic until – inspired by Gillett, Marcus and others who'd written books – I embarked, aged 20, on a book of my own, a half-baked study of "Pop" as aesthetic and sensibility. Researching this ill-thought-out treatise took me to New York in September 1979, mainly to buy used rock books at the famous Strand Books store on Lower Broadway. (Years later my professional life came full circle when I gave a reading there and clocked Richard Goldstein, whose *Greatest Hits* anthology I'd bought on that 1979 visit.) At the end of the week I made a cold call to Davitt Sigerson, who'd also been at Oxford and was writing smart pieces about soul, funk and disco for *Black Music* and *Melody Maker*. He was droll and gracious, sending me back to London with an introduction to *Maker* editor Richard Williams, whose book about Phil Spector had seeded an early fascination with that diminutive megalomaniac. Richard was good enough to pass me over to the charming Ian Birch, for whom I wrote my first-ever piece: an omnibus review of two Gladys Knight & the Pips compilations.

I could say I never looked back from this validation. In truth, it's been 40 years of stress, anguish and only periodic exhilaration – so much so that I wonder if I might not have made an easier life for myself. But every time I've tried to break away and do something more grown-up or lucrative, music has dragged me back to articulate what it does to me: to make "sense" of it. Whether or not Walter Pater was right to state that "all art constantly aspires to the condition of music", he certainly spoke for me. Music has been a constant companion since I stood on those chairs at five and "conducted" Bach and Beethoven. It is almost always playing in my head, sometimes to the point of torment. (I'm struck by the words of Norwegian writer Jon Fosse in Erling Kagge's *Silence In The Age of Noise*: "Whoever does not stand in wonder at [the majesty of silence] fears it. And that is most likely why [...] there is music everywhere, *everywhere*".) More than even this, I suspect, music is a proxy for emotion itself: it is *the way I feel,* dissolving the rationalisation of feeling and enabling me to experience joy, desire, pain, loss, sadness, defiance and gratitude that might otherwise remain out of reach. Indeed, it almost seems to me the *point* of music that it frees us from the constrictions of thought and plunges us into Van Morrison's "inarticulate speech of the heart". In the greatest music there is always something transcendent and, dare I say it, divine. Hence my title, filched with thanks from Josh Homme. (*Seinfeld* obsessives will note the origin of my *sub*title, from Season 6's 'The Doodle'.)

God Is In The Radio pulls together 50 pieces about the music I've loved the most – the singers and players whose records have shaped me for over 50 years. The only ones missing are those I've written about in other books: Prince, Love, Big Star, Tom Waits, Todd Rundgren, The Band, Joni Mitchell, Led Zeppelin. I'm grateful to the editors who either assigned the subjects or gave in to repeated entreaties to let me take a crack at them. The pieces are essentially those I wrote for *NME, The Times, The Observer, The Independent, The Guardian, Tracks, MOJO, Uncut, eMusic, The Word,* and *Rock's Backpages* – as well as for projects by Doug Aitken and Charles Moriarty – but with what I trust are improving tweaks and corrections.

My thanks are due to commissioning editors Tony Stewart, Richard Williams, Mat Snow, Caspar Llewellyn-Smith, Paul Lester, Michael Azerrad, Anthony DeCurtis and Michael Bonner. Thanks also to my agent Matthew Hamilton and to Omnibus' David Barraclough for making this happen; to Imogen Gordon Clark for seeing it through to completion; and to Lucy Beevor for her very diligent copy-editing. Additional thanks go to Richard Wootton, Jane Rose, Mick Houghton, Shane O'Neill, Ted Cummings, Pete Cook and Martin Smith; to the Rock's Backpages team (Mark Pringle, Martin Colyer, Tony Keys, Paul Kelly, Jasper Murison-Bowie); to my beloved and deeply musical wife Natalie; to my amazing sons Jake, Fred and Nat (and my amazing stepsons George and Fred); and to my dear sister Tam, my brother Ben, my niece Alice and my nephews Wilf and Chan ... all of whom have shared momentous musical experiences with me over the years.

London, March 2021

One
Short Cuts

1 What's New
Frank Sinatra

Album bought in London in 1984

VOGUE SAYS OF Frank Sinatra that "the Voice is leading cool moderns back to emotion". Glancing about me at the well-heeled sentimentalists and legend-seekers at his London Arena show, it was hard to spot any moderns at all. We could as easily have been about to witness a heavyweight boxing contest as a performance by the greatest pop singer of the 20th century. So why do we come to see him? Because there's some twisted pleasure in hearing the burnt-out shell of vocal genius? Because, for odd moments, we hear the ghost of his greatness? Or just because he's Sinatra?

Fortunately, the experience is not entirely grotesque. If the hipster movements are stiff, there's enough rhythm and resonance in his singing to keep us hanging on his sometimes uncertain words. The swing classics are easier for him than the ballads, but one applauds the bravery of 'My Heart Stood Still', a Rodgers & Hart song he introduces with the concern of a music historian. He makes little attempt to disguise his scorn for the trite pop of songs such as 'Strangers In The Night', telling the audience, "I didn't like this song when I first heard it, and now I positively hate it." For the most part he romps through the obvious numbers, kicking off with 'Come Fly With Me' and following up with the inevitable irony of 'You Make Me Feel So Young'. 'The Lady Is A Tramp', 'For Once In My Life' and a semi-spoken 'Come Rain Or Come Shine' follow in quick succession. On 'Foggy London Town' and 'Mack The Knife', he hits his stride, though the best singing of the night comes with the patriarchal braggadocio of the Rodgers-Hammerstein 'My Boy Bill'.

From the scrawny, callow Sinatra of the Forties to the paunchy elder statesman of Vegas glitz is a long way to come in one career. One wishes, of course, that he'd simply metamorphose back into the voice of his Capitol years and give us immaculate renditions of 'What's New?' or 'One For My Baby'. The saloon-song ritual that precedes 'Angel Eyes', complete with cigarette and barstool, has become worn and tired, and the head voice falters painfully. If the Sinatra of the Forties was a violin, and the Sinatra of the Fifties was a viola, the voice of 1990 is a battered cello.

In the final analysis, is he a cynical fat-cat or a tormented artist in a tuxedo, raging at what he can no longer do? And when he does "face that final curtain", as he's threatened to do for a mighty long time, will this music die too?

The Times, 1990

4

2 In Between The Heartaches
Burt Bacharach

Box set sent by Rhino Records in 1998

PAINTED FROM MEMORY, Elvis Costello's collaboration with Burt Bacharach, isn't just timely: it's indicative of a generally enhanced perception of Bacharach's standing. Like all the man's true fans, Costello's had enough of him being patronised as the Godfather Of The Bachelor-Pad Set. True, there are loungecore moments on *The Look Of Love*, a three-CD box intermittently sprinkled with yuk like Bobby Vinton's 'Blue On Blue' and Paul Anka's 'Me Japanese Boy I Love You'. But anyone who can't hear past the cocktail-piano kitsch to what Costello accurately calls Bacharach's "sense of darkness" and "romantic doubt" surely has cloth ears.

For here's the point: as missing links between Rodgers & Hart and Lennon & McCartney, Bacharach and his principal lyricist Hal David transcended the conventions of Teen Pan Alley so effortlessly that their cool neoclassical peaks – 'Make It Easy On Yourself', 'Don't Make Me Over', 'Anyone Who Had A Heart' and so many more – tower over even the best songs of Doc Pomus and Mort Shuman, Gerry Goffin and Carole King, and Barry Mann and Cynthia Weil. Only Jerry Leiber and Mike Stoller, whose work lay almost entirely outside the pop-ballad realm anyway, fully deserve to stand alongside them.

A child prodigy inspired by Ravel, Bacharach did things with chords and time signatures that nobody else working in pop has even attempted. Think of the sudden key change in the middle of 'Do You Know The Way To San Jose?' – *"In a week, maybe two, they'll make you a star"* – and ask yourself which other pop/rock tunesmith (unless it's a Burt fiend like Jimmy Webb or Thom Bell or Arthur Lee) would even contemplate doing it. Here's another amazing thing: a 34-year-old veteran of the cabaret circuit – working at the time as a conductor-accompanist to Marlene Dietrich – suddenly, in the early Sixties, begins writing complex ballads for the voices of Jerry Butler, Chuck Jackson and Lou Johnson, polished Black baritones who could handle the long legato phrases Burt heard in his head, and hence rise to the challenge of his always unpredictable melodic twists. Is there any more perfect pop-soul record than the unsung Johnson's original 1964 version of '(There's) Always Something There To Remind Me', a recording whose considerable thunder was undeservedly stolen by the shoeless Sandie Shaw?

After the uptown soul men came the incredible diva. Just as Bacharachian balladry offered a counterpart to Spector-esque pomp, so Dionne Warwick's cerebral soprano defused the deep-soul sobbing of so many Sixties sirens. Not for her the hysterical melisma of much gospel, even if she was steeped in the stuff. She knew Bacharach's music lay in some uncharted land that separated Carole King from Stephen Sondheim, which is why so many Burt/Dionne jewels ('Alfie', 'Here I Am') sound more like songs from musicals than hits you'd have expected to hear on mid-Sixties AM radio. Among the welcome semi-obscurities that make *The Look Of Love* essential listening are several forgotten Warwick masterpieces: the majestic 'In Between The Heartaches', the retake of the Drifters' 'In The Land Of Make Believe', a little miracle from 1972 called 'The Balance Of Nature'. Aside from Warwick, the box gives us Dusty's breathy 'Look Of Love', Cilla's histrionic but irresistible 'Alfie', and the Carpenters' velveteen '(They Long To Be) Close To You'. Even when the voices are blanched and the melodies a touch trite – Jackie DeShannon's 'What The World Needs Now', B. J. Thomas' 'Raindrops Keep Falling On My Head' – we're talking perfection. Stretching that argument to the limit are Bacharach's own recordings, rendered in what he himself described as an "earnest, rumpled baritone". Best of these by far is the 1971 album track 'Hasbrook Heights', a jauntily ironic hymn to American suburbia.

It is customary to write off Bacharach's work of the late Seventies and Eighties. The Patti LaBelle/Michael McDonald hit 'On My Own' is routinely dismissed as glutinous LA soul when it is actually a peerless duet that more than redeems the slush of 'Arthur's Theme' and 'That's What Friends Are For'. As for present-day Burt, one can only hear the closing 'God Give Me Strength' as one of the most wrenching things either he or Costello has ever done. Time to say a little prayer of thanks – make that a *massive* prayer – that the man was ever born.

MOJO, 1997

3 Cry To Me
Bert Berns

CD sent by Universal Records in 2002

HE WAS, wrote Jerry Wexler, "a paunchy, nervous cat with a shock of unruly black hair". He looked like a vaguely disreputable cross between Gene Vincent and Denholm Elliott. He liked the company of gangsters, boasting that he'd run guns and dope in the Havana of the 1950s. But Bert Russell Berns was also a master of symphonic soul, of the uptown New York sound that combined cascading orchestration with drenching gospel vocals. He made the kind of records Bacharach and David might have made had they ventured down to Stax, or Pomus and Shuman down to Muscle Shoals: stupendous singles like Betty Harris' 'Cry To Me', Solomon Burke's 'Goodbye, Baby (Baby Goodbye)', Ben E. King's 'It's All Over' and Freddie Scott's 'Are You Lonely For Me'. In partnership with Jerry Ragovoy, he wrote and produced orgasmic soul ballads by Garnet Mimms and Erma Franklin, whose scorching 'Piece Of My Heart' has been covered by everyone from Big Brother & the Holding Company (1967) to Shaggy (1997). "He was a great writer, a great man," said Burke. "'Cry To Me' [1961]… was really soul music. It wasn't like pop at that time, it wasn't country, it wasn't like R&B. The only way it could be classified was soul music. That's when it all started." High praise from a man who, according to Jerry Wexler, actively disliked the cocky, street-smart Berns.

Berns had learned his smarts in the Bronx, where he was born to Russian immigrant shopkeepers on November 8, 1929. He studied classical piano as a child, and possibly even attended the famous Juilliard music school. Employment during the Fifties came in a variety of forms: work as a salesman, as a music copyist, and finally as a session pianist. Smitten with salsa, he headed south to Cuba and soaked up the *quajira* rhythms of Havana – rhythms that would come to serve him well in the early Sixties. (Wexler remarked that Berns made a virtual cottage industry out of the chord changes to 'Guantanamera'.) Returning to New York at the end of the Fifties, he took a job as a song-plugger with Robert Mellin Music, down the road from the Brill Building on Broadway. Under the pseudonyms "Bert Russell" and "Russell Byrd", he wrote songs – and even recorded them – for labels like Laurie and Wand. With Phil Medley he wrote 'Twist And Shout', a song massacred by Wexler and Phil Spector when they produced a sorry version for Atlantic vocal group the Top Notes, then revived by Berns himself when he produced the 1962 version by the Isley Brothers (covered in turn by the Beatles). Other early hits included the Jarmels' 'Little Bit Of Soap' and the Exciters' 'Tell Him'.

Work for Atlantic began in late 1960. "He just came off the street one day and started demonstrating songs to me," Wexler recalled. "He had so many ideas and licks that I said, 'We're gonna produce some records together'." Taking over the Drifters from the departing Leiber & Stoller, Berns produced 'At The Club', 'Saturday Night At The Movies' and the group's last great single, 'Under The Boardwalk' (1964), with its sombre Berns-Wexler-composed B-side 'I Don't Want To Go On Without You'. For Burke, he produced 'Cry To Me', 'The Price' and 'If You Need Me', and co-wrote 'Down In The Valley' and 'Everybody Needs Somebody To Love' (a song Burke described as "our gospel march"). Wexler even put new signing Wilson Pickett together with Berns for one single, the gloriously misjudged 'Come Home, Baby'. "Bert had Pickett crooning, something like Ben E. King, and it was a flop," Wexler said. In 1963, fate brought him together with Philly-based writer-producer Ragovoy, and he wound up splitting the royalties on the sublime lamentation that was Garnet Mimms & the Enchanters' 'Cry Baby' – backing vocals courtesy of Cissy Houston and the Warwick sisters. "Bert was a meat-and-potatoes four-chord basic kinda guy with a street feel that other people would have killed for," Ragovoy told Al Kooper. "I think his talent far exceeded mine, but he couldn't really hear past four chords, and comparatively I was sophisticated. So I would come up with a fifth chord, and he'd give me that look and say, 'What is that, *bebop?*'" After more Mimms beauties – 'It Was Easier To Hurt Her', 'I'll Take Good Care Of You' – Ragovoy took uptown soul to an almost delirious extreme with Lorraine Ellison's volcanic 'Stay With Me' (1966).

Booming drums, mournful horns, gospel keyboards, wailing female vocals: these were some of the ingredients Berns utilised to produce such sobbingly cathartic sides as 'Cry Baby', 'Cry To Me' and Ben E. King's 1964 masterpiece 'It's All Over'. There's a lot of raw despair in these records, but it's a despair held in check by the craft of the arrangements. "I never met anyone who understood pop so well," Nik Cohn wrote in *A WopBopaLooBop ALopBamBoom*. "He was an identikit American record man, canny and tough and flash, always money-conscious… he wasn't a beautiful person, but he was intelligent, articulate and he made some good lines."

Take another little piece of his heart.

MOJO, 1998

4 Didn't I Blow Your Mind This Time
Thom Bell

Review copy sent by Phonogram Records in 1979

THE STYLISTICS were a permanent fixture on the British pop charts of the early Seventies. Every tenth record coming out of my radio seemed to be another creamy hit by the Philadelphia vocal group. But when you're 12 years old, and half in love with Marc Bolan, the last thing you want to hear is a seraphic falsetto backed by oboes and bassoons – not to mention 12 violins, four violas and two cellos. No less ubiquitous on Britain's weekly *Top Of The Pops* in their silk-spun Afros and ruffled tuxedos, the group embodied everything that was icky and comically formal about the imported soul music of the day. To teens waiting for Noddy Holder to appear and bawl 'Mama Weer All Crazee Now', the Stylistics seemed as cheesy as the umpteenth road edition of the Drifters entertaining the scampi-and-chips set at Batley's Variety Club.

So how is it that this former glam-rock urchin – that would be me – came to adore the great hits the Stylistics chalked up in that long-unsung decade?

11

Why do I now agree with Prince – who covered it – that 'Betcha By Golly Wow' is the loveliest love song ever written? Why does 'You Make Me Feel Brand New', with its gloriously corny sitar, make me well up with love for my *inamorata*? How come I even retain a sweet-tooth soft spot for the tacky 'Sixteen Bars', and for 'I Can't Give You Anything But My Love', a song that sat atop the UK singles chart for what felt like the entire summer of 1975? At least part of the reason must be coming to realise – as any true fan of Black American pop must – that the Stylistics' producer/arranger/ co-writer, Thom Bell, was *the* great genius of the sub-genre known as "symphonic soul"; that the songs he wrote with white Jewish lyricist Linda Creed represent the melodic peak of the fabled Philadelphia Sound. For the records he made with the group – and with the Delfonics, the Spinners, Deniece Williams and others – were as close as soul music came to the subtlety, complexity and sheer beauty of Bach or Mozart. From the fanfare intro to the Delfonics' 'Ready Or Not (Here I Come)', via the stunning charts he wrote for the O'Jays' 'Back Stabbers', to the intricate harpsichord phrases that grace Ronnie Dyson's 'Give In To Love', Bell's ever-daring arrangements make clear the classical training he received after moving to America from his native Jamaica as a child. (For the record, he also wrote orchestral charts for Jerry Butler's 'Only The Strong Survive', Billy Paul's 'Me And Mrs. Jones', and Harold Melvin and the Blue Notes' 'If You Don't Know Me By Now'.)

When Bell met the Stylistics in 1972, he'd already been working as a pianist, arranger and producer in Philly for over a decade. After a stint at Cameo-Parkway, home to Italian-American pretty boys of no discernible talent, he worked for Chubby Checker and then for Stan Watson's Philly Groove label, where he struck Delfonics gold with 'La La Means I Love You' and the majestic 'Didn't I (Blow Your Mind This Time)'. Influenced by such "beat concerto" masterpieces as Little Anthony & the Imperials' 'Goin' Out Of My Head', Bell matched the vision and sophistication of Burt Bacharach, Jerry Ragovoy, Teddy Randazzo and Charlie Calello. Meanwhile the Stylistics had been going since 1968, with a line-up comprising Herbie Murrell, Airrion Love, James Smith, James Dunn, and lead singer Russell Thompkins, Jr., possessor of a voice as unrepentantly girly, as unmacho as the Black male voice has ever been – the missing link, one might almost say, between Little Anthony, Al Green and Prince. Bell took this voice and all but exaggerated its fey quality. Where the group's first hit 'You're A Big Girl Now' sounded Black – closer to the Chicago vocal group sound, or to Philly-soul pioneers the Intruders – 'Betcha' and 'Brand New' left the ghetto behind. They were, dare one say it, slightly white. And when Bell and Creed wrote the hilariously naff 'Rock And Roll Baby', it was tantamount to admitting as much. "There have been quite a few where people have said, 'Huh? R&B? What are you getting at?'" Creed recalled in 1975. "'You Make Me Feel Brand New' is different from what people think of in the context of an R&B tune. I don't think that we write R&B, but that's beside the point."

Like 'Betcha By Golly Wow', the Stylistics' other smashes ('You Make Me Feel Brand New', 'I'm Stone In Love with You', 'You Are Everything') were sugar-sweet – buppie bubblegum, you might say. They were also more artless than either Bell's work with the Delfonics or his dazzling arrangements for such Philadelphia International stars as the O'Jays. But they were effortlessly lovely, platforms for angelic harmonies. Over a bed of Rhodes piano, Bell sprinkled harps and woodwinds, then gave everything a wash of sweet strings. 'People Make The World Go Round', meanwhile, was the Temptations' 'Papa Was A Rolling Stone' filtered through Bacharach and David, its chorus like a classic mid-Sixties hit by Dionne Warwick. (Bell made his debt to Burt and Hal overt when he had the Stylistics cover Dionne's 'You'll Never Get To Heaven'.) Where Bell went on to make further classics with the Spinners ('I'll Be Around', the euphoric 'Rubberband Man'), with Warwick herself ('Then Came You', her gorgeous duet with said Spinners), and with Deniece Williams (1982's 'Waiting By The Hotline'), the Stylistics themselves fell into the hands of schlockmeisters Hugo & Luigi – sometime producers of Sam Cooke – and proto-disco overlord Van McCoy. They chalked up huge hits in Britain, but thereafter languished in their native country. Worse, they fell out with each other, Thompkins becoming the sworn enemy of the fellow members he saw as his musical inferiors.

Some will accuse me of playing the Guilty Pleasures card here, but – like Prince – I'm wholly sincere in my love of the sweet-soul classics the Stylistics made with Bell. In the age of 50 Cent and Chamillionaire, they offer a tenderness and a vulnerability – a beauty – that the world will always sorely need.

eMusic, 2007

5 Natural Woman
Aretha Franklin

Album bought in London in 1975

"SUMMERTIME, AND the living is easy…" So ring out the words of Aretha Franklin's backing singers as they warm up the crowd for the entrance of soul's most royal highness. It is indeed summer and therefore hard to move in the USA for music festivals, many purporting to be gatherings of "blues" singers and most of *those* sponsored by Camel or Budweiser. The Rockport Rhythm and Blues Festival, staged on the hallowed ground of Fort Adams State Park in Newport, Rhode Island, at least has the distinction of being sponsored by a manufacturer of footwear.

We're all living in a House of Blues culture now. "Blues" – a lazy umbrella term that now seems to include R&B and Sixties soul – has become a touchstone of rootsy authenticity in America, bringing middle-aged white people out into the broiling sun for events like these. Soul monarch she may be, but for these sunburned folks in their Buddy Guy T-shirts, Franklin is still the haughty mama who told her man to 'Think' in *The Blues Brothers*

– the righteous matriarch of church congregation and soul-food parlour. Franklin herself bears no relation to that matriarch: dolled up in an insane wedding cake of a dress with a pair of enormous wings that envelop her like candyfloss, she plays the diva to end all divas. "The undefeated, undisputed champion of the world", is how blues-fest impresario Quint Davis introduces her, tactfully omitting the word "heavyweight". The surprise is how much fun Franklin proceeds to have in the hazy Newport sun, and the gusto and skill she brings to her singing. Dispensing with the candyfloss wings, she opens with a Sly Stone medley that yokes 'I Want To Take You Higher' to 'Dance To The Music', complete with Was (Not Was)-style "boom-chakka-chakkas" from backing singers the Ridgeway Sisters. Standard show biz stuff, but done with conviction. The real gems, though, come with the ballads Franklin essays a little further into the set.

Her tendency for some years has been to over-sing – to give us three or four notes where one would do. But listening to '(You Make Me Feel Like A) Natural Woman' and a particularly fine 'Angel' made me think that perhaps the melismatic overkill of the Whitney Houstons and Mariah Careys has convinced even Aretha of the virtues of simplicity. Not that the swooping command of the voice has in any way diminished: all the power is still there. It's just that when she tackles 'Angel' – and even new ballads like Jermaine Stewart's 'Here We Go Again' and Puffy Combs' 'I'll Never Leave You Again' – her technique is altogether less showy than it was. She also looks happier onstage. Where her regality was once undermined by her vulnerability, and her cuddliness by a distinct coldness, she now seems like a queen reborn. When she gets happy during the extended gospel closer 'Testimony', she trots herself across the stage like a frisky teenager. The woman I watch backstage signing autographs and chatting amiably with fans is unrecognisable from the housebound recluse of the Eighties.

"Is my hair still standing?" she asks at one point during her set, worried the heat has flattened it. The hair isn't standing, but it doesn't matter. What matters is that the Queen of Soul, the most awesomely gifted female singer in the history of R&B, is doing more than going through the motions. She's giving it all she's got.

The Observer, 1997

6 Dangerous Liaison
Eddie Hinton

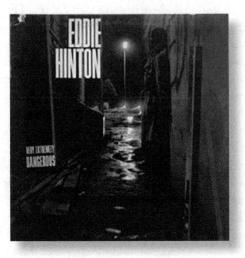

Album bought in Nashville in 1985

IN THE WORDS of Jerry Wexler, Eddie Hinton was always "the guy who would be next year's big thing". Says Wex, "he would sit out on the back porch of Muscle Shoals with Bob Dylan, and we all knew he was about to make the record that would blow everybody away." That was 15 years ago, and it took Hinton another seven to deliver a single incredible album of scorched southern soul called *Very Extremely Dangerous*, by which time he was a disturbed, drunken wreck of his former boyish self who needed all Wexler's powers of patronage to be allowed near a studio at all.

If you've never heard *Very Extremely Dangerous*, you're missing out. For Hinton's is simply the Blackest white voice ever committed to vinyl, the result of hours of tortured screaming and obsessive imitation of Black singers such as Otis Redding, Bobby Womack and Wilson Pickett. Redding in particular haunts the album – a version of 'Shout Bamalama' uncannily apes Otis' early Little Richard style – while Womack's laid-back cosmic preaching seeps into

16

the beautiful 'Get Off In It'. (Womack had just recorded Hinton's song 'A Little Bit Salty' in the same Muscle Shoals studio.)

Hinton's story is one of inexplicable self-destruction and fall from grace; the tale of a gentle southern boy mutating into a kind of R&B-obsessed werewolf. "He got in on the LSD trips and it messed him up," says Dan Penn, himself one of the original blue-eyed soul men. "Something snapped up there, and he sort of got an obsession with sounding like Otis. He was a clean-cut kid when I first met him, but now when he drinks he gets to hollering and staring, and you don't want him in the house." Today, Hinton is to be found in the city of Decatur, in northern Alabama, an hour's drive due east along the Tennessee River from Muscle Shoals. Eighteen months ago, drunk and destitute, he was spotted outside a Salvation Army Hostel by old friend Johnny Wyker and installed, *gratis*, in a tiny one-room apartment in the town. All he had on his person was a sheaf of country songs he'd been trying to peddle round Nashville. One, intended for Poco, became the title track of the *Letters From Mississippi* tape that Wyker produced in 1985 – a grungy, Alex Chilton-ish collection of garage-soul anthems with dotty love lyrics and hoarse, bleeding-throat vocals.

To get to Hinton, we proceed via Wyker, who skilfully arranges an interview time when his friend is too broke to start another drinking spree. Sober, the man is sweet, if mildly disturbing. You sense the impending madness alcohol would unleash, but his memory is clear and his diction almost quaintly naive. "I was born in Jacksonville, Florida," he says, "but I moved to Forth Worth, Texas, and finally to Tuscaloosa, Alabama, at the age of five. I remember I was curious from an early age about how the Negroes lived, and I remember hearing rhythm 'n' blues guys on the radio. John Lee Hooker became my biggest idol." As a Tuscaloosa teenager, Hinton played in party bands the Spooks and the Minutes, bawling Bo Diddley and Jimmy Reed songs at University of Alabama fraternity parties and playing side gigs with Wyker, whose Rubber Band scored a regional hit in 1965 with the oft-covered 'Let Love Come Between Us'. It was at a Minutes date in Nashville that Hinton ran into Marlin Greene, co-producer of Muscle Shoals hits by Percy Sledge. "Marlin liked what I was writing and said he could get me some work if I moved to Muscle Shoals. I'd been on the road for a year and I was tired, so I moved there in February 1967 and started playing on sessions. The first one I played was Ted Taylor's 'Feed the Flame'."

Having notched up one hit with Greene (Sledge's 'Cover Me'), Hinton began collaborating with Shoals writer Donnie Fritts. Together they wrote Sledge's mournful 'You're All Around Me' and Dusty Springfield's seductive

17

'Breakfast In Bed', journeying up to Memphis to sit in on Dan Penn's Box Tops sessions. Back in the Shoals, he met his idol when Otis Redding came to produce Arthur Conley's *Shake, Rattle & Roll* album. He also played on sessions by Joe Tex. "Tex was the first guy I learned from in terms of trying to imitate the American Negro idiom," he says, simulating a vintage Tex cackle to make his point. "Then I was a gopher at the first Aretha Franklin session at Fame. That's where I met Dan Penn and Jerry Wexler. I spent a long time with Dan, learning how to write and playing on his productions in Memphis. I also played lead guitar on Elvis Presley's 'Merry Christmas, Baby' when James Burton couldn't make the session."

Penn and his wife Linda remember Hinton as a kind of kid brother. Linda recalls fondly how he'd watch television at the foot of her bed while she slept. For them, the change happened in 1969, after he returned from a week in London, where he'd overdubbed strings with the LSO for an ambitious *Sgt. Pepper*-ish concept album by singer Jim Coleman. "I spent about two years on that project. Phil Walden [Otis' original manager and founder of Capricorn Records] got me a deal with Warner Bros., but they thought it was too shaky and dropped it." While he continued doing session work at Muscle Shoals Sound – playing on records by everyone from Lulu to the Staple Singers – Hinton's behaviour became increasingly manic and unpredictable. Moving to Nashville in 1971, he was used by producers John Richbourg, Buddy Killen and Norbert Putnam, but got drunk on one session too many and fell out of favour. "In about 1972, I started working on Negro gospel records. I had in my mind that I should go back to an earlier root if I was going to make any money using R&B idioms. I believed a Caucasian singing Negro music could make a lot of money. But the main reason I chose it was because I liked it."

Sadly, no one was willing to put up with Hinton's behaviour for long enough to record him in his own right. In 1975, "borrowing money and trying to perfect my craft as a songwriter", he settled in Fairview, Tennessee, recording demos that eventually found their way to Phil Walden in Macon, Georgia. The Allman Brothers' manager hired him to work in the Capricorn studio – Jerry Wexler says he was literally just cleaning the place out – and then, in July 1977, succumbed to Wexler's plea that Hinton be given a shot at a solo album. "Well, I was a happy man then, 'cause I could just stay home and drink beer rather than have to go down to the studio. We recorded the album in November, in Muscle Shoals, most of the tracks done live besides a few horn and tambourine parts. 'Shout Bamalama' was the first song I'd done a good demo on, with Dan in Memphis. I started out singing like Otis to try to get to sing like Sam Cooke, but I just kind of dropped the Cooke thing. I like Shirley Caesar, Joe Tex and Wilson Pickett. That's the main sound I try to stay with." As bad luck would have it, Capricorn Records went down the tubes just as *Very Extremely Dangerous* was picking up sales. (It did about 20,000 without Hinton even going on the road to promote it.) Relocating to the Shoals and then to Birmingham, a few hours south, he formed a touring combo called the Rocking Horses with his wife Sandra. They gigged around Georgia, the Carolinas and Virginia before he disbanded the group and moved in with his mother back in Birmingham. To make his beer money, he stacked tins in a dog food plant.

So how does Hinton now spend his days? Mainly sitting around drinking beer and Pure Grain Alcohol in his apartment; occasionally cutting grass in a friend's mother's yard. He says he's writing a novel, "a kind of space odyssey patterned after Mark Twain and Hermann Hesse… I've got about 27,000 words and I need 10 or 15,000 more". It's doubtful Johnny Wyker will be able to do much with his friend's washed-up career, especially in a town as remote from the business as Decatur. The folks in Muscle Shoals have lost patience with him, so there's little hope of his receiving quality production again. Meanwhile, *Very Extremely Dangerous* grows in reputation as a cult album. Last year, Dave Marsh found Nils Lofgren and cronies yelping along to it backstage after a Bruce Springsteen show. They were as dumbfounded as I was to learn that Hinton was white.

Soul Survivor, 1987

7 Simply Beautiful
Al Green

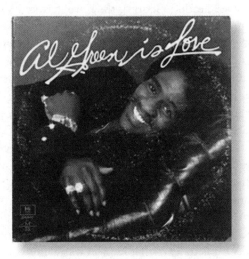

Album bought in London in 1981

"GENN'LMEN, WE JUST havin' church here..." Six words which – directed at myself and a fellow southern soul buff at Memphis' Full Gospel Tabernacle Church by its chuckling, irrepressible pastor – still cause me to blanch after 15 years. In truth, the sight of two pale Englishmen sat stiffly at the back of his church was probably no great novelty for the Reverend Al Green. Our 1985 visit to the white A-frame structure in the city's Whitehaven district – shouting distance from Elvis Presley Boulevard – was an obligatory stop on any musical tour of Memphis. For these particular tourists, moreover, there was a supplementary pilgrimage to the Royal Recording Studio, the "windowless cave" where Willie Mitchell cut the tracks that made Green a Black pop superstar. "We spent a lot of time softening Al's style," Willie told us. "Originally he wanted to sound like Sam & Dave, but I told him we had to tone him down and get his range up. I knew he could cross over. When we were big with 'Let's Stay Together', I was up in Detroit and I heard

the Bee Gees' 'How Can You Mend A Broken Heart?' on the radio. So I brought the song back to Al in Memphis. He laughed in my face and said, 'That shit is *country*, man!' I said he didn't understand what we were going to do with it.'"

We went to worship in Memphis because we too had succumbed to the spell of those records, lost ourselves in both the breathlessly sexy curlicues of Green's singing and the earthy, boxed-in crunch of Mitchell's sound. For me, 'I Didn't Know' on 1975's *Al Green Is Love* was the most ecstatic eight minutes of slow deep soul ever recorded. And it wasn't even deep soul *per se*. It was – like all the records the two men made together with those virtuosi of understatement, the Hodges brothers – a supernal blend of downhome and uptown, lo-fi southern grit and whipped-cream Philly topping. It was a key sound of the early Seventies, as intrinsic to my adolescence as T. Rex or Roxy Music. Like Sam Cooke and Marvin Gaye, Green "crossed over": almost everyone I know has, at the very least, a copy of his *Greatest Hits*, many more than own a *Best Of* Otis Redding. Where Redding was fundamentally one-dimensional, Green was a changeling, a shapeshifter who – within a single performance of a song like 'Simply Beautiful' or 'I'm So Lonesome I Could Cry' – could flip from comedy to tragedy, godliness to lubricity, male to female, and back. He was a one-off, which is why one has looked forward to his "story" for so long.

Like Cooke's and Gaye's stories, Green's autobiography – *Take Me To The River* – is a narrative of internal conflict, of sin and salvation, guns and God: *"strong as death, sweet as love"*, as he sang it on a little-known masterpiece from 1974. In this instance, it wasn't the singer holding the gun but a deluded New Jersey housewife who shot herself dead after hurling a pan of boiling grits over his back: *"The Rev. Green, in the bathroom, with the grits…"* Turns out that this shocking night in October 1974 wasn't quite the watershed moment in his CV we've been led to believe. *Take Me To The River* takes pains to stress that he was already on his way back to his redeemer when the unhappy Mary Woodson entered his life. Yet it encapsulates the way he's spent much of his life torn between his love of God and his love of women. "There's no use trying to deny the obvious," he notes. "There's something about me that women find very attractive."

Predictably, a lot of *Take Me To The River* is delivered in this bland, pseudo-conversational style, one beloved of as-told-to ghosts. It's strange how everyone – from sanctified soulsters to heavy-metal mutants – ends up with the same "voice" on these printed pages. So many tomes read like treatments for Lifetime biopics, with their pat anecdotes and cosily reductive homilies. I'd rather have heard the slightly nutty voice – part Little Richard, part Prince – of the real Reverend. Then we might have had a book to stand alongside Chuck Berry's *My Autobiography* or even Charles Mingus' *Beneath The Underdog*. Too often one can feel writer Davin Seay filling in missing details in Green's "voice". Too rare are any real moments of revelation, or just plain old insight. Even the accounts of how the famous Hi sound came about are undermined by self-contradiction: one moment Green claims that "softening" his vocal style was his idea, the next he gives Willie Mitchell the credit.

As Craig Werner notes of Green in *A Change Is Gonna Come*, the Last Soul Man's return to the ministry "brought the deep soul tradition full circle", taking the music out of the pop marketplace. Today we make do with the ersatz emoting of Macy Gray and Shelby Lynne, music that references Green but seldom wrestles with the agonies of choosing between church and roadhouse. We will never hear his like again.

Rock's Backpages, 2000

8 Who's Gonna Fill His Shoes
George Jones

Single bought in London in 1982

IN THE DAYS before hats and hi-tech rednecks, country music was a soap opera – and George Jones and Tammy Wynette were its Dirty Den and Angie Watts. Twenty years on from their messy divorce, they've joined forces for a last trawl through their brazenly autobiographical hits. More Nancy Reagan than Hillary Clinton, Wynette is frail but dignified after a long illness, reaching for high notes with a slight grimace. But trooper that she is, she can still belt 'em out like a cowgirl howling at the moon. "I may not be the best," she says, "but I *am* the loudest!" She sings the hell out of 'Stand By Your Man' – "written in 20 minutes, and we been defendin' it ever since" – and dredges every drop of heartbreak from tearjerkers like 'Till I Can Make It On My Own'.

Many of us have waited twenty-odd years to hear Wynette's ex-husband sing live. Did Sinatra really say George Jones was "America's second greatest singer"? If he didn't, there's still time. Initially the feeling is one of

23

mild disappointment. The weird hair architecture is in place, but there's a diffidence in his singing. Just our luck that when ol' No-Show finally shows, he's only gone and picked up a throat infection. He hits his stride on James Taylor's 'Bartender Blues', laying our fears to rest. With Jim Buchanan's fiddle weaving through every vocal phrase, the Possum lets loose his inimitable swoops and slides, dropping to a sudden deep baritone and then just as suddenly soaring into his airiest tenor range. The artistry is utterly instinctive, the precision almost uncanny. That he scarcely seems aware of the beauty of his singing only makes it the more spellbinding: he is a singer like Hendrix was a guitar player. Nowhere is his brilliance more evident than in the medley of ballads that begins with 'I'll Share My World With You', takes in 'Window Up Above' and 'The Grand Tour', and winds up with 'Walk Through This World With Me'. Nothing is over-sung; every note seems to dance within the swirl of his bizarre vocal lines. It's transfixing. And when he gets to 'He Stopped Loving Her Today', a deathly hush spreads through the auditorium. This is better than anything we'd hoped for.

If anything mars the performance, it's only Jones' peevishness at the way contemporary Nashville puts its old-timers out to grass. Along with the periodic references to "kids" and "whippersnappers", there's a mournful rendering of 'Who's Gonna Fill Their Shoes', with its nods to departed heroes, and a double-barrelled blast through '(I Don't Need No) Rockin' Chair'. The duets portion of the evening is a letdown after Jones' solo set; all the mock-bickering in the world can't change the fact that these famous voices aren't blending tonight, not even on 'Golden Ring' or 'We're Gonna Hold On'. Jones himself is clearly unhappy, clutching at his throat and complaining about the monitors. "Should we apologise or what?" he asks his ex. They conclude with 'Someone I Used To Know', then quit while they're still (just) ahead. At least one fan spills out into the damp night knowing he's witnessed something transcendental. A little Tammy goes a long way, but you could listen to George Jones for all eternity.

MOJO, 1995

9 Gone Solo
Sandy Denny

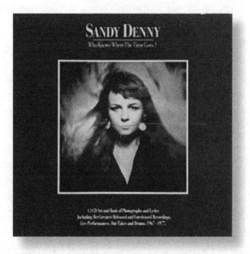

Box set sent by Rykodisc Records in 1985

WHAT, HYPOTHETICALLY, would have happened had Sandy Denny tried out for I*TV's Voice UK*? Would Rita Ora and Ricky Wilson and will.i.am and Sir Tom Jones have turned at the sound of her artless and piercing mezzo-soprano? Or would they have deemed it too natural, not showy or melismatic enough? And if any of them *had* turned, would they have been disappointed by the dumpy, unglamorous gal in the floral smock and bell-bottom jeans who stood there in the glare? Perhaps the questions are unfair; perhaps the swivelling foursome *would* have responded to Denny's voice, as so many have since she started out in the folk dens of southwest London. (Jones, one assumes, would have been aware of her anyway.) They might have thought, "Thank God for singing that's human and real, that doesn't treat music as a gymnastic exercise".

A woman who transcended folk-club purities to become one of the great singer-songwriters of the Seventies, Alexandra "Sandy" Denny was as vulnerable as she was commanding. Fairport Convention fiddler Dave Swarbrick nicknamed her "Boedicia", but producer Glyn Johns – who oversaw the Fairports' 1975 album *Rising For The Moon* – thought her "a rather sad character and quite disturbing". Her stock was low at the time of her death in 1978. Punk and post-punk had laid waste to ladies in smocks who sat at pianos and sang of sea captains and sweet rosemary. Revered by her folk peers, and by a subsequent generation of American troubadours, she hadn't made the mark she should have with the sequence of great solo albums that began with 1971's *The North Star Grassman And The Ravens*. Those collections included some of the best songs and performances of the era – 'Late November', 'Next Time Around', 'It'll Take A Long Time', 'Listen Listen', 'No End', the exquisitely soppy 'Like An Old Fashioned Waltz' – but they weren't Carole King, and they certainly weren't Lynsey de Paul. For the most part they were broodingly poetic, grandly sweeping ballads, sometimes smothered in strings though generally interspersed with contrasting moods: Denny could sing jazz or country as well as she could sing traditional folk. "When I sit down at the piano, the words come in their thousands," she said in 1972. "Doomy, metaphorical phrases, minor keys, weird chords… and I can't do a thing about it."

Like John Martyn, her labelmate on Island Records, she was an often-infuriating mix of mystical artistry and boozy bonhomie: one of the lads, as many interviewees make clear in Mick Houghton's respectful and affectionate biography *I've Always Kept A Unicorn*. The pubs of Wimbledon, where she grew up, have always boasted their share of dissolute middle-class bohemians like her, but few of them can break your heart with a single verse of 'Bruton Town'. Out of suburban drabness and art-school rebellion came the fully formed power of her voice – an instrument that, as Pete Townshend noted, was almost free of vibrato. "When other singers try to sing like Sandy," folk doyenne Shirley Collins tells Houghton, "they throw their voices at top lines, rather than just singing them." Wise words from one who knows.

She was a kind of siren-next-door. "She sang about serfs and noblemen with the naturalism of a woman describing everyday life," Greil Marcus wrote in *Rolling Stone*. "And she sang about everyday life as if from a perspective of a woman a thousand years gone." On early recordings of songs such as ex-boyfriend Jackson C. Frank's 'You Never Wanted Me', Denny is as assured and charismatic as, in reality, she was shy and self-doubting. Recruited by the pioneering Fairports, she found a perfect creative foil in the brilliant Richard Thompson, using the group to master public-domain songs like

'Matty Groves' and to hone her own songs, among them the effortlessly melancholic 'Who Know Where The Time Goes'. Rarely a careerist, she was always restless. After the traumatic shock of drummer Martin Lamble's tragic death after the band's tour bus veered off a motorway, she lurched from the Fairports to Fotheringay – whose 'Banks Of The Nile' is hailed by Houghton as her defining performance – and back to the Fairports, whose 'One More Chance' is another peak of her oeuvre. As the years rolled on, her core unhappiness manifested in dysfunctional attachment – to adulterous Australian husband (and former Fairport member) Trevor Lucas, mainly – and eventually in chronic alcoholism and cocaine abuse. While never wreaking the public havoc that Joplin or Winehouse did, she was a mess nonetheless. The unravelling of her life in the cut-off Northamptonshire village of Byfield was something we already knew from Clinton Heylin's earlier biography *No More Sad Refrains*, but not something known or honestly acknowledged by those involved in her career when she was alive. Reading Houghton's account of how Lucas abducted their baby daughter Georgia surely supports his contention that he was trying to save the baby's life. The next time Denny drove drunk into a ditch with Georgia in the back could have killed them both.

I've Always Kept A Unicorn – a line from Denny's archetypal piano ballad 'Solo' – is rich in insight from those who loved and despaired of her. While never over-embroidering the story, Houghton patiently builds it through the intelligent and sensitive recall of everyone from Richard Thompson to *The Guardian*'s Richard Williams. He also draws on interviews that Denny gave to publications such as *Melody Maker*, which twice crowned her Best Female Vocalist Of The Year. (Never a rock chick *per se*, her rousing duet with Robert Plant on Zeppelin's 'The Battle Of Evermore' lent her a status that served her well – though she was never paid a penny for the session and never asked for one.)

What would have happened had she not died? Would she have weathered the slick, synthetic Eighties and emerged on the other side of them, as more fortunate veterans did? It's horribly poignant to read in one of this book's footnotes that her friend Judy Collins – one of many who recorded the beloved 'Who Knows Where The Times Goes' – quit drinking the day before Denny's death, and has been sober ever since. It's difficult, though, to picture a happy ending to the life of someone who could so recklessly endanger the life of her own child. Putting it as kindly as one can, Denny simply never grew up. *"I'm a dreamer"*, she sang in 1977 in her last great song. *"I'm a schemer with an eye for a show..."* And therein lies the enigma of so much great art. Sandy Denny's best songs are so powerful and so healing – such cathartic outpourings of sorrow and joy – that one can't help but attribute a kind of wisdom to them. They enable us to bear the pain that Denny, apparently, could not.

The Guardian, 2015

10 Changing Trains
David Bowie

Album bought in London in 1975

IN THE DAYS of vinyl album sleeves, rock music was always a synesthetic experience, and David Bowie's *Station To Station* is nothing if not white: a white-out of cleansing and purging, if also of cocaine euphoria. *Station To Station* is also a bit red (the lettering) and a tad orange (the tangerine RCA label). White seemed right for Bowie in 1975/76, at least until the Thin White Duke talked ill-advisedly of fascism and Hitler, and you wondered if it was the White of Aryan supremacy he meant to convey. Which, of course, it wasn't: half the Duke's group was Black.

Bowie's entire career has been a journey from station to station, and his tenth album remains one of the most impressive of his musical junctions: intense, passionate, focused, surging and urgently funky – stripped-back, too, just as its iconography is stripped-back and monochromatic after the hypertrophied dystopianism of *Diamond Dogs* and the funky-but-chic hustle of *Young Americans*. It is also a miracle, given the physical/chemical state of the Skeletal White Duke in the Los Angeles of 1975. (Was there ever a less Californian rock god?) "I heard it and I thought it was brilliant, absolutely mind-blowing," recalled former Deep Purple bassist Glenn Hughes, at whose LA pad Bowie crashed in May and June of that year. "I was amazed how he could come up with that, having been in complete psychosis." Compounding the ill-health and paranoia was Bowie's megalomaniac conviction that rock was dead, that his future lay instead in directing films. "Me and rock'n'roll have parted company," he announced rather grandiosely to interviewer Tina Brown, two months before starting work on *Station To Station*.

Excessive cocaine use is seldom beneficial, but it was especially deleterious for the boy from Bromley, a charming if rather affected fellow until stardom and coke turned him into a paranoid, cadaverous maniac whose fleshless hand Aretha Franklin refused to shake at the Grammy awards. Joni Mitchell once observed that cocaine "seals off the heart", and there are few more heartless albums than *Young Americans*, which may be hip and slick but is also – as its maker admitted – a pointedly "plastic" record. By contrast, *Station To Station* is *not* plastic, and there are good reasons for that. The first is producer Harry Maslin, who knew a thing or two about crafting a massive rock sound in the studio. The second is guitarist Frank Madeloni, whose cartoonish moniker "Earl Slick" was as perfect as the blazing, blaring Gibson licks he played over the core funk unit of Carlos Alomar (rhythm guitar), Dennis Davis (drums) and George Murray (bass). "I got some quite extraordinary things out of Earl," Bowie told Kurt Loder in 1990. "I think it captured his imagination to make *noises* on guitar, and textures, rather than playing the right notes." More important than either of these, though, was Bowie's own desire to move away from the darkness of decadence and towards the light of – dare one say it – intimacy: "*Stay, that's what I meant to say or do something/ But what I never say is/'Stay this time'/I really meant to so bad this time…*"

So often I've heard *Station To Station* spoken of in terms of decadence – of *spiritual enervation* – but it never sounded like that to me. (Maybe I'm just perverse: I don't find Bowie's subsequent album, *Low*, very downbeat.) It's true there are darkness and occultism on *Station*, but all its urges are towards hope and healing; they really *aren't* "the side-effects of the cocaine". 'Word On A Wing', for instance, is *literally* a prayer for redemption, a beseeching to be rid of black magick and Kenneth Anger pentagrams and the horrorfest of cocaine hallucinations: "*Lord, I kneel and offer you my word on a wing/And I'm trying hard to fit among your scheme of things*". *Station To Station* is Bowie seeking a return to his better nature, desperate to flee the malnourished fakeness of Hollywood Babble-On. Hence the explicitly religious allusions to the Kabbala and the Stations of the Cross, the metaphors of journeying and changing. *"Got to keep searching and searching/Oh, what will I be believing and who will connect me with love?"*

The album opens with the phased and irresistibly exciting sound of a train engine. For Bowie, there seemed to be a correlation between rail travel and ch-ch-ch-changing as new stations loomed in the distance. How perfect that his return to London from mainland Europe in early May 1976 was aboard the *über*-romantic Orient Express – and how unfortunate that he had to mar the homecoming with a wave he claimed was misconstrued as a *Heil Hitler* salute. A confused and often silly chap Bowie was, but what a musician! By that, I don't mean a great guitar player or even a particularly great singer; I mean a man with a profoundly instinctive talent for organising rhythms and melodies. The exhaustive and exhausting work he put into *Station To Station* at Hollywood's Cherokee Studios, shortly after playing the made-for-Bowie role of Thomas Jerome Newton in *The Man Who Fell To Earth*, belied his apparently fragile state. For this is magnificently muscular music, at least on the towering rock-funk disco of its most powerful tracks. It's true that lead single 'Golden Years' could just about have lived on *Young Americans*, while 'Word On A Wing' and the cover of the Johnny Mathis/Nina Simone standard 'Wild Is The Wind' – two tracks which alliteratively mirror each other as hymnal slow-burners – are as fey and crystalline as they're ardent and heartfelt. But 'TVC15', 'Stay', and the album's epic title track are among the most supercharged items in the whole corpus of Seventies rock. They're Bowie, out on his own, streaking away from sagging balladeers and bloated prog-rock virtuosity.

In interviews, Bowie talked of his musicians as hired guns who owed him no allegiance, but both Davis and Murray would play with him for another five years, and Alomar was making cameo appearances with him as late as the 2003 album *Reality*. Augmented on *Station To Station* by Slick and by the barrelhouse-*moderne* piano of Roy Bittan, the Alomar/Murray/Davis unit made for a fearsome engine-room. "Was there ever a funkier white man?" a colleague asked recently when 'Stay' fired up on Spotify. Arguably, but few have funked this convincingly without Black musicians behind them. Bittan's addition to the *Station* band was interesting in the light of Bowie's unlikely penchant for the pianist's boss, Bruce Springsteen. Moreover, you wonder whether the white-heavy sleeve of the latter's breakthrough 1975 album *Born To Run* might not have influenced all that white space on the cover of *Station To Station*. Or indeed the sound of *Station* itself, which –

though deficient in Springsteen's post-Van-Morrison rock'n'soul swagger – is similarly urgent and romantic.

What, indeed, *is* the sound of *Station To Station*? Is it something like Springsteen + Mott the Hoople + ABBA keyboard flourishes + sub-Sinatra "crooning" + Gibson Les Paul guitar? Is it, as Bowie intimated in contemporary interviews, an amalgam of American dynamics and the cool suaveness of the "European canon" he cites on the title track: Sigma Sound meets *Lou Reed Live* meets Kraftwerk? Or is it, in the words of *Creem*'s glam-o-phobic reviewer Lester Bangs, "an honest attempt by a talented artist to take elements of rock, soul music, and his own idiosyncratic and occasionally pompous showtune/camp predilections and rework this seemingly contradictory *mélange* of styles into something new and powerful that doesn't have to cop futuristic attitudes or licks from Anthony Newley and the Velvet Underground because he's found his own voice at last"? That is certainly how *I* heard the album as a 16-year-old who'd never been totally sold on Ziggy Stardust or Aladdin Sane. It was the first Bowie LP I truly fell in love with.

Whatever *Station To Station* is, it's a singularity in the Bowie discography, a bridge between the apocalyptic pseudo-rock of *Diamond Dogs* (or the glistening disco of *Young Americans*) and the more mechanised Europa of *Low*'s first side. (There's a faint premonition of the elegiac electronica on its *second* side in the dying strains of 'Word On a Wing'.) It's an album he remains proud of, and one he implicitly harks back to on *Heathen* (2002) and *The Next Day* (2013), his two best records of the past 30 years. Though he's described it as "extremely dark", he's also talked of *Station To Station* in terms that suggest it was a rebirth. "I do feel like I'm starting over again in a way," he told Robert Hilburn of the *Los Angeles Times*. "I think there's a certain maturity now." To Lisa Robinson in *NME*, he made it plain the album was partly about thawing out and becoming vulnerable. "It's nice to know," he said, referring to himself in the third person, "that behind the callous, cold, iceman-cometh Bowie, he's really pretty uncertain about what he's doing. I think that's poignant and very tender." To *Phonograph Record*'s Ben Edmonds, he added: "I think the previous albums were of a colder emotion, and this is one of a warmer emotion. It's got some kind of Godhead recognition, a feeling of empathy about it…"

One might almost say that by the time he'd finished his starkly expressionist "Isolar" tours of 1976 – the Thin White Duke as Sinatra-meets-stonefaced-Buster-Keaton – the Duke in question had fattened up and become human again. Once he was in Berlin with his new best pal Iggy

Pop, the tainted Bowie of LA was as dead as a vampire with a stake through its heart. For Ian MacDonald, *Station To Station* was no more nor less than "an exorcism of self, of the mind, of the past". And for Cameron Crowe, who'd witnessed Bowie hallucinating bodies falling from the sky, the album was the "diary of a life saved, set to a soundtrack of vision and soul". Look at the sky: life's just begun...

From Doug Aitken's Station To Station project, 2013

11 Gimme Friction
Television

Album bought in London in 1977

BEFORE THE Sex Pistols, there was New York's Lower East Side: trash aesthetes with short hair, kinky vixens in B-movie stilettos. Kids with minor drug habits and slim volumes of symbolist verse. Pre-punk "punk rock" was Gotham's reaction to smug denim California and prog-pomp stadium blowout. The new Bowery Bop was about immaculate posing, streetcorner nihilism. It was railroad-apartment art-rock out of the Velvets, Stooges, Dolls, with a side order of *Nuggets* garage psychedelics. If Patti was the tomboy boho icon – all hairy armpits and Rimbaud – and the Ramones the inner-suburban drongos peddling cartoon ramalama, for us pale and interesting boys Television were the ones to watch: cool and arty, monkish Apollos to Patti's riot-grrrl Dionysus. Tom Verlaine (*né* Miller) had slunk into NYC in 1968 from small-town Delaware with his pal Richard Hell (*né* Myers), the pair forming the Neon Boys with ace drummer Billy Ficca circa '72. Waves were made once the newly christened Television put CBGBs on the map in '74. Lou and Bowie dropped by; Lennon dropped the name. By

December of that year, Brian Eno was producing demos of 'Prove It', 'Friction', 'Venus De Milo' and 'Marquee Moon'.

Island's Richard Williams nearly signed the band, but Verlaine wasn't thrilled by Eno's sound. "He recorded us very cold and brittle, no resonance," the singer-guitarist recalled in the late summer of '76. "We're oriented towards really strong guitar music… sort of *expressionistic*." Verlaine also knew that Hell, who was already singing 'Blank Generation' but wasn't the world's most disciplined bassist, would have to go. The two-part Ork single 'Little Johnny Jewel', released in October '75 and included on *Marquee Moon (Expanded)* as a bonus track, came closer to Verlaine's blueprint for the band: lean, nervy, with (yes) "expressionistic" guitar, like Barry Melton on sulphate. Given that seminal 45, it's amazing to think another 18 months elapsed before the major-label *Marquee Moon* finally saw daylight with a new TV line-up of Verlaine, Ficca, Richard Lloyd (guitar/vocals) and Fred Smith (bass).

When Nick Kent drooled at length in *NME*, pale boys sloped off *en masse* to purchase *Marquee Moon*. In the Robert Mapplethorpe portrait on the cover, Verlaine – his swanlike neck bearing a prominent, slightly scary Adam's Apple – proffered … *what?* The sound we'd all been waiting for through the years of rock's otiose decline? That was certainly what the album represented for *me*. Indifferent to much UK punk, I buried myself in the album's eight songs for months, thrilled by its taut dynamics, its quivering guitar interplay, and by Verlaine's jarring, alienated imagery. *("I recall how lightning struck itself…", "Broadway looked so medieval…")* Thanks in part to Stones/Zeppelin engineer Andy Johns, it still sounds flawless – everything melodic four-piece/two-guitar art-punk *should* be. The driving, almost danceable 'See No Evil' is the perfect opener, a sharp declaration of intent (*"What I want… I want now!"*). Verlaine's pinched, petulant voice isn't to everyone's taste, but it's perfect for this punk poetry of existential unease. "Many of my songs seem to be obsessed with defining or expressing a sensibility," he told me in 1984. "People who've stuck with me for a while tend to point to a few songs that somehow define that sensibility – 'Venus', 'The Fire', 'Breakin' In My Heart', 'Penetration', 'Clear It Away'. Again this struggle to articulate, or even to say why one is happily inarticulate. It says a lot about dealing in a non-verbal realm all the time." 'Venus' sits marvellously between 'Evil' and the similarly charged 'Friction'. As skew-whiff as it is – well, *you* try falling into the arms of Venus de Milo! – it's a song filled with breathless wonder, a vision of Manhattan as a sort of neon playground. (*"You know it's all like some new kinda drug…" "I fell sideways laughing…"*) At the end of the vinyl Side One was

'Marquee Moon' itself – a ten-minute epic in an era of 40-second gob-rants, set to a weird white skank of a groove, climaxing in a fantastic ascending Verlaine/Lloyd jam that still sounds like some Avenue A take on the sparring of Jerry Garcia and Bob Weir or Neil Young and Danny Whitten.

Vinyl Side Two kicked off with 'Elevation', another slice of electric rock'n'roll that – with its sudden stops and rhythmic lurches – sounded like no electric rock'n'roll one had ever heard before. Pretty boy Lloyd's 'Guiding Light' at first stuck out like a sweet finger in a fistful of sore thumbs, its plaintive appeal (*"Guide me through the night…"*) anomalous in context. Yet its simple glistening beauty shines on. The flip, sarcastic 'Prove It' harked back to the earlier New York pop era of Dion via solo Lou Reed – always a Televisual crowd-pleaser, but the least interesting song on the record. 'Torn Curtain', rounding the album out, was superb: deep and mournful and packing one of Verlaine's tensest solos.

The sophomore 1978 offering *Adventure* never stood a chance after *Marquee Moon*. But the simple fact is that its songs were not, and still aren't, as daring or convincing as 'Venus' or 'Elevation'. Some are downright dull. 'Glory' and 'Days' are pleasant to the point of blandness, chiming 4/4 "rock songs" of no great distinction. One feels the life's gone out of the group; in hindsight we know it wasn't a happy camp – Verlaine the cerebral control freak at spiteful odds with peevish junkie Lloyd, Smith and Ficca striving to keep the peace. (The body language of the group portrait – a *Marquee Moon* second take of sorts – says it all.) 'Foxhole' has a bit of grit to it, but its war imagery is hackneyed and its riffology ordinary. 'Careful' is a yawn. 'Carried Away' is better – prettier – but limp next to 'Torn Curtain' or 'Guiding Light'. 'The Fire' is redolent of latter-day Mercury Rev but never develops into anything striking. 'Ain't That Nothin'', veering into vaguely Tom Petty-meets-*Kill City* territory, at least has some meat to it – big riffs, strutting vocals. (It was the only track I played more than five times when *Adventure* came out.) 'The Dream's Dream', closing the record out, attempts to repeat the drama of 'Marquee Moon' but drags along the ground like a wounded animal.

There we have it: the legend of Television, who occasionally manage to put their differences aside to earn a few bucks but whose London show a couple of years back left too much to be desired. At a time when NYC is once again making so much of the running – and when Television can be heard in the sound of the Strokes, Yeah Yeah Yeahs, Interpol *et al.* – the reissue of *Marquee Moon* couldn't be more timely. TV have proved it all over again.

Uncut, 2003

12 Forbidden Love
Chic

Album bought in London in 1979

SO FEW and far between are the live performances that made any real impression on me that they stick out in the memory like skyscrapers rising over shanty towns. There was a historic Little Feat show at London's Rainbow in '75 – a passport from teenage glam-pop to a hairy new world of slide guitars and denim dungarees. There was a breathtaking Prince gig at New York's Ritz in 1981. There was R.E.M. at the Marquee in '83, Todd Rundgren at the Hammersmith Odeon in '75, ABBA at the Albert Hall in '77. Rickie Lee Jones' 1992 show at London's Dominion was so great the entire audience stood for 20 minutes demanding her return. There aren't too many more. Most "gigs" make me wish I was curled up in bed with a mug of cocoa and a new Elmore Leonard novel. But one show swept me off my feet and transported me to a higher plane of musical ecstasy.

I'd been a Chic freak from the instant I first heard 'Everybody Dance' and Norma Jean's 'Saturday' in 1978. Chic's best tracks were sassy and smart, but also – it seemed to me – full of a deep yearning. I was in New York when it was the Disco Mecca of the universe and Chic's 'Good Times' was the anthem of the streets. Even in this ostensibly euphoric work, you could hear an undertow of sadness: the desperate wanting-to-believe that life really *was* "clams on the half-shell... and roller skates, roller skates!"

Back in London that autumn, I learned that the group were playing Hammersmith on the night I was due to return to Oxford for my final year there. Though I knew they were a proper band (*qua* band) and not just an anonymous disco unit, I still didn't quite believe they were capable of playing a... well, a "gig". Few of my friends understood my predilection for disco – they were all too busy listening to useless "new wave" groups – so I went alone and lost myself in a throng of suburban soul boys and girls. I'd steeled myself for disappointment. Any fears the genius of their records would forsake them onstage were banished within seconds of their first song. Do I remember what it was? No, but I know I completely lost myself in the dancefloor mantras of 'I Want Your Love', 'My Forbidden Lover', 'My Feet Keep Dancing' – entrancing, heartbreaking loops to which I could have swayed all night. I know that the way Nile Rodgers and Bernard Edwards locked together on 'Le Freak' and 'Dance, Dance, Dance' – with Rodgers chipping and chinking over Edwards' bubbling bass runs and Tony Thompson's tight-as-a-gnat's-ass drums – was a thing of unearthly groovesomeness. I know that Alfa Anderson and Luci Martin were the epitome of erotic Jazz Age grace, swaying and sashaying as they purred their songs of forlorn love. I know that Jill Furmanovsky took a picture of the four of them at the show which still brings that magic night back to life.

Afterwards, sky-high on the euphoria of the "gig", I drove up to drizzly, cloistral Oxford in a clapped-out Mini – back to the musty world of essays on Tennyson and mopey walks across quadrangles. Trapped in a house with a man who only wanted to listen to Madness, I had no one with whom I could share my epiphany. But those *were* the good times.

Unpublished, 1998

13 The Eternal
Joy Division

Album bought in London in 1980

HAVE JOY DIVISION finally come in from the cold? After years of
compilations with forbiddingly monolithic titles like *Still*, *Substance* and *Permanent*, a four-CD box called *Heart And Soul* is a slight surprise. Perhaps it
is actually a small joke: played next to similarly titled hits by the Cleftones
(1961), Exile (1981), Huey Lewis (1985), T'Pau (1987) and No Sweat (1990),
Joy Division's 1980 track 'Heart And Soul' may be one of the most heartless, soulless songs ever recorded. "Heart"? "Soul"? The whole point of
Joy Division was their implicit opposition to the blustery, chest-beating
emotion on which so much rock music is predicated. Forget T'Pau – Joy
Division weren't on the same planet as U2. They sounded like the Doors
or the Stooges, but the Doors or Stooges playing in some claustrophobic
Salford disco in a dystopian future. Theirs was an "other" world; Burroughs'
Interzone or Gibson's Sprawl via Pere Ubu's dub housing, and it was mostly
about loss and darkness. "Joy Division," remarks Bernard Sumner in Jon

Savage's accompanying essay, "was about the death of my community and my childhood… the death of optimism, of youth."

Part idiot savant, part epileptic saint, singer Ian Curtis was less a would-be rock messiah than a character who'd wandered out of the pages of Kafka or Dostoyevsky. With his alienated, deadpan voice and prosaically "literary" lyrics, Curtis was interested not in exhibiting emotion but in describing the husk – the *ghost*, one might almost say – of feelings that have passed. This does not mean his strangely blank singing does not produce emotion in the listener. Precisely the opposite: it tells us a great deal more about his inner turmoil than all of Bono's handwringing tells us about Sarajevo. One of the many interesting things about *Heart And Soul* is the way it allows us to hear again how Curtis' voice gradually found itself over the course of 18 months. To go from the half-hearted Strummer pasticheur of the Warsaw songs ('Warsaw' itself, 'No Love Lost') to the nervy David Byrne/Alan Vega burbling of the *Factory Sample* tracks ('Digital', 'Glass'), and thence to the oddly mid-Atlantic, Mark E. Smith-meets-Stan Ridgway voice of *Unknown Pleasures* is to relive the rapid growth of a stylist whose technique was almost a Brechtian device. No less fascinating is the development of Joy Division's sound from punk rock to "modern dance" music that's at once Gothic and industrial. Hearing the May 1978 RCA and March 1979 Genetic demos of songs they would later re-record with Martin Hannett ('Interzone', 'Shadowplay', 'Transmission', 'Insight', 'Ice Age') makes it clear just how much Hannett "cooked" the band's raw post-punk noise. On the demo versions, the guitars sound like guitars and the drums sound like drums; by the time they've been through the Hannett mangler (or at least delay unit), they barely sound like rock'n'roll at all.

Oh, the power of despair! The allure of the heart of darkness! How we've all been there, and how the immense gravity of this music still sucks us in – the big, surging songs, like 'Disorder' and 'Transmission'; the desolate, glacially beautiful ballads, like 'New Dawn Fades' and 'The Eternal'; the songs that scarcely *are* songs, like 'Candidate' and 'Insight'. There's something so invigorating about the crude rhythms and primitive post-punk arrangements of these tracks, even clothed as they are in Hannett's post-*Low*/*Idiot* textures and effects. (Dig Steve Morris' jerky 'Be My Baby' drum pattern on 'Atmosphere', the apex of Hannett's futurist-Wall-of-Sound production. Dig 'Love Will Tear Us Apart', for that matter, with its blatant quoting of the Crystals' 'And Then He Kissed Me' in the fadeout…) Often there are no real chords here at all, just the bare bones of a melody coming from the pulsing distorto-thrust of Peter Hook's bass. At other times ('Colony', 'Dead

Souls', 'Twenty Four Hours'), Sumner's frenzied scything fleshes out some of the most intense music ever captured on tape. Those who never saw Joy Division play had better brace themselves for the furiously exciting live material on CD 4, taken from 1979 shows in Manchester and Bournemouth and a February 1980 gig at London's Lyceum. Bootleg quality it may be, but it pisses over the live half of *Still*. (Among other rarities of particular note on *Heart And Soul*: a Piccadilly Radio Session version of 'Atmosphere' – then called 'Chance' – that shows the group groping for the grandeur of Hannett's production; and a rehearsal tape of the heartbreaking 'Ceremony', with a muffled, barely audible vocal by Curtis.)

"The procession moves on, the shouting is over..." How different Joy Division sound from today's northern heroes – from brash, megalomaniac narcissists like Oasis and the Verve. What would Ian Curtis have made of that debauched twerp Richard Ashcroft, I wonder? No matter. *This* is the way. Step inside.

MOJO, 1998

14 Boys Keep Swinging
Associates

Album bought in London in 1982

BILLY MACKENZIE never fitted into the round hole of Eighties pop. With his beret and his whippets, and the dimpled smile that hid his sadness and madness, Dundee's finest fruitcake was just too odd, too buccaneeringly brilliant to compete with the likes of Spandau Ballet and Duran Duran. Transported back to 1980 by the thrilling drive of 'The Affectionate Punch', it's difficult not to feel burning indignation at the way Billy's talent was so pitilessly sidelined by the *Smash Hits* generation. Even when the kids put the delicious 'Party Fears Two' on *Top Of The Pops*, they clearly didn't see they had a genius in their midst. With darkly handsome multi-instro talent Alan Rankine making echoey Cocteau-esque soundscapes behind him, Billy Mac took the exultant Eno-fied Euro-funk of Bowie's *Low/'Heroes'* period kicking and swishing into the indie Eighties – no wonder the first single here is the locally released cover of 'Boys Keep Swinging'.

The new *Singles* compilation reflects the three distinct phases of the Associates' life. First come the extraordinary early singles: futuristic, almost haughtily uncommercial – distant cousins of Scott Walker's more *outré* experiments. Next come the glossier and prettier hits from the scintillating *Sulk*. Finally we have the rather damp and mechanical stuff from *Perhaps* and beyond – the sad sound of compromise with WEA's suggestion that Mackenzie write something more, uh, "commercial". You feel the soul draining out of the poor fellow. (There's a sort of sense in covering 'Heart Of Glass' and 'Love Hangover', yet both smack of defeatism to me. Fortunately, most of the hackwork is on CD2, so you can ignore it.)

"Beauty drips from every pore," Billy almost sobbed on the brilliantly strange 'Q Quarters'. Certainly it drips heartrendingly from such unclassifiable masterpieces as the desperate 'Tell Me Easter's On Friday' and the almost hysterical 'Kitchen Person'. Mackenzie's Caruso-via-Bowie voice may be one of swoonsome artifice, but how one misses a man prepared to take such highwire risks with his vocal cords. He should never have had to take his own life. He was no Ian Curtis, after all: more than any of the New Romantic charlatans of the period, he embodied sexy fun, mercurial glamour and sheer *joie de vivre*. Bring him back to life by buying *Singles*.

Uncut, 2004

15 I Remember That
Prefab Sprout

EP sent by Kitchenware Records in 1984

A THIRD OF the way through a rare outing to the capital, Paddy McAloon dedicates the lovely, little-known 'Dragons' to the spouse of his keyboard player Jess Bailey. Unsurprisingly, everyone guffaws as McAloon realises his gaffe: wives and dragons should not co-exist in the same sentence. "You can see why we don't play live very often," he mutters with a forlorn smile. But then Prefab Sprout are not, never were, about "the live experience". There's no pumped-up showmanship here, no surging guitar riffs. (Well, one: as McAloon prepares to fire up 'Faron Young', he advises us to listen closely lest we miss it.) Moreover, Prefab Sprout – starting with that accursedly silly name – may be less cool than they've ever been. Yet still we turn up to hang on Paddy's every curling word and heart-melting chordal shift.

I remain convinced that people who don't "get" McAloon are dolts without a musical bone in their bodies. For these benighted souls, he is too courtly a lover, too lacking in angry guitar grit. They're people genuinely

44

bothered by the fact that the Hermit of Tyneside currently resembles Karl Marx crossed with Roky Erickson. "Why the hair? Why the beard?" he responds to a flimsy jibe from the back of the stalls. *"Because I'm worth it!"* And he is. To be sure, the sound is a little bare. There are just the four men, *sans* new mom Wendy: faithful old retainers Neil Conti and McAloon's brother Martin, and the very adept Mr Bailey. We miss the breathy sheath of Wendy's interpolations and the silken layers of studio Sprout. Yet McAloon, sore of throat, proceeds to deliver two hours of crystalline masterpieces: songs like the first album's 'Couldn't Bear To Be Special', with its elegant minor chords out of Bacharach via Becker & Fagen; like 'Life's A Miracle', a song of pure love couched as ironic muzak and wrapped in rapture; like the glimmering, starry-eyed opener 'I Remember That'. And we *do* remember it.

As a pop nation, we've become woefully suspicious of the song-as-spell – as microcosm of life and capsule of emotion. Britpop left us with nothing but stale posturing and burnt-out husks of form. And those who defend dunderheads like Noel Gallagher sneer at Paddy McAloon as some yuppie hangover of Sunday-supplement Geordie soul because they can't feel the tender hurt and eager magic of his songs. But to paraphrase the closing, masterful 'Prisoner Of The Past', this Eighties ghost is here to stay. He survived the blast.

MOJO, 2000

16 Come As You Are
Nirvana

CD sent by Geffen Records in 1994

EVEN NOW, a decade on, *Unplugged In New York* sounds so bare and desperate. Before a fawning audience of industry ladder-climbers who'd probably have applauded him taking a dump onstage, Kurt Cobain sounds utterly alone in the world. The weirdest thing about the record is that it's just another *MTV Unplugged* album – like Eric Clapton's, Neil Young's, Mariah Carey's. And yet the MTV logo on the cover is a hollow corporate joke. In the belly of the music-television beast, with key grips and dolly boys flitting around, Kurt Cobain is Christ on the cross, a squillion miles from being a telegenic star.

He hadn't wanted to do *Unplugged* in the first place, and who could have blamed him – the format was already a cosy cliché. As Ben Thompson wrote on the album's release, "the whole *Unplugged* ideal – music as a living history lesson; hey, it's acoustic and therefore real – seems antithetical to everything Nirvana were about." Contempt aside, the acoustic template for the show scared the crap out of Kurt. He knew how exposed he'd feel up there on his stool. He also knew how hard it would be to mask the averageness of his guitar playing without his Fender and fuzzbox. Twenty-four hours before the taping he made a pathetic attempt to sabotage the event by announcing he wouldn't play. No one believed him. As the throng of vultures and voyeurs trouped into the studio, they were greeted by the setting for a wake. Black candles and Stargazer lilies bedecked the stage: *Six Feet Under – The Musical.* Not inappropriate, really: five of the six non-originals Cobain chose to sing during the taping were about death. The set was a virtual requiem for a man who hadn't yet died, a beautiful boy-man who looked – in his cardigan and Converses – like an old ghost.

The grinding, claustrophobic *In Utero* had appeared only two months earlier. *"Teenage angst has paid off well"*, went the opening lines of 'Serve The Servants'; *"now I'm bored and old."* A black-hearted anti-*Nevermind*, *In Utero* made plain the faithless agony Kurt was in. Pre-empting the legions of Emo frauds who clogged up the charts after his death, he had lost his belief in everything – including music. He sang three songs from *In Utero* in New York: 'Dumb', 'Pennyroyal Tea' and 'All Apologies'. Penultimate number 'Apologies' sounds mildly jaunty even if it isn't. 'Dumb' is kinda dumb. But 'Pennyroyal Tea' is emblematic of the album's weary bleakness – its death-wishfulness. *"Give me a Leonard Cohen afterworld,"* he sings on 'Tea', *"so I can sigh eternally."* 'Polly' was already disturbing on *Nevermind* – and unplugged, to boot – but its creepy ennui sits perfectly here between 'Dumb' and 'On A Plain' (for all that Bob Dylan said, it proved Cobain had "heart"). Other *Nevermind* stalwarts – 'Come As You Are', 'Something In The Way' – sound muted and almost folksy in this faux-campfire setting. (No surprise that 'Teen Spirit' fails to make an appearance here.) But then *Unplugged In New York* is nothing if not anti-muso. Though Cobain, Grohl and Novoselic are joined by former Germ Pat Smear, as well as by cellist Lori Goldston on eight tracks, this is hardly Sting In Concert. It's admirably low-key and lo-fi, even drab in spots – acoustic grunge that plods along with a steady 4/4 thump. Bowie's sad, plangent 'Man Who Sold The World' doesn't break stride. Nor does the Vaselines' 'Jesus Doesn't Want Me For A Sunbeam', despite featuring Novoselic on accordion. A mordant inversion of a gospel staple, Eugene Kelly's 'Jesus…' is an interesting choice for the set, especially when one learns that MTV exec Amy Finnerty had breathlessly reassured Cobain that "these people think you are Jesus Christ". (Just what *did* the suicidal Cobain feel as he croaked the irreligious lines *"Don't expect me to cry/ For all the reasons you had to die"*?)

The best, or at least the bleakest, is saved for last. Written by folk-blues man-myth Leadbelly, 'Where Did You Sleep Last Night' – aka 'In The

Pines' – is Cobain's very own Americana classic, a harrowing howl of jealousy that taps into all that disturbing swamp-country undertow we've feasted on: *"In the pines, in the pines/Where the sun don't ever shine/I will shiver the whole night through"*. Kurt could be singing about heroin withdrawals but it hardly matters: when his voice leaps an octave to shriek its unswerving question, the blood curdles. Nick Cave eat your heart out. Which leaves the three-song mini-interlude featuring Phoenix's Meat Puppets. Gangling desert punk-poets, brothers Cris and Curt Kirkwood were early hardcore heroes of Cobain's, who invited them on tour and selected not one, not two, but *three* of their songs for the MTV set. 'Plateau', 'Lake Of Fire' and the ultra-melodic 'Oh Me' – from 1984's *Meat Puppets II* – are all superb and worthy of rendition by Cobain. Behind this selfless gesture, though, one detects the guilt of The Indie Kid Who Made It Big – the boy who wanted to be famous but also didn't, and who found that success did little but confirm his despair. Why did Kurt Cobain succeed where Curt Kirkwood remained so obscure? "I feel so incredibly GUILTY," Cobain wrote in his overhyped journals, "for abandoning my true comrades who were the ones who were devoted to us a few years ago…" If his anguished scribblings tell us nothing else, they make it clear just how tormented he felt about his fame – and how ambivalent he felt about rock'n'roll itself. "I feel," he writes early on in the journals, "there is a universal sense amongst our generation that everything has been said and done." But this is why Cobain still matters so much: his suicide remains the most powerful of antidotes to the spurious, specious rebellion packaged by today's record industry. As Air's Jean-Benoit Dunckel puts it: "Rock music is no longer about being a rebel. It is a product being sold by huge companies. If you want to be a rebel, don't be a rock musician – be a human rights campaigner or something."

For Cobain, grunge in its original inception was/is a rejection of nostalgic classic-rock cliché. But he also knew that grunge itself was guilty of bad faith – witness Pearl Jam and Smashing Pumpkins. Always the subtext in his journals is: How can we keep rock'n'roll alive as something *real*? With the implicit rejoinder: *Maybe we can't.* "Hey hey, my my," wailed Neil Young at the start of the song Kurt quoted in his suicide note, *"rock and roll will never die."* But from our vantage point in 2002, Kurt's death looks like the last gasp of rock conviction in our flattening, hyper-mediated society. And *Unplugged In New York* remains the most sobering of swansongs.

Uncut, 2004

17 Deaf School
Queens of the Stone Age

CD bought in London in 2002

ONCE IN A blue moon, an album happens along that relights your fire and brings moribund rock back to life. The odd quasi-supergroup that is Queens of the Stone Age – Josh Homme, Nick Oliveri, Dave Grohl, Mark Lanegan – has made just such a record with *Songs For The Deaf*, a 60-minute sonic voyage packed with crunching guitars, brooding riffs and high desert humour. QOTSA are a southwestern Nirvana on a bed of Black Sabbath, ZZ Top and Blue Öyster Cult, via Metallica – with a healthy splash of Red Hot Chili Pepper sauce for added melodic zest. Call it cactus grunge, call it stoner hardcore: the fact is no one else is writing driving metallic grooves quite like 'First It Giveth', 'Sky Is Fallin'' or 'Song For The Dead'.

Like the Chili Peppers (of whom, on 'No One Knows' and 'Go With The Flow', they are arguably a beefier version), Queens are the supreme antidote to the bad-faith rage-by-numbers of 99.9% of the nu metalheads out there. (As head Pepper Anthony Keidis put it in a recent *Spin*, "I don't think any of those conservative, ultra-aggro rap-metal bands had the funk influence or punk-rock energy that we had…") Queens reinvigorate rock with muscle and sinew, guitars that sound like proper late Sixties/early Seventies Gibson SGs – Tony Iommi out of Johnny Echols. Driven by the merciless Grohl and elevated by haunting Homme/Lanegan harmonies, they are utterly their own band: what Jane's Addiction were to HM/"hard rock" a decade ago, Queens are now. They sound like a rock band from the time when rock was still dazed and confused, their root groove as much Alice Cooper/Mott the Hoople as Zeppelin/Sabbath. 'Do It Again' is a slab of glam boogie; 'God Is In The Radio' is mordant ZZ Top and a neat aside on the hilarious airwave links that connect *SFTD*'s tracks (courtesy of guests that include Casey Chaos and Twiggy Ramirez). The opening motorik chugger 'Millionaire', meanwhile, is this album's feel-good hit of the (very late) summer.

QOTSA's drugs'n'debauchery *shtick* is a smokescreen for their intense musical commitment: the passion that infuses *Songs For The Deaf* makes that abundantly clear. What other band would Lanegan – one of the great grunge voices, and a man as steeped in Bobby "Blue" Bland as in grunge itself – conceivably have joined? (Lanegan's vocal on 'Hangin' Tree' is pure whiskey and holy ghost, Gun Club via Screaming Trees…) The Oliveri-sung 'Another Love Song' is the sole odd-song-out here – a Sixties garage-punk homage with underwater guitar, Farfisa organ and pounding stomp beat – but it's seamlessly succeeded by the pounding 'Song For The Deaf', which starts with an ominous Metallica bass line and settles into a relentlessly evil groove, overlaid by twin-lead diddling.

Dark and blood-red, mysterious and magnificent, *Songs For The Deaf* is a statement of belief in music's power to sidestep the numbing formulae of radio fodder – to deliver heavy metallic sounds that deliver us from dullness. It's good to *hear* again.

Rock's Backpages, 2002

18 The Hunter
Björk

CD bought in New York City in 1997

I HAVE A TEN-year-old who loves OutKast and Kanye West but recoils in horror when I play my favourite albums by Kate Bush or Mary Margaret O'Hara or Joanna Newsom. I don't take my son's distaste too personally. I suspect it's all about his pre-adolescent need to reject The Feminine as vulnerable, hysterical, deranged. More grating to him than anything is Björk, whose music I have adored ever since an A&R man sat me down 20 years ago to play an advance copy of the Sugarcubes' 'Birthday'. (I guess by 1987 I was ready for The Feminine.) Hearing the sheer burst of life from Björk's lungs on 'Birthday' left me humbled. There was a raging playfulness and a sexual exuberance in her voice that made a mockery of the sterile, codified pop of the late Eighties. A few years later I reeled from the entrancing martial groove of 'Human Behaviour', the opening salvo of her solo *Debut*. 'Violently Happy', Björk called herself, and I believed her.

In the beauty and urgency of her melodies and rhythms, Björk defined the eclecticism of the early Nineties. At once primal and postmodern, she created a lush language of beats and textures that had at least something in common with the Bristol sound of Massive Attack and their kin – not least *Debut*'s producer Nellee Hooper. But where British acts were constrained by cool, the Icelandic Björk was fearless and thrillingly intuitive. She took risks no Brit would have dared to, flirting with disaster (or at least ridicule) as she chased peaks of ecstasy and lost herself in the oceanic delirium of sound. Merely as a singer, she was brilliantly unhinged. Her voice seemed to issue from the volcanic core of her being, in Simon Reynolds' words "a mad jumble of astonishment, elation, rapture, dread, awe". As Bush or Rickie Lee Jones had done before her, she sang at moments like a possessed child, pursuing melodies with a gut instinct, opening out vowels with her odd phrasing and impish intonation. The sound of her open throat, the tongue thrust out, was unforgettable. In an age of stodgy Britrock, Björk's music was an enchanted forest. On the sophomore *Post*, the storming 'Army Of Me' laid waste to those who dismissed her as an exotic kook. But the album also gave us the riffling beats and reveries of 'Hyper-Ballad' and 'Possibly Maybe'. *"I'm going hunting for mystery,"* she confided on 'Cover Me'. A year later she let a motley crew of remixers – from Deodato to Dillinja – loose on *Post*'s tracks and released the very extreme results as *Telegram*.

Increasingly, Björk has blended electronica with more organic instrumentation, particularly harps and string octets. 1997's *Homogenic* was sombre and elemental, 2001's *Vespertine* intimate and glimmering. Increasingly, too, she's straddled the worlds of street culture and highbrow art, aligning herself with the hippest artists, photographers and fashion designers. Collaborators from LFO's Mark Bell to laptop geeks Matmos have helped her to create a kind of Björkworld, while her marriage to artist Matthew Barney cemented her status as an avant-garde icon. As pompous and narcissistic as the art world can be, her music remains deeply felt even at its most abstruse. *Medulla*'s 'Who Is It', nestled among such extreme pieces as 'Ancestors' and 'Where Is The Line', is phenomenal: a mad collage of skittering mouth rhythms, oozing bass synth and sheer beauty that's unlike anything I've heard in western pop.

The new album *Volta* offers the usual dizzying mix of styles and guests. Who else could bring Timbaland and Toumani Diabaté to the same table ('Hope'), or duet so affectingly with Antony Hegarty (on 'The Dull Flame Of Desire', adapted from a 19th-century Russian poem) before getting it on with Congolese troupe Konono No. 1? *"I have lost my origin,"* she sings on

'Wanderlust', *"and I don't want to find it again"*. She never ceases to amaze. In a culture where every new retrograde guitar band is still hailed as The Next Big Thing, we badly need our Björks – our mutant divas, our high priestesses of multi-new-media. I continue to worship her war on orthodoxy, her refusal to dilute the polymorphous perversity of her music. Even if it does send my boy running for the hills.

eMusic, 2007

19 The Revivalist
Gillian Welch

CD sent by Almo Sounds Records in 1996

DETACH YOURSELF for a minute, and this here is a pretty rum scene. A raw, callow-looking couple, straight out of a Depression-era Walker Evans photograph, are singing plaintive mountain songs in a bar in, of all places, Chicago – not commonly renowned as a bluegrass town, even if it *is* home to Freakwater. They are doing it, moreover, to the wild applause of folks who sport combat boots and dye their hair, most of whom seem to know these songs – the song about the V-8, the song about "the dead baby" – by heart and only want more of what the lanky girl and bony boy do so very, very well. Not only do their voices blend superbly – the girl's stark, vibratoless alto shadowed by the boy's soft tenor – but their guitars, a 1935 Epiphone for the boy, a big reddish-brown Guild for the girl, also intertwine with unearthly neatness. They sing beautiful, chilling songs like 'By The Mark', 'Orphan Girl' and 'One More Dollar', and the place is simply transfixed. They rev it up a little

54

for 'Pass You By' and 'Tear My Stillhouse Down', and the effect is no different.

The girl is Gillian Welch, the boy David Rawlings. Together they're responsible for the outstanding country-music debut of 1996. Produced in Los Angeles by T Bone Burnett, *Revival* features legends James Burton and Jim Keltner; mostly it's just Gillian (hard G) and David, performing quietly together as they do onstage tonight. Since its release last spring, the album has received across-the-board raves and taken them from the Bluebird Café in Nashville, where they live, to the Purcell Room in London. At a time when the profile of bluegrass in America has never been higher – when an Alison Krauss can make the Top 20 Album Chart and you can't move for summer festivals dedicated to the genre – they are becoming one very hot property. They met in 1989 when auditioning for a country band at Boston's prestigious Berklee College of Music (where both studied), Welch the adopted daughter of Hollywood television composers, Rawlings a Rhode Island native who'd come late to the guitar in 1986. "We both passed the audition," says Welch. "Mainly we played Bob Wills and Buck Owens stuff in the band. Sometimes we'd play a little recreational bluegrass. It wasn't till later that Dave and I first sang together, just the two of us. We started doing traditional tunes and realised our voices together sounded okay. Especially as it seems to be a little less common in bluegrass to have the lead on top, with a baritone harmony below. You're a little more used to hearing lead with a tenor harmony on top. It meant that – hard as we tried to copy a Stanley Brothers song – it always ended up sounding different." A move to Nashville in 1993 was based on the pragmatic decision to base themselves in a music town. "I'd lived in the Bay Area," Welch says, "so I had a feel for what it would be like to stay in a non-industry city, and to try to come up through the local scene. I'm definitely glad we went to Nashville. It's been a good place for us."

The couple's first big break came with a writing deal at Almo-Irving, in turn leading to Welch's signing to Almo Sounds, the post-A&M label formed by Herb Alpert and Jerry Moss in 1994. Welch signed as a solo act for the simple reason that it's harder to market a duo. "I did an in-person audition for Jerry in the summer of '94," says Welch. "Flew to LA and sat in his office and sang. I knew things were going well when he was singing along to 'Orphan Girl'. And then we made the record about a year later. Didn't meet Herb till a bit further down the road, although he and Jerry came to see us play at this real neighbourhoody bluegrass dive in Nashville called the Station Inn." The venue was also where Burnett caught them the first time, offering his services as a producer, should they ever want one. "We talked to nine other producers after we signed our deal," says Rawlings. "But we kept coming back to T Bone, because that was who we felt the most in tune with." In the end there wasn't much production to be done on the record, though the duo gives full credit to Burnett for adding just enough contemporary feel to the arrangements to rescue it from the cobwebs of Carter Family arcana. The dragging rockabilly groove of 'Pass You By' and the spooky Patsy Cline-meets-Cowboy-Junkies feel of 'Paper Wings' are two of the album's highlights. "We started with the arrangements Dave and I had been playing, recording them live to mono," says Welch. "Did about a week of that, and then brought in Jim Keltner and [bassist] Armando Campean, plus James Burton on… other stringed things! I feel like T Bone kind of pushed us to experiment somewhat. We tried some wackier stuff, and then most of it got pared down again."

The resulting album has been a priceless gift to citybillies searching for some midway compromise between Alan Jackson and Will Oldham: far from the glitzy big-hair mainstream, but not too twistedly *outré* for the traditionalists. Do they see themselves in any way as part of today's "alternative country" scene? "We're probably over on one edge of it, if there's such a thing as a spectrum," says Welch. "But when people say to us, 'Don't you feel oppressed in Nashville?', we're like, 'Well, not really'!"

But is it not ironic – some have even suggested disingenuous – that a couple of middle-class Berklee graduates are reviving stark gospel tunes and murder ballads while Nashville slides ever nearer to Vegas shlock?

Rawlings, who has clearly been asked some form of this question before, gives it due reflection. "I tend to think that this kind of music is… is, you know, art. And I think you can make art out of it if you love it. In the Sixties it was the exact same thing – the people who played folk music weren't people from the backwoods. But if you really want to authenticate it in some way, Gillian was singing Woody Guthrie's 'Ramblin' Boy' at eight years old! And I've spent quite a lot of time outdoors! Doing rural things!"

MOJO, 1997

20 A Rose Through The Concrete
Mary J. Blige

CD bought in London in 2005

"WE LOVE YOU, MARY!" The shouts float up from isolated pockets in the plush auditorium housed within Columbus Circle's glitzy Time Warner building. Mary J. Blige has just wrung every last drop of pain from 'Not Gon' Cry', the Babyface song she contributed to the 1996 film *Waiting To Exhale*, and it's left her lost and little-girlish on stage, unsure whether to replace the protective sunglasses she's briefly removed. *"We love you, Mary! We love you!"* The reassuring yelps are a natural response to the honesty of Blige's emotional confusion, and to the narrative of self-destruction and redemption her career represents. "The Queen of Hip Hop Soul", as MJB has for some years been dubbed, is a beguiling mixture of imperiousness and vulnerability, a bitch goddess who shows us the wounded child inside. We hear the rawness of her pain in a voice that foregoes the showiness of modern R&B divas. Blige, in fact, isn't a diva at all: she's a street queen, a tomboyish everywoman from the projects who, for over a decade, has

57

spoken not only for women but for all survivors of urban poverty and violence.

Blige is quintessential East Coast, NYC R&B. When her sometime mentor André Harrell introduces tonight's live memory-lane trawl through Mary's key songs, he borrows the timeless image of "a rose growing up through the concrete" from Ben E. King's ghetto poem 'Spanish Harlem'. Something about Blige touched Harrell deeply when years ago he heard the yearning in her 1989 mall-booth recordings of Chaka Khan's 'Sweet Thing' and Anita Baker's 'Caught Up In The Rapture'. He saw the hurt in her anger, the residue of her loveless and abusive childhood. "We were able to take Mary's pain," he has said, "and make it a platform."

Born in Savannah, Georgia, in January 1971, Blige was raised in the notorious Schlobohm Projects of South Yonkers, a place where, in her words, people lived "like crabs in a barrel". The absence of her father was compounded by sexual abuse she suffered as a child. On her own from the age of 17, she was signed to Harrell's MCA-distributed Uptown label in 1991, releasing *What's The 411?* the following year. The opening cut, 'Leave A Message' – a succession of phone messages from her answering machine over a slick drum-machine groove – made it instantly clear that Blige was street rather than chic. Meanwhile the wistful 'Reminisce' and 'You Remind Me' hinted at the loss and melancholy behind much of hip hop's aggression. With the help of his pushy lieutenant Sean "Puffy" Combs, Harrell moulded Mary into a post-buppie icon of urban Black aspiration: modern R&B's own Aretha Franklin, musical mother to Beyoncé and all her sisters. The fact that she wasn't conventionally cute made her all the more charismatic. After a decade of Whitney Houstons, she was the perfect female figurehead for the new convergence of soul melodicism and hip hop attitude, togged out in combat boots and baseball caps. Her "keepin'-it-real" stance became an emotional touchstone for urban African Americans, who fetishised her pain and welcomed the elision between her life and her art. "They think this is entertainment," Blige told *Ebony* two years ago. "This Mary J. Blige thing is not entertainment. This is my life and I put it out there on the line for everybody."

1994's *My Life* was a kind of manifesto for her pain, equal parts despair and hope. Tracks such as 'Be Happy' and 'I'm Goin' Down' spoke of the dreams and self-destruction of the girl who'd felt ugly in school and didn't get noticed by boys. Women lapped it up, clinging to the album as an articulation of their own sorrow. For younger female R&B artists like Destiny's Child, *My Life* was life changing. Her music became more sophisticated when MCA brought in Jimmy Jam and Terry Lewis – the legendary writer-producers behind the Human League's 'Human' and Janet Jackson's 'Control' – to work on 1997's *Share My World*. 1999's *Mary*, with its stark monochrome image of Blige in profile, pushed her closer to the pop mainstream and featured cameos from George Michael, Elton John and Eric Clapton. It even boasted a ballad – the divine 'Give Me You' – from the hand of power-balladmeister Diane Warren.

Behind the scenes, the Queen of Hip-Hop Soul was in alcoholic-narcotic meltdown, angry and damaged. "Nobody around me loved me or cared for me," she has said. "Somebody actually told me, 'Girl, you young. It's okay to drink and sleep around.' I'll never forget that. That's where my life was, spinning out of control – drinking and drugging, staying up for days and days and days. The way I was living, I should have been dead." Volatile relationships with such fellow artists as Jodeci's K-Ci Hailey contributed to Mary's plummeting self-worth. Only when she met and fell in love with industry veteran Kendu Isaacs did she clean up her act, the result being the repentance and resolution of *No More Drama*, its title track a stormingly emotional testament to her recovery. (She has said she quit drinking and drugging after the death of singer Aaliyah in August 2001.) Performing 'No More Drama' at the 2002 Grammy awards, Mary burst into tears as the song concluded. "I know it sounds like something everybody says, but I had to like me and I didn't," Blige told *Newsweek*. "I was drinking, which was something people in my family did all my life, so I thought that was the answer. But it just blinded me to what was really going on in my life and in my career." With Blige's sobriety has come the charge that she's lost her edge, that she's too ensconced in domestic bliss to make the powerful music of her cocaine heyday. 2003's underperforming *Love & Life*, which reunited her with the tycoon formerly known as Puffy Combs, was regarded as a disappointment. Understandably, Blige was peeved that people who'd invested so much in her pain couldn't feel pleased for her newfound happiness. Her new album *The Breakthrough* continues in the vein of therapy-through-song.

At the Rose Hall's invitation-only celebration of her 15-year career, she starts tentatively, reaching back to her euphoric block-party classic 'Real Love' but remaining distant in her shades and her black uber-hooker garb. For all the innovations in sound and style in Black pop of the last decade, the presentation of R&B live hasn't changed greatly since the Eighties, with the musicians arranged conventionally behind the star: the band-leader keyboard dude, the beefy drummer playing micro-fills-within-fills, the four backing singers in a line of black Armani suits, the three-piece horn section, the overly flashy guitarist. If she tears through the bourgeois sheen of Eighties soul, one still hears the scatting and melisma of Anita Baker in her vocal digressions. Her range is impressive, spanning low contralto notes and arching Aretha wails. As she sings 'My Life', 'I Love You', 'I'm Goin' Down' and the Rufus-ish 'Love I Never Had', she warms up, pulling off the sunglasses so we can see the feeling in her eyes. The cathartic 'No More Drama' lacks the concentrated agony of its shattering performance at the Grammies (or on *Later… With Jools Holland*) but still makes the hairs stand up on my arms. With the buoyant, swaying 'Family Affair', she gets the audience on its feet, shouting along with her like a gospel congregation. "Don't need no hateration, holleratin' in this dance for me," she sings as she stomps about in her giant platforms. "Let's get it percolatin', while you're waiting, so just dance for me…" It's party time at the Rose Hall.

"I feel like I'm a new artist," she announces before a final song that looks back over her life and namechecks the music that made her a star. The years of gin and cocaine are behind the happily married 34-year-old, whose standing has suffered in the era of the R&B starlets she inspired. The "broken street kid" – her own words – has become Aretha's Natural Woman, still raw and flawed but weary of her own rage. We love you, Mary.

The Observer, 2005

21 I Want You
Rufus Wainwright

Review copy sent by DreamWorks Records in 2004

LAST YEAR, Rufus Wainwright was a guest on Tom Robinson's BBC 6 Music radio show, fielding questions about music, life and celebrity while pointedly avoiding allusion to his host's former incarnation as the author of 'Glad To Be Gay'. Yet he managed to be splendidly catty about David Bowie, implying the former Z. Stardust had felt threatened by the flamingly out-there R. Wainwright. Tetchy queen that he can be, how great to have a truly gay, unapologetically effeminate *star* at last. No sly closet clues required for *this* diva with his lispy intros and flouncing campery. But it's so much more than that: spawn of Loudon and Kate McGarrigle, Wainwright has ten times the talent of an Elton John, or even of a Jobriath. This torch-song troubadour, with his pink-pound passion and drag-queen melancholia, is one of the most compelling singer-songwriters working in pop today. With his effortless tenor voice – *bel canto* with an edge of petulance – he's Thom Yorke reborn on the stage of La Scala. Part-throwback to a golden age of post-folk auteurs of which his parents were a core part, he has veteran mentor Lenny Waronker to thank for shepherding him through three stunning albums to get to his new *Want Two*.

When Wainwright came out with his self-titled debut in 1998, it was clear he possessed craft and sophistication in spades. Here was a beautiful voice singing songs with artful arrangements, aided by the likes of Jon Brion and the venerable Van Dyke Parks. What wasn't clear was how he would get played on radio, a dilemma that 2001's *Poses* partially solved by dispensing with the palm-court Parks factor and replacing with it with bluesy guitars and Propellerheads collaborations. "I thought we would attempt to make a more poppy record," he told me on its release. "It was essential to show that I can get up from behind the piano and that I'm actually pretty compatible with other people of my age out there." What was reassuring about *Want One* (2003) was the sheer spectrum of its palette. Wainwright's talent hadn't contracted in pursuit of the commercial rewards his narcissism demanded: he'd stayed faithful to his swooning muse, to a place where Radiohead interfaced with Mahler. Here was pouty self-pity, delicious pathos and searing intensity, all bathed in resplendent orch-pop. The album confirmed that he was more than a mannerist: that however much a mask his bruised glamour-boy persona was, there was a real ache in his ravaged heart.

Want Two is more and even better of the same. Echoing the cover of *One*, *Two* gives us the other side of Rufus' androgynous split-self: an armoured knight for *One*, on *Two* he's a bereft and possibly ravaged damsel, laid out on a bed of straw. On 'The Art Teacher', he sings in the guise of a Desperate Housewife (wearing a "uniformish pantsuit sort of thing") harking back to a schoolgirl crush on the man who'd led her around the Metropolitan Museum looking at "Rubens and Rembrandts". On the baroque 'Little Sister', with its ornate ballroom string arrangement, he dresses up memories of early musical education with sibling Martha and asks her to *"remember that your brother is a boy"*. Elsewhere he is gleefully Queer: the Second Coming of 'Gay Messiah' (*"No, I won't be the one/Baptised in cum"*), the power breakfast of 'Old Whore's Diet', featuring Antony Johnson (who repays Rufus' cameo on *I Am A Bird Now*'s 'What Can I Do?')

With its scraped-viola intro and impassioned Arabic feel, 'Agnus Dei' serves as a sort of overture, Rufus soaring like a louche monk over swelling strings and rippling pianos. Single 'The One You Love' sets off like something by early Eighties Squeeze before flowing into a declaration of ambiguous devotion as glisteningly pretty as 'Grey Gardens' or 'I Don't Know What It Is'. Though it'll never happen, wouldn't it be grand to see

Rufus in the Top 20? The album's keynote feel, though, is of what literary critic James Wood calls "measured lament": the sound of Wainwright at the piano, *"tired of waiting in restaurants/Reading the critics and comics alone"* ('Peach Trees'), *"bruising from you"* ('This Love Affair'), or simply *"waiting… for the present to pass"* ('Waiting For A Dream'). If *Want One* was all seedy Gotham glam, *Want Two* is the aftermath of that album's restless wanderlust. Most moving of all is 'Memphis Skyline', an elegy for another beautiful boy blessed with more than attitude and exhibitionism. *"Always hated him for the way he looked/in the gaslight of the morning,"* Rufus croons of Jeff Buckley, to whom the song is a plangent homoerotic tribute: *"So kiss me, my darling, stay with me till morning…"*

This album brims over with beauty.

Uncut, 2005

22 Love Among The Ruins
Burial

CD bought online in 2019

IF *I'M* WRITING about dubstep, it must surely be over as a trend. I don't even know what dubstep *is*, and I'm not sure I need to. It seems to be a term for the skippy, jittery South London dance sound that came out of UK garage and "two-step" – the latest mutation of the sound that produced the Streets. I loved Mike Skinner, and for some reason checked out last year's debut by Burial, whose name suggests pantomime metal morbidity but who instead seems to be an anonymous young man from South London making records in his bedroom while harbouring no desire for personal attention: a laudable stance in this age of feverish exhibitionism. "I can't step up, I want to be in the dark at the back of a club," he said in a recent and rare interview. "I don't read press, I don't go on the internet much, I'm just not into it. It's like the lost art of keeping a secret, but it keeps my tunes closer to me and other people."

In truth, I checked out *Burial* because a bunch of other armchair rock critics had drooled over it. Still and all, I'm glad I did, because verily it blew my little mind. Like some creepy fusion of *Wu-Tang Clan Forever* and Massive

Attack's *Mezzanine*, the album was scary and beautiful at one and the same time, a conjuring of urban alienation that simultaneously craved redemption, questing for love among the tower-block ruins of the new dystopia. For every dark articulation on the record ('Wounder', 'Gutted'), equal weight was given to a longing for light ('Prayer', 'Forgive'). At a time when not just London but numerous British cities crawl with feral gangs in hoodie sweatshirts stabbing and "happy-slapping" each other, the sound of *Burial* captured the hopelessness, isolation, and dread we all live with now. This was interior dance music, aural solipsism, soundtracks for the shadows. There was a mechanised, disembodied beauty in pieces like 'Night Bus', with its splashing rain, and 'Broken Home', with its echoey synth motifs. Much of the album was predicated on a nostalgia for the loss of innocence – and of anonymity – in the UK dance scene, a place where (in Mike Skinner's words) the weak became heroes. "I love [...] old jungle and garage tunes, when you didn't know anything about them, and nothing was between you and the tunes," Burial says. "I liked the mystery; it was more scary and sexy, the opposite of other music."

Burial's follow-up, *Untrue*, haunts the same Ballardian cityscapes as its predecessor but is musically richer – in places even oddly exultant. There are more voices, muffled snatches of diva mantras that sound like sad ghosts, and a raft of heart-melting melodies. The hymnal grace of the opening 'Archangel' (*"If I trust you/If I trust you/If I trust you…"*) sets the tone for an album whose dystopian dolor is deeply touching. *"I envied you,"* the male voice cries on 'Near Dark' before admitting he *"can't take my eyes off you"*. The distorted vocals of 'Etched Headplate' fold around each other with a kind of sad desperation, while the album's textures recall the cerebral beauty of early Aphex Twin and his techno disciples. There's nothing glitzy about this sonic world: one of *Untrue*'s tracks – an amorphously beautiful sketch – is called simply 'In McDonald's'. Another bears the title 'Dog Shelter'. Closer to the bone is 'Homeless', whose busy rhythm is undercut by the muted anguish of its floating vocal lines. The title track, like *Burial*'s 'U Hurt Me', is an unsettling statement of reproach to a faithless lover. 'Raver', finally, is a requiem for the scattered hopes of Generation Ecstasy, set to a pulsing 4/4 house groove.

Had Burial been prepared to stick his head above the parapet, his debut might have been dubstep's *Original Pirate Material*. But *Untrue* confirms that the self-styled "rubbish superhero" wants his music to remain a kind of private experience, untarnished by media attention to its creator. For that he deserves our unconditional admiration.

eMusic, 2007

23 Drawn To The Blood
Sufjan Stevens

CD bought online in 2015

IN AN INTERVIEW with *The Quietus* in October 2010, when music streaming was still in its infancy, Sufjan Stevens opined that technological change "kind of allows us to be less anxious about the album as an event and its considerable aesthetic and economic leverage... I think the album can now be much more casual." It's ironic, therefore, that five years later Stevens released an album that *demands* to be treated as an event. A kind of gentile *Kaddish* for his bipolar drug-addicted mom, who died in 2012, *Carrie & Lowell* is a work of great art and deep feeling that's elevated Stevens to the front rank of American singer-songwriters. Following a series of artful, playful experiments with choral/orchestral writing, electronica and even Christmas songs, he'd made a record one might almost call confessional. I haven't been able to stop playing it, glutting myself on its piercing lyric precision and pellucid sorrows, since its release in March. And I sense I'm not alone in my response to the serene, intricate beauty of songs such as 'Fourth Of July', 'Drawn To The Blood', 'All Of Me Wants All Of You', 'No Shade

In The Shadow Of The Cross' and 'Carrie & Lowell' itself. Trite though this sounds, the album is genuinely one of those "long players" that's hard not to follow through from start to finish.

It's true that, in the same *Quietus* interview, Stevens said he didn't think people had altogether "lost the capacity for patience and long-term investment". Clearly he hasn't lost it himself, or he wouldn't be performing *Carrie & Lowell* in its entirety – and almost, though not quite, in its original running order – on his ongoing European tour. There was certainly nothing casual about the presentation of the music at London's Royal Festival Hall, ranging as it did from gossamer softness to what one can only describe as full-blown "progtronica". This was a spectacular and beautifully lit show, however dressed-down Stevens insisted on being – no angel wings tonight – and however understatedly tasteful the contributions of his five instrument-switching accomplices (Casey Foubert, Steve Moore, Dawn Landes and James McAllister, plus special guest Nico Muhly). Much of the music was hymnal, the experience close to religious: it shouldn't surprise anyone familiar with Stevens' singular version of Christianity that home movies of his mother – and from his own childhood and youth – were projected on to long vertical panels behind him that suggested nothing so much as stained-glass church windows.

I have no doubt Stevens' music could sound a mite precious to the uninitiated – *"light as a feather, bright as the Oregon breeze"*, as he sings on 'Should Have Known Better'. But there is such weight to the hushed and careful intimacy of his picking, the seraphic rapture of his singing. As a melodist he is a modern master, even when he opts to deviate from the album's unplugged delicacy. 'All Of Me Wants All Of You', a song of ecstatic strummed melancholy on *Carrie & Lowell*, unexpectedly becomes a slice of minimalist electropop on stage yet loses little of its sweetly desperate pain – even with hunky Sufjan throwing little dance shapes to the song's new swaying groove. 'Fourth Of July', exquisite centerpiece of an album shot through with loss and grief, also undergoes a dramatic transformation in concert. Where the original version ends with the haunting but muted repetition of the phrase *"We're all gonna die"*, here the line is delivered with a thumping, defiant insistence, building to an intense and Mogwai-esque climax. Later in the set, after triumphantly revisiting the synth-heavy 'Vesuvius' from *The Age Of Adz*, Stevens speaks for the first time and riffs hilariously on the subject of our unavoidable demise – "the privilege of our anxiety about dying", as he puts it – with bleakly funny namechecks for Sylvia Plath, the *Book Of Job* and the *Tibetan Book Of The Dead* and references to his hippie parents' belief that we're all just a sort of "celestial fungus". Stevens' eloquence reminds one that he is, *inter alia*, something like the Dave Eggers (a pal) of American Indie. Loosened up by his monologue on mortality, he becomes endearingly silly on 'To Be Alone With You' and even mildly flirtatious with singer/instrumentalist Landes on *Seven Swans'* ineffably perfect 'The Dress Looks Nice On You'.

As if we needed reminders of how great and how unique he already was before *Carrie & Lowell*, Stevens also dusts down 'Chicago' – his encore – and "my murder ballad" 'John Wayne Gacy, Jr.', two highlights of 2005's beloved *Illinois*. Belatedly he completes the slightly re-sequenced *Carrie & Lowell* with its last track 'Blue Bucket Of Gold', bringing the song to a mind-blowing climax that sees Muhly ascend to the Festival Hall's mighty pipe organ, high above the stage. "Sorry, we kind of went into a trance there," Stevens mutters as we recover.

"What's the point of singing songs / If they'll never even hear you?" Stevens asks at the end of *Carrie & Lowell's* 'Eugene' (evidently realising there's a point after all). His music is a kind of incantation, an extended prayer for redemption and for the willingness to forgive. It sears and then heals the anxious human heart. And there's not a hackneyed rock riff in earshot all night.

Rock's Backpages, 2015

24 Have One On Her
Joanna Newsom

CD bought online in 2010

THERE AREN'T many contemporary musicians I'd stand in the pissing Wiltshire rain at summer's end to hear: I'm too ancient to care too much about Next Big Things (or most of the *last* ones, for that matter). So much sounds so samey, so patched together from old building blocks. And then there's Joanna Newsom.

What *is* this combo of harp plinking and faux-naïf girlishness; this voice whose Melanie-meets-the-McGarrigles timbre has proved to be archetypal musical Marmite? I've always been partial to the Kook brigade – a chain of fearless females stretching from Nyro to Björk via Bush, Mary Margaret O'Hara and more – but not even they quite danced on *this* high wire. I heard the voice – was it on one of Peel's last shows, or on the late Robert Sandall's *Mixing It?* – and straightway embraced it as, yes, mannered but, no, not precious or twee, as Newsom's detractors claim it is. I heard it as real, true to its own emotional shtick, fully engaged and immersed in the girl's strange and gorgeous melodies. What could we call the style that then evolved on 2006's *Ys* [pronounced "Eeese"] to become a tingling hybrid of Björk's *Vespertine* and Van Dyke Parks' *Song Cycle*? "Chamber Americana", maybe? The story goes that Newsom's then-squeeze Bill ("Smog") Callahan turned her on to *Song Cycle*; that Parks was then hired to write string and woodwind arrangements for such *outré* pieces as the closing 'Cosmia'. Some deemed Parks' micro-baroque decoration excessive, but to me it exquisitely complemented the Mills College graduate's sonic filigree.

For the closing Sunday set on End Of The Road's Woods stage, Newsom is accompanied by, among other things, violins – played by a pair of brilliant women who play all kinds of other obscure instruments too. The equally brilliant male players *also* frequently switch to other unusual instruments, though they additionally supply the more conventional rock elements of drum kit and electric guitar. (I suppose the point is that this isn't rock music at all. I'm standing in the dark Larmer Tree drizzle because Newsom has so beautifully broken free of rock's terminal tropes – and also of the many "alternative" music forms that have become their own generic traps and cul-de-sacs.) I'm confident she will astonish me, even if she plays the rolling and relatively orthodox piano pop of *Have One On Me*'s heavenly 'Good Intentions Paving Co.'. The latter turns out to be the last song of a breathtaking set characterised by intense concentration: dazzling beauty and complexity, high drama and virtuoso passages more thrilling than any pounding rock discharge. She's a strange sprite: part Faerie Queene, part California Girl, with her beaming smile and her "thank you so *much*" after every round of applause. But there's nothing fey or ethereal about her singing or her playing – mainly at the harp that sits centre-stage, sometimes at the grand piano at the back (for 'Good Intentions', 'Waltz Of The 101st Lightborne' and more). Every interlocking part of her songs is so precise and considered, every long knotty vocal line unspooled with such passionate conviction. It's not like I don't get how odd Newsom's voice is. But it's come a long way from the ditsy Appalachiana of *Milk-Eyed Mender*: it's the human voice as theatre, a sound as rich and beguiling as any singing I know, whether it's tackling the convoluted swirls of 'Cosmia', the crazed nursery rhymes of 'Monkey And Bear', or the slowly unfurling ecstasy of *Divers'* 'Time, As A Symptom'.

Maybe it's just because I'm growing old and slowing down that the work of women like Björk and Newsom feels so much more fluid, intuitive and exuberant than the constrained music of their male counterparts. All I can say is that Newsom – kooky or otherwise – possesses a talent that's unfettered but never pretentious. She's a poet and songstress whose voice soars and carries me into the lowering English sky: into the cosmic mystery that all the greatest music intimates.

Rock's Backpages, 2016

25 Mourning And Melancholia
Grizzly Bear

CD bought online in 2012

ON A DAMP Sunday night in the unlovely London satellite town that is Kingston-upon-Thames – and all for a paltry £12 – I got to see the greatest American rock group of the last decade play for a whole glorious hour. It reminded me of why one cares about "rock" at all. Sometimes I think I no longer do.

Grizzly Bear – launched 15 years ago on a wave of bands with similarly bestial monikers – are an unFab-looking Foursome who've made several of the best records ever to come out of the US. They could be a random quartet of white Brooklyn hipsters, skirting middle age, politely wry and super-smart. You wouldn't, looking at them, expect the astonishing music that pours so passionately out of their speakers on the small stage of Kingston College's Arnold Cottesloe Theatre.

Their songs, like their sonics, their textures, their voices, aren't like much else I've ever heard in "rock" (though I'll concede there are stray echoes of *Surf's Up* and *Big Star Third* in there). They blaze with not just beauty but delicious intricacy, overlapping splashes of melody, archness but sweetness, emotion that's never cheap or crass. It's true the Bear's peak moments may be behind them. Commercially they may not top 'Two Weeks' or have Jay-Z and Beyoncé come see their show. Yet *Painted Ruins*, the latest album by Ed Droste, Daniel Rossen, Chris Taylor and Christopher Bear, is no less lovely or transporting than 2009's *Veckatimest* or 2012's *Shields*, and the songs from it performed tonight are, without exception, sublime. The same intimate intelligence, and the same sense of wonder, inform the gorgeous 'Mourning Sound' and 'Three Rings' as inhabit *Shields'* 'Sleeping Ute' and *Veckatimest's* 'While You Wait For The Others', both also aired tonight. The contrasting but equally tender singing of Droste and Rossen is wonderfully underpinned by Rossen's treated guitars, by the subtlest keyboard padding (much of it supplied by part-time Bear Aaron Arntz), by Taylor's craggy Rickenbacker bass, and by emphatic Christopher Bear tom-tom patterns that suggest immersion in the sonic scaping of the late Martin Hannett (no rote timekeeping *here*).

Unlike too many rock shows these days, Grizzly Bear's 60 Kingston minutes are accorded a respectful, almost awestruck silence during their songs: I heard no attention-deficit chatter, rather a surrender to the waves of sound, the loose bliss of the playing, the spacey reverbed textures, the almost jazzish unfurling of the melodies. This is a kind of angelic post-post-rock, fey yet frenzied when it needs to be (e.g. the squalling freakout that brings *Shields'* 'Yet Again' to its climax). With seven minutes to go, they do the only decent thing and finish with *Shields'* slowly exploding finale 'Sun Is In Your Eyes', a song of soaring hope that has us all rapt. There are bigger Bear shows coming up: make sure you see at least one of them.

Rock's Backpages, 2017

Two
Long Players

Feel the music in the air
Find a song to take us there.
It's paradise when I lift up my antenna
Receiving your signal like a prayer…

**The Beach Boys, 'That's Why God
Made The Radio', 2012**

1 God Is In The Radio
The Beach Boys

Album bought in Sudbury, Suffolk, in 1973; signed in Los Angeles in 2012

THIS CAN'T be right. Five golden-throated singers of paeans to California's endless-summer sunshine have gathered at Hollywood's hallowed Ocean Way studios to discuss their half-century journey from the LA suburb of Hawthorne, and… *it's raining.* The group whose peppy anthems of surfin' and *"bushy, bushy blond hairdos"* made Southern California a state of mind for Sixties pop culture have parked their Bentleys in the grey drizzle and scurried into the legendary studio they used when it was still known as United Recorders. (Half a block east on Sunset is the old Western studio – now Cello – that was all but a second home to Brian Wilson when he masterminded the run of classics that climaxed with the aborted psych-pop opus *SMiLE*. "Lotta history between these two buildings," says Bruce Johnston, who joined the Boys for the first time in 1964. "*Everybody's* recorded in these studios.")

As I arrive, Brian Wilson is sitting alone in the big room where the Beach Boys are making their new album – the first since 1985 to feature both Wilson and the band's ageless figurehead Mike Love. The only member to have arrived on the dot for a two o'clock group interview, Wilson could be Dustin Hoffman's Rain Man on a deserted railway platform. Up close, he looks blank and flat and almost not there, an Adult Child whose autistic aura is only heightened when his bandmates wander into the room. Not quite offsetting his spooky catatonia is the chatty affability of Johnston, a Santa Barbara multi-millionaire in tasselled loafers. To his left is the tiny and gentle Al Jardine, who frequently comes to Wilson's rescue with an arm around the shoulder and a tender "*You* remember that…" To Wilson's left, significantly, sits Love, guardedly courteous beneath his perennial Beach Boys baseball cap. Next to him, finally, sits the most unassuming of the quintet, the deferential David Marks, whose cheerful 14-year-old grin stood out in the best-known early Beach Boys photos.

Perhaps someone should have put out two more chairs to mark the absences of Dennis and Carl Wilson, the younger brothers whose very different voices and personalities were so central to the Beach Boys' collective character. When their names are first spoken – as they must be when the group's 50th anniversary is the central subject – a heavy silence descends on the five men. For who, back in 1975, would have imagined Brian Wilson – 300-plus pounds of addictive dread – outliving either of them?

THE SAGA of the Beach Boys is an archetypal American fable of talent, promise, madness, tragedy and sporadic redemption. A group which should have been an ephemeral spasm, a spike in a passing pop fad, against all odds made some of the most extraordinary American music of the last century: anthems religious in their choral beauty, divine in their harmonic perfection and layered complexity. And then it all went disastrously wrong.

Brian Wilson heard things in his head that startled those who'd pigeonholed the Beach Boys as purveyors of teen radio fodder. Long before the symphonic boldness of *Pet Sounds* and the kaleidoscopic swirl of 'Good Vibrations', he was secreting tiny melodic signals in otherwise innocuous songs about beaches and girls. "They were… at the outset, the very emblem of obviousness," Geoffrey O'Brien wrote in *Sonata For Jukebox* (2004). "Our journey consisted of finding, in the heart of that obviousness, what was most secret." Anyone with half an ear hearing 'Lonely Sea' or 'In My Room' – or

'The Warmth Of The Sun', or the joltingly beautiful intro to 'The Little Girl I Once Knew' – instantly sensed that Wilson was up there with Bacharach and McCartney, and even with George Gershwin, whose *Rhapsody In Blue* had enraptured him as a boy. Still, jumping from 'Surfin'' to 'Surf's Up' in four short years was miraculous, as even Mike Love knew.

It's hard to unpick the dysfunctional mess of the Beach Boys narrative without dredging up the sub-story of Love's hostility to Wilson's unfurling musical ambitions circa 1965. The stiff body language of the two men as the question is put to Mike – "Do you think you've had an unfairly bad rap over the claim that you asked Brian not to, er, mess with the formula?" – speaks a small volume of denial or shame. "I've never been against experimentation," he says, looking me straight in the eye. "I made barnyard sounds like everyone else. But I *am* commercially very competitive. What that means is that if 'Good Vibrations' went to No. 1 and 'Heroes And Villains' didn't, then I say – in my own crass commercial way – that I prefer a No. 1 record to one that comes in at 48 *[it actually reached No. 12]*. If I said 'Don't mess with the formula', I don't recall it and I don't believe it's true."

Wilson says nothing as Love defends himself, closing his eyes and zoning out of the conversation. It is impossible to know whether he feels or remembers anything at all about an issue that's preoccupied Beach Boys fanatics for decades. Four years ago, when Love suggested to me that "all that 'Mike's the bad guy' stuff comes from writers who weren't there", it made me question the received version of the schism that ruptured the group, especially when I re-read the long conversation *Crawdaddy!*'s Paul Williams undertook in 1968 with Wilson acolyte David Anderle – the source for much of the conjecture about how *SMiLE* unravelled – only to find that Anderle had actually spoken *up* for Love. "[He is] continually being accused by Brian of being mercenary, soulless," Anderle told Williams. "[It's] very untrue – Mike is a very soulful person."

Given what happened over the ensuing 15 years to Wilson (and to the drug-crazed Dennis), it's hard not to feel some sympathy for the guy who simply wanted to keep the summer alive. "The Beach Boys brand serves a great purpose for what it does," says Jeff Foskett, Wilson's musical director for over a decade and a key member of this reunited Beach Boys. "It's summertime fun, cars, girls, and it's never left the American psyche. And the reason for that is that Michael has kept the brand and the logo in the forefront of the people's mind." Yet the tension between the striped-shirt conservatism of the surfin' Boys and the baroque adventures of the acid-soaked *SMiLE* songs goes to the heart of what makes the group so fascinating. For uniquely the Beach Boys have long juggled two very different audiences. One is the heartland America that hears the group's California cheerleading as a kind of patriotic songbook. The other consists of the pop geeks obsessed with the minutiae of Wilson's Wrecking Crew sessions at Western and Gold Star – along with the *noir* factor that was Dennis Wilson's relationship with Charles Manson. Among these geeks are the artists who've produced such brilliant Beach Boys pastiches as 'My World Fell Down' (Curt Boettcher), 'Mr. Wilson' (John Cale), 'Lower California' (Jack Nitzsche), 'She's Not Worried' (the dB's), 'At My Most Beautiful' (R.E.M.) and 'Let's Hope That Nobody Finds Us' (Lewis Taylor). With the release last year of the sumptuous *SMiLE Sessions*, perhaps there is at last some closure around the myth of Wilson's thwarted brilliance. "It brought back very pleasant memories of when we did it," he says. "And it brought back some of the drugs that I took. Not quite as happy."

As the "reformed" Beach Boys gear up in February for a new album and a 50-date US tour, there's every incentive for the five men to balance their entrenched populism against the radical risk-taking of their greatest music. "The Beach Boys' history is that of conflicting agendas and egos," says film director Oren Moverman, who is currently working on a Wilson biopic, "but the dynamics of any family at a later stage in life are sometimes more rational. Only Brian and Mike and the people that immediately surround them understand it."

"Mike is a great frontman, plain and simple," says Jeff Foskett. "That's why getting back together – with Brian's love of the recreation of the music in its exact form and Mike's outgoing personality and all his stage banter – is going to make it a really fun show."

NO DOUBT IT'S being partly staged for my benefit, but the spine nonetheless tingles as I sit next to Wilson in Ocean Way's control room, watching as he steers his bandmates through the backing vocals for a new song called 'Shelter'. Through the glass we see Love, Marks, Jardine and Johnston as their all-but-flawless *"Dee-dee, dee-de-dee"* harmonies are punched in by a ProTools engineer. The fill is simple enough, but only Wilson could have heard it in the way it fleshes out the flow of the song's melody. And when he sits me down at the console to play lead radio track 'That's Why God Made The Radio', there are chord changes in it so beautiful – and so *un-obvious* – that you instantly know he's still got a gift for pulling beauty out of the ether that almost no one else in the formal pop tradition has equalled. "I heard the song a long time ago," says Jeff Foskett. "When Bruce and Alan and Michael walked into the studio and heard it for the first time, they all just flipped." In the track's yearning, cascading chorale one hears echoes of Beach Boys masterpieces from 'All Summer Long' to 'Sail On, Sailor' – not to mention that other "God" song once cited by Paul McCartney as the most perfect pop record ever made.

God must have made the radio for the young Brian Wilson, who heard everything from Gershwin and the Four Freshmen to the Crystals' 'Uptown' on the family radio in Hawthorne. Sometimes the lanky dreamer drove north to visit his cousin Mike Love in Baldwin Hills, and the two teenagers would sit together listening to Johnny Otis' show on KFOX. "We'd get kicked out of the house because the music was too loud, and my dad had to get up at 5.30 in the morning to go to work," says Love. "So we went out and listened to the radio in Brian's Nash Rambler." If Love was besotted by the Black R&B records Otis played, the Beach Boys' first A&R man at Capitol Records, Nik Venet, described the group as "pure white trash, West Coast hillbillies". For Venet, as for British pop writer Nik Cohn, the Beach Boys were unwitting exponents of the same Pop Art that LA's Ferus Gallery avant-garde were piecing together from the iconography of custom cars and hamburger stands. Hipped to beach culture by canny scouts like Kim Fowley, Venet saw surf pop as the unmediated voice of Aryan Californian teens.

Also paying attention was Bruce Johnston, a rich-kid crony of Fowley's similarly entranced by R&B. "I was just going over to Swami's in San Diego with my surfboard, and I heard 'Surfin'' on the radio," he says. "I thought, 'Now my sport has a voice'." That Brian famously did not surf did not prevent him – with the help of his lyricist collaborators (chiefly Love, Roger Christian and Gary Usher) – from snaring the subculture perfectly. Such was the irony of the outsider-looking-in – alone "in my room", in Guy Peellaert's timeless depiction in his *Rock Dreams* – who saw exactly what it was that defined the scene. Though only drummer Dennis of the five Beach Boys could ever have been called a sex symbol, the group was the closest thing America had to a homegrown Beatles. Soon their records were even being compared to those of the Scouse invaders. Wilson, however, was hopelessly unprepared for the hysteria engendered by 'Surfin' USA', 'Surfer Girl', 'Fun Fun Fun', 'I Get Around', 'Don't Worry, Baby', 'Help Me Rhonda' and 'California Girls'. After a breakdown in December 1964, he decided he just wasn't made for the times, opting to stay in LA and concentrate on making records.

81

With the others away on panty-wetting tour duty, the head Boy – whose 'I Get Around' had voiced the need to *"find a new place where the kids are hip"* – fell in with a cast of mystics and scenesters. He wrote 'California Girls', of all things, after his first acid trip, and already the most striking thing about it was not the rather trite song itself. "'California Girls' was brilliant," says Mike Love. "You could hear the origins of *Pet Sounds* in its intro." If the Beatles' *Rubber Soul* was the first album to make a case for pop as a maturing art form, 1966's *Pet Sounds* was a quantum leap into the unknown – an LP that took doo wop, surf, Spector, MOR and even Charles Ives, and out of them created a symphonic new sound using what Ian MacDonald described as "a polyphonic palette of wide range-spaces and innovative voicings". Yet when Wilson and Love played it to Capitol, the label's Karl Engemann told them, "Gee, guys, that's great, but couldn't you do something more like 'Surfin' USA'?" "Capitol were so into *Pet Sounds*," says Bruce Johnston, "that two and a half months later they released *The Best Of The Beach Boys*. But thanks to the Beatles and everybody else freaking out over *Pet Sounds*, the album found its place."

"There's an old Maharishi wisdom that says the name contains the form," says Al Jardine. "And it's a little difficult to evolve beyond 'The Beach Boys' because you get typecast with a particular kind of music and that name follows you. I'm not saying it's a bad name, it's just that writing *beyond* surf and cars isn't necessarily easy." Written *way* beyond surf and cars was the mind-boggling 'Good Vibrations', one of the most ambitious pop productions of all time. "It was not a rock'n'roll record," Brian states for the record. "I consider it to be a pop record." Says Mike Love, who wrote its lyrics: "It was so non-derivative. There are so many songs that sound like a homogenisation of things that went before, but when I heard *that* track I said, 'Oh my goodness, that is so unique'." Though Love was not averse to Wilson's experimentation in the studio, he was perturbed by his cousin's new circle of friends: turned-on types like Anderle, Danny Hutton, Michael Vosse, Tandyn Almer, Loren Schwartz and Van Dyke Parks. "There was a time when there were people within the group – and *around* the group – who were involved with drugs," he says. "And there were those of us that did not participate in some of the stronger formulations – meaning Alan and Bruce and myself. Maybe I felt out of it because I didn't want to take LSD. There were a lot of people at the time who thought that was the way to go and the way to unleash creativity, and perhaps it was. But the side effect of certain things was not good."

Wilson pipes up at this point to state that it was Parks who turned him on to LSD and amphetamines. "We wrote 'Heroes And Villains' on uppers," he says, adding – in finest *idiot savant* style – that "I'm not sure, but I think the Beatles took psychedelic drugs too." Al Jardine instantly disputes Wilson's claim about Parks, adding in a near-whisper that "I wouldn't say that".

"Well, if that's Brian's recollection…" Love interjects.

Given that Parks has continued to badmouth Love over the years, hidden agendas may be jutting through here. The real issue is surely whether Wilson's mental and psychological problems were caused by chemicals, or whether their true underlying cause was the emotional and physical abuse he and his brothers had suffered at the hands of their tyrannical father Murry.

Was *SMiLE* too far out? Did Wilson fly too close to the sun with 'Cabinessence', whose "acid alliteration" caused Love to bridle at Parks' lyrics? Fast forward to the bed-bound, cocaine-crazed agoraphobe of the mid-Seventies and you'd be forgiven for assuming so. Yet Wilson's long hibernation had an unexpected upside: from the lysergic DIY doo wop of *Smiley Smile* (1967) to the serene eco-rock of *Surf's Up* (1971), the Beach Boys albums after *Pet Sounds* made the Brother Records-era group more of a cogent pop-rock entity than it had ever been. Even if the albums sold poorly, magical tracks like 'Little Bird', 'Our Sweet Love', 'Feel Flows', the darkly fatalistic "Til I Die', 'Sail On, Sailor' and Carl's superb 'The Trader' – along with re-recorded *SMiLE* songs like 'Wonderful' and the godlike 'Surf's Up' – make it plain that the Beach Boys' best days were far from behind them. "I think if you combined the best moments from those albums, you'd have had a record that was ahead of *all* of them," says Bruce Johnston. "My favourite Brian-at-the-controls album is of course *Pet Sounds*, but my favourite *band* album is *Sunflower*. I love it because we all just threw our best stuff in it."

"Dennis and Carl really started coming into their own as songwriters on those records," adds Al Jardine.

"Each of them had his own thing to say," Wilson agrees. "Like, Dennis did 'Forever' and 'Be Still', where Carl would do 'Long Promised Road'. Carl would write songs like mine, but he took it a step further too." When Dennis went on to make 1977's remarkable *Pacific Ocean Blue*, it was as if he'd taken the mantle from his troubled older brother. With the release of the costly but rewarding *Holland* (1973, the year of Murry Wilson's death), an augmented Beach Boys reinvented themselves as an actual rock band, one foot in the oldies-radio demographic and the other in the beardy world of CSNY and the Grateful Dead. "It became hip to go to Beach Boys concerts," says Johnston. "We played with the Dead at the Fillmore

East. Our audience got a little longer-haired." For the Beach Boys, the mid-Seventies were a frustrating hiatus. When various false-start "Brian Is Back!" campaigns finally delivered something like a coherent album – 1977's faux-naif *The Beach Boys Love You* – every paid-up member of the Wilson cult on the planet prayed that pop's greatest melodist was on the mend. He wasn't. His life may have been saved by Eugene Landy, the controlling therapist entrusted with the task of pulling him out of his narcotic quagmire, but the rescue came at a heavy price. Wilson was still visibly damaged, if not permanently traumatised, when I watched him make his comeback at New York's Beacon Theatre in 1999.

It is possible that, behind the scenes, his second wife Melinda is as controlling as Landy was. It seems unlikely, however. "You can say what you like about her," says Jeff Foskett, "but Brian certainly wouldn't be in the positive head space that he's in now without her formula of however she helps him to lead his life." It was unquestionably Melinda who got Wilson to a place where he could even *contemplate* resurrecting *SMiLE* in the astonishing concerts he gave in 2004. "He has managed to keep the deeper-listening audience very happy over the years," says Johnston, long a part of Love's touring Beach Boys. "Mike and I, when we do our thing, probably go a little more *hits*, but we do try and take a dive in, though not as deep as Brian and his incredible musicians do." Exactly which version of the Beach Boys wins out on the forthcoming album and tour will not alter the fact that the curtain is coming down on the group's extraordinary story. "They belong to the past," says Oren Moverman. "We're witnessing the end of the era of nostalgia – the farewell tour not just to the Beach Boys, but to the whole idea of longevity and survival. It's a long goodbye."

HAS PEACE finally broken out in the Beach Boys' ranks? Is the 50th anniversary album-and-tour proof the hatchets have been buried? And shouldn't the new version of 'Do It Again' be called 'Doing "Do It Again" Again'? "Believe it or not, we love each other," David Marks says with a smile. "As long as we were all alive and healthy, I thought it was inevitable we would get back together and do this again."

"It's not really so outlandish an idea," Love concurs. "First of all it's the 50th anniversary of the Beach Boys, which is a remarkable milestone. Second of all, we're able to sing and do our parts, and it's pretty cool to come into the studio where Brian has structured these harmonies. It's just like old times."

"I can tell you this," Jeff Foskett confirms. "There's been nothing but graciousness and good vibrations every time we've been in the same room. There hasn't been one time when anybody has said any snitty things or taken a swipe at somebody – not even behind the glass." For the moment, then – with the deaths and divorces and lawsuits firmly behind them – harmony reigns between the five Beach Boys as it once reigned in their greatest music. California is dreaming again.

MOJO, 2012

2 That Demon Life
Keith Richards

Album bought in London in 1973

"DON'T BE MISLED!" shouts the faded 8" x 8" flyer propped up on a baby grand piano in the mansion Keith Richards is renting in an affluent suburb of Toronto. *"HEAR THE REAL, AUTHENTIC, RHYTHM & BLUES SOUND – THE ROLLING STONES!"* "Yeah, Brian wrote that," the guitarist smiles at my side. "There were all these other bands who he felt weren't the real thing, and he sort of wanted to make the point that we *were*." I can't quite prevent the thought flashing through my mind: just how "real" and "authentic" would the Rolling Stones seem to Brian Jones in 1997? What would the great Lost Boy of Sixties pop make of his old playmates, now at the helm of a mobile rock'n'roll institution that coins it to the tune of millions at the box office? Would he, through his foggy haze of booze and barbs, be appalled by the very fact of their survival, calling out Richards and Mick Jagger for the steely careerism that's kept them afloat for almost four decades?

If he did, he certainly wouldn't be alone. It is bracing to recall that the Stones' run of shows at London's Earl's Court 21 years ago was seen by many as the last straw, the point at which a rancid decadence had set in and made a mockery of all our rock dreams – to remember, indeed, that 1976's *Black And Blue* was described by Lester Bangs as "the first meaningless Stones album". (How many more have there been since then? One shudders to count.) Even I, attending my first Stones gigs at the age of sweet sixteen, could see how Earl's Court was a sham, a shadow, a charade hideously inflated into a carnival like the hydraulic phallus that accompanied them on that joyless procession through Europe. And yet here we are, some of us, two decades on, unable fully to let go of the Stones and what they mean to us. Clinging to them because no one – not the Beatles, not the Who, not the Velvets or the Stooges or Led Zeppelin or anyone else – ever made rock'n'roll music of such demonic intensity and sensuality. And wanting to reclaim at least part of rock's terrain for them after four years of Britpop Beatlemania.

But then I ask myself: am I actually alone with this? Am I the only sad fuck who still *wants* something from them? Is there anyone else out there who wants to tear off Mick Jagger's masks and reach through to the blues-besotted boy of 1961 – to extract a precious drop of sincerity from that ageless grinning baboon? Or has everyone else just packed up and gone home? I dare say they have. But I shan't apologise for my abiding love, or for taking an interminable train ride up to Toronto to talk to Richards about the predictably patchy, inevitably unsatisfactory *Bridges To Babylon*; and about the US tour for which the group had just begun rehearsing; the ongoing love-hate affair between the Glimmer Twins; the timeless glory of the 25-year-old *Exile On Main Street*; those modern upstarts Oasis and Prodigy; and the Rastafarian busman's holiday that is his side project *Wingless Angels*. I still say the Stones have intermittently made great rock'n'soul music in the last decade – on the Richards solo album *Talk Is Cheap*, on the second half of *Steel Wheels* – and even on *Bridges To Babylon*. If you thought Richards was a spent force, check out the last song on the new album, a six-minute ballad that's as gruffly moving as 'All About You' or 'Slipping Away' or 'The Worst' or any of the man's other croaky, country-soulful musings on loss and devotion. The song, aptly enough, is called 'How Can I Stop'.

"Welcome to Doom Villa," grunts Joe, the vast cockney minder who keeps guard outside the bizarre building Richards has chosen for his lodgings in Toronto. Part Vegas cathedral, part nouveau riche dreamhouse, the house provides an oddly suitable habitation for the leathery relic who emerges from one of its many chambers at teatime on a sunny September afternoon. Ageing like a fine wino, here he comes now: the first and last rock star, Beelzebub-in-the-snug, feet bare, words curling and unfurling in a voice that's Roly Birkin QC crossed with Danny, demented dealer of *Withnail And I*. On the table there's a tumbler of radioactive orange liquid that could well be Sour Mash and Tango.

Twenty-five years after he was infamously busted in this city, how does Richards find Toronto? *"Teronno?"* he answers in fluent Keithspeak. "Hmmm. If and whenever I think about it, it's actually been very good to me. Immediately after the bust, it was sort of, 'Whoops! Sorry!' And they did kind of pay for it. In the end, I was coming up here so often for the court appearances that it was like my new gig: you know, 'Forget the music, put the tie on and go up to Toronto!' But the other thing I always think about Toronto is that that's when I realised the experiment had gone on long enough. There's a point where you realise you can't handle it, and you either go over the edge or you do something about it. So it was like, 'Boink! You're gonna climb the walls one more time and then you ain't doin' it no more.'"

At a certain point, he seemed to turn from being the wasted, demonic Keef to being the genial, lovable man we know today. Was that essentially when he put down the dope? Or was there always a nice guy underneath? "There's a demon in me, and he's still around," he says. "Without the dope, we have a bit more of a chat these days. It's more of a truce. It's been twenny-odd years, and there's been families not brought up under stress like the first lot, God bless 'em… it all came out all right, thank God, and now there's a granddaughter thrown in. Marlon, he's had a weird life. My upbringing compared to his was very mundane, it was a cap and a satchel, whereas his was buzzing around in a Bentley, waking his dad up with a broom because, y'know, he's got that *shooter* under the pillow."

It's been nice getting to know the soulful, vulnerable Richards of 'Locked Away', 'Thru And Thru', 'How Can I Stop'; this is some of the most affecting music any Rolling Stone has made. "Well, I wouldn't have been able to write songs like that 10, 15 years ago. I guess a lot of the earlier stuff is just a hard shell: 'Before They Make Me Run', and so on. Although never forget that one of the first ones was 'Happy', which should explain some of the lines on this face. Even on the dope, when the cops are waking you up again, you somehow have to laugh."

I take a big risk and ask if it hurts that few people take the Stones very seriously anymore. "I… I suppose you get to accept the fact that you're now covering several generations," he says. "You look out at the audience, and you're seeing your whole life before you. It's not so concentrated as it used to be, and that sort of spreads the angle of who you're touching. But I find it very heartening for myself that I get a lot of stuff from 13-year-old would-be guitar players, because my theory is that the only thing you can put on a musician's headstone is 'He Passed It On'. Personally, that makes me feel very warm."

Does he take the Zimmer-frame jokes personally? How come Black singers in their fifties never get the abuse the Stones do? "At the beginning of the Voodoo Lounge tour, we all sensed people were all coming to see if we could still make it for two hours. But these boys are a lot tougher than you think. We're all late bloomers, you know what I mean? We thrive on it." Does he ever, in the middle of a gig, think back to the Ealing Blues Club and ask himself, "How the fuck did we get from there to here?" "You occasionally look at your feet and think, 'This is the same old shit'. When you're up there, you're always doing the same gig. And you're hoping to get to that place where your fingers are doing things you *know* they can't do. When you surprise yourself, you rise about three feet off the ground and you see Charlie rising above his drum kit. For a minute you get that buzz where a band just gels for a magic few moments."

Would he have become such a big star without Jagger's drive and obsession with business? "Probably not, but I doubt *he* would be a star without *me*. And believe me, his business head is greatly exaggerated. Alright? Just leave it at that." So all the "Mick's the brains/Keith's the soul of the Stones" clichés irritate him? "Yeah, because I haven't been playing this game without watching what's going on, and sometimes wishing he wouldn't get into it. Because my best weapon business-wise is a silent Mick, one that I could *unleash*. Which is the way Andrew Oldham and I basically designed all of our business moves right from the beginning. You just threaten to be unleashed on these people."

Nils Lofgren called him "the greatest rock'n'roll songwriter", but most people think of Richards primarily as the guitarist, the foil to Jagger. Does he ever resent not being ranked alongside the supposed geniuses of pop? "I hate pretension," he says. "I understand its appeal to other people, but I try to avoid it at all costs. The overblown and the pretentious – you can kill me with that shit. At the same time, the only plaque I ever keep around is my Songwriters' Hall of Fame plaque signed by Sammy Cahn on his death bed. The other big thing for me was Hoagy Carmichael calling me just six months before he died. I mean, I used to listen to that Tin Pan Alley stuff and it went right through me. But once you become a songwriter, and you start to listen to how songs are constructed, you realise how good those guys were. To a certain extent it's a craft, but a lot of it's just inspiration. If there's such a thing as art, it's what turns music into the best vehicle for expression you could possibly have."

AT THIS POINT, sadly, we are interrupted by Jane Rose, the manager whom Mick Jagger fired in 1981, and who subsequently dedicated herself to the career of Keith Richards. She is reminding him that the Stones are due to make a live-by-satellite appearance on the MTV Video Awards in an hour. One hour later, I am back in my hotel room watching the aforesaid awards with a mixture of rage and perverse delight in the insane unpredictability of such televents: Fiona Apple spouting garbage about "following yourself" as she receives her award for Best Newcomer; Busta Rhymes co-presenting an award with Martha Stewart, doyenne of American upper-middle-class life-styling; a stiff Sting warbling 'Every Breath You Take' as Puff Daddy leads a gospel choir through an arrangement of his zillion-selling 'I'll Be Missing You'; Madonna dolled up like some governess and lecturing the world, *pace* Princess Di, on the evils of celebrity junkies – this from the exhibitionist responsible for *Sex* and *In Bed With Madonna*.

Queasy with nausea at the hypocrisy of contemporary pop culture, I realise just how remote from this shiny new world the Rolling Stones now are. It's almost as if there are two parallel music streams out there, the stream that is MTV's youthquake discourse and the reverential, cummerbunded one that is the Rock & Roll Hall of Fame. And I don't know what I have to do with *any* of it.

AT 10.30 p.m., a ripple of applause breaks out and quickly builds inside a tiny Toronto bar called the Horseshoe Tavern. The Stones are stumbling on to the minuscule stage to play one of their "secret" gigs. It's really them, ten feet away in a place the size of the Half Moon in Putney. Is this the Pub Rock revival? Judging by the hopelessly unfashionable attire of dear Ron Wood, you'd be forgiven for thinking so. Jagger is wearing an expensive yellow shirt and looking as unnaturally skinny as ever. You still can't take your eyes off him, even if you look at him with an uneasy mix of fascination and revulsion. Next to him, cranking out the chords to 'Little Queenie', Richards is an unreconstructed Seventies rocker in cartoon shades and a leopard-spot silk shirt. Behind the two men, wearing that perpetual look of vague puzzlement we've come to know so well, is Charlie Watts. Flanking the foursome are Daryl Jones, laying a bedrock of rock-solid bass beneath his employers, and a waistcoated Chuck Leavell behind a keyboard.

A couple more songs in – 'Honky Tonk Women' and a surprisingly exciting '19th Nervous Breakdown' – and it strikes you that this is a cracking little band. After two decades of hearing the Stones in colosseums, it is good to hear them in a joint where they can actually hear *each other*. Even when they move on to the sub-AC/DC grind of 'You Got Me Rocking', they sound tight and cohesive. Richards smiles throughout, clenching the strings and drawing his guitar into his body at that curious angle he favours. When they play 'Little Red Rooster', they could be the resident blooz band in Anytown USA – or the UK, for that matter. It's funny to think of the thousands upon thousands of R&B bar bands who simply wouldn't do what they do if it hadn't been for these guys. As the set continues, there are constant random shouts for Richards and Watts – *"Wuuurrgh Keeeef! Eeeaagh Chaaawlie!"* – but none for Jagger. Does it actually hurt Mick, I wonder, that nobody loves him? I watch him sing the one new song in the set – the awful ersatz-soul number 'Out Of Control' – and notice how he sort of *hurls* the song at us, working up a whole pantomime of gestures and expressions to sell it: *"The drunks and the homeless/ They all know me..."* Of course they do, Mick. And I think to myself that the point is this: Mick wants to be Black, but Keith Richards *is* Black. Mick wants to be loved, but Keith and Charlie *are* loved.

For the last song, 'Jumpin' Jack Flash', Richards hunkers down with his knees bent, stabbing out the riff as Jagger peels off his shirt to reveal the pale, scrawny torso that hasn't gained a roll of fat in 25 years. A slight commotion starts in the crowd, and I realise I've underestimated Mick. He may never write a lyric as great as 'Jumpin' Jack Flash' again, but he's still tapped into that primeval evil – the imperial cool and lewdness of the Seventies rockocracy. And when the band comes back on to encore with 'Brown Sugar', augmented by stout and redoubtable saxophonist Bobby Keys, I remember again why that devilishly sassy record was the first single I ever saved up my own hard-earned shekels to acquire: because Jagger and Richards were the evil hedonists who'd dragged me out of my glam-pop teen idyll into the frenzied, libidinous world of rock'n'roll. Because they were my gods. My demons.

*

TWO AND A half weeks later, the Stones are about to entertain 54,000 people in a sold-out Soldier Field, home to the Chicago Bears. Taking shelter from a blustery wind that swirls in off Lake Michigan, a forlorn huddle of hacks is scarfing down canapes in a white marquee and debating whether the start of the Stones' thirteenth tour of North America actually means anything. Having reacquainted myself with Robert Greenfield's track-marks-and-all account of the band's infamous 1972 jaunt (recently reprinted as *A Journey Through America With The Rolling Stones*), I feel hardpressed to attribute any great cultural significance to the spectacle we're about to witness. For all the clichés trotted out in the American press about baby boomers reliving their wild youth for an evening, the Bridges To Babylon tour – sponsored to the tune of several million dollars by phone company Sprint – inevitably smacks of hollow ritual. It doesn't help that the fans sloping into Soldier Field are indistinguishable from the kind of jocks and *hausfraus* who attend Bears games, even if they *are* bedecked in the usual Stones regalia. Everywhere I look I see the redundant symbol of Jagger's tongue lolling lasciviously from his pillowy lips. "Maybe it was the corporate logo of the Western world, the leer and pout that follows you down the street," surmises Don DeLillo of the image in his new novel *Underworld*. "[Klara] liked to watch him dance and devil-strut but found the mouth a separate object, sort of added later for effect."

Among the freeloaders circulating in the media marquee is local heroine Liz Phair, whose revered *Exile In Guyville* album was written as a track-by-track response to the beloved *Exile On Main Street*. I ask her what resonance the band's latest trawl of America's sports stadia could possibly have for a 30-year-old female singer-songwriter. "I'm throwing in my lot for the type of music they represent," she says. "*Exile On Main Street* changed the face of music for me forever – to me, they're rock'n'roll at its highest visceral level. Even though they're from a generation before me, it's still about the emotion of the lyrics and of Keith's chords. I would love to be moved tonight."

Let us disregard the two Whores Of Babylon – gigantic inflatable creatures of the kind that now seem unavoidable at stadium gigs – that wobble pointlessly on either side of the set designed by Mark (PopMart) Fisher. Let us disregard the Midwestern rabble who would rather hear 'Under My Fucking Thumb' ten times than hear 'Sister Morphine' or 'Shine A Light' even once. (I know this because 'Under My Thumb' easily won a cybercast vote on the Stones' website, trouncing even 'Gimme Shelter'. What can you say, really?) And let us forgive the hash the band make of songs like 'Anybody Seen My Baby' – co-credited now to k.d. lang and Ben Mink, whose 'Constant Craving' Jagger and Richards realised they'd subconsciously pilfered for the song's chorus. The heartening news is that the stadium-sized Stones in late September 1997 sound like a band. It's Richards who strolls on first, clad in a floor-length leopard-spot coat that makes him look like a Wild West teddy boy; and it's Richards (dispensing this time with the hair dye) who fires us into the opening 'Satisfaction'. But look for a moment at Jagger behind him, Jagger who for once is wearing a sharp suit and not some idiotic leotard-and-football-shirt-with-ballet-shoes ensemble. Listen to how the guy is actually *singing*, and *thinking* about what he's singing, not just shamelessly shaking his tush at the jocks and boomers.

And how about this: you can *hear* every one of Charlie Watts' miraculous drum fills, *hear* the crag-like foundations of Jones' bass, *hear* some separation between Richards' and Wood's guitars. My God, even 'It's Only Rock And Roll' – the second song – sounds good tonight. Methinks the $3 million dB sound system is paying off handsomely. "Da Bulls, Da Bears and now Da Stones," says Jagger in failsafe ingratiation mode, and the jocks howl with delight. But then he adds that "we have very warm memories of Chicago, when we first came here", and almost sounds like he means it. Can it be… no, surely not… that Mick is actually *feeling* something? There follows a bunch of songs I particularly loathe – 'Ruby Tuesday', 'Let's Spend The Night Together', and (a little later) the inevitable fucking 'Thumb' – but when Jagger and Richards put their arms round each other during '19th Nervous Breakdown', and when Jagger says "I'm feeling pretty good, I must say… this is sounding excellent", it's hard not to feel genuine pleasure. Several velvet frock coats later, he sings 'Miss You', accompanied by images of the dear departed – Lennon, Garcia, Zappa and Duke Ellington among them – on the huge circular vid-screen that hangs centre-stage like an enormous gong. When he introduces the band, from the be-turbanned Bernard Fowler to former Beach Boys sideman Blondie Chaplin, the entire stadium resounds with a long *"Keeeeeeeeeeith"* before Mick even gets to him. Buoyed by this, Richards turns frontman and sings 'All About You', the bittersweet ode to Anita Pallenberg that closes *Emotional Rescue*. The whole band seems to be emotionally on board for this slice of transmuted southern soul, and Fowler and Lisa Fischer flank him for the last verse, cushioning his fragile voice with their rich harmonies. I'm open-mouthed, astonished that something like this can even *happen* at a Stones gig.

With a nod to U2's PopMart show, Jagger returns to lead the core of the band – Richards, Watts, Wood, Jones and Leavell – along a walkway to a tiny stage in the middle of the stadium. Ripping through 'Little Queenie', 'Let It Bleed' and 'The Last Time', they're suddenly the beat combo of 1965 again – a nostalgic sleight-of-hand, to be sure, but one that works. For a moment they're really ours again. Back on the main stage they perform towering versions of 'Tumbling Dice' and 'Sympathy For The Devil'. The sound is still taut and gripping, a zillion miles from the mush of recent tours. 'You Can't Always Get What You Want' starts with just guitar, hi-hat and trombone, and finishes with a walking jazz bass line as a snowstorm of confetti is loosed on the crowd from the tops of the lighting rigs. By this point during the average Stones show, I reflect, I have usually fallen asleep. An encore of 'Brown Sugar' and a few hundred fireworks later, we are swarming out into the starless night.

"I don't know if it's the same night but it's the same show, the same city," says Acey in DeLillo's *Underworld*. "The same motherfucking band of emaciated millionaire pricks and their Negro bodyguards."

That demon life's still got me in its sway.

MOJO, 1997

3 Further Up The Road
Bobby Bland

Album bought in London in 1982

TWENTY-FIVE years ago, searching for the extant spirit of southern soul music, I made my way to a former Pepsi-Cola warehouse in an unlovely industrial zone of Jackson, Mississippi. It wasn't exactly Stax or Fame, but I'd come to meet the men who ran Malaco Records – and to find out how they'd carved out the canny commercial niche that was the label's sound. Tommy Couch, Wolf Stephenson and Stewart Madison turned out to be the best kind of white southerners: amiable, amusing, loquacious. I liked hearing them talk about Ole Miss and Mississippi Fred McDowell.

Best of all was the story of how – almost by accident – Couch and Stephenson had stumbled on the formula that gave Malaco its winning streak: a cheaply recorded album by veteran Z.Z. Hill that included 'Down Home Blues' (1981) and enabled them to sign such fellow soul survivors as Johnnie Taylor and Denise LaSalle. "The success of that record attracted other artists," Stephenson told me that grey fall morning. "They were people who'd been out there and been well-known, but had absolutely no place to get a record out." Said Madison, the label's financial director: "We just happened to take a chance with what we liked. We didn't understand disco, so we didn't *do* disco."

That year, 1985, Malaco's passion for old-school R&B came full circle with the signing of Bobby "Blue" Bland, the king of the southern blues ballad, as seminal a figure in the genesis of soul music as Ray Charles or Sam Cooke or James Brown. Bland's 1962 classic *Two Steps From The Blues* had been the first album Couch ever bought. Now, almost a quarter century later, he had this heavyweight champ on his own label. Moreover, Bland's Malaco debut followed in the footsteps of Hill and Taylor and sold by the truckload to a hitherto-forgotten market of middle-aged African-Americans that had long idolised him.

Bland's signing to Malaco had more than a little to do with the label's legendary septuagenarian promo man, Dave Clark, who'd seen him singing in his native Tennessee long before he'd become part of the loose Memphis aggregation known as the Beale Streeters. Clark knew the veteran singer was miserable at MCA, an impersonal corporation that had swallowed up ABC-Dunhill – which in turn had swallowed up the Duke-Peacock stable where Bland enjoyed his long streak of great R&B hits through the Sixties. He telephoned the big man known as "the Lion of the Blues" and put out feelers. "When ABC got put over to MCA, I got kind of put on the shelf," Bland told me when Couch brought a Malaco live revue over to London in the summer of 1989. "They weren't behind me, and I thought it was best for me to make a move as soon as possible. Dave was a friend of mine and we had worked together for a lot of years. He called and asked if I had a record company. I said, 'No.' He said, 'Are you *thinking* about a record company?' I said, 'No.' So he said, 'Well, how about coming to Malaco?' So I said, 'Okay, Dave, let's give it a shot.' And so here I am. And Malaco has been very nice."

When he performed that night in Hammersmith, Bland's voice was undiminished in its power and its subtlety. He sang his classic Duke hits – 'Further Up The Road', 'Turn On Your Love Light', 'I'll Take Care Of You', 'Stormy Monday', 'That's The Way Love Is', 'Ain't Nothing You Can Do' and more – along with some of his new Malaco material. All of it made the hairs stand up on one's neck. It also made the point that he'd never sounded like anybody else on earth – and that, despite Greil Marcus calling him "the most sensitive and original blues singer of the last 40 years", he was never really a blues singer in the first place. "I would not like to be classified as just a blues singer, because I do a variety of lyrics on the ballad side," he told Charles Shaar Murray in 1982. "In my early days I did the harsh blues kind of thing, but I really wanted to do the softer stuff." He went on to claim that his biggest influences were not just Billy Eckstine and Brook Benton – and Nat "King" Cole, naturally – but Andy Williams, Tony Bennett and even Perry Como ("because he shows no strain whatsoever when he's doing a song"). Though he covered Z.Z. Hill's 'I'm A Blues Man' – referring in the lyric to Hill, who'd passed away in 1984 – his voice had as much to do with the precision of a Como as with the fervour of the Reverend C.L. Franklin, whose gargled roar he'd incorporated into his delivery. "He is a screamer without being a shouter," wrote jazz critic Gary Giddins; "always in control and never crackling into a desperate B.B. King yell." So unusual was the combination of delicate diction and cavernous timbre in his larynx that some of his early employers advised him to give up singing altogether and return to the cotton fields of Tennessee.

If you listen to the vast body of tracks Bland recorded in the Sixties with mentor-producer Joe Scott – tracks adorned and sometimes saturated by brass and strings – the prevailing mood is closer to cabaret than to juke joint. "It was the brass that gave me a kind of an identity," he told Peter Guralnick in 1975. "Joe liked the trumpets, you know, same as I have now." Unlike many of his peers, Bland was singing better in his late fifties than he'd sung in his early thirties. "The voice is mellower and much richer and quite settled," he told me on that London visit. "I try very hard to get the point over strongly with what I do now. I think a lot more when I'm singing than I would if I was 25 or what have you, because I don't have to worry about how the voice actually would be. Now all I have to concentrate on is how much sleep I should get – or would love to get. Overall I feel pretty good singing now."

For Bland, Malaco was a retro dream come true. If the production was slicker than it had been in the Sixties, the material and the approach to the music put him straight back in his blues-ballad comfort zone. On *His California Album* (1973) and *Dreamer* (1974), ABC-Dunhill had updated the Bland style to make it more accessible to a white audience – Whitesnake even scored a heavy-metal hit in 1978 with his 'Ain't No Love In The Heart Of The City' – but Malaco went straight for the Black vote by reviving the southern-soul template of the Sixties and early Seventies. "I think our sound still has that flavour of early Chips Moman in Memphis, or Rick Hall at Fame," Couch told me. "The sound is technically better today, everything is a little more sophisticated, but that's still what we do best." Augmenting a pool of musicians from Mississippi and Muscle Shoals – Malaco had recently acquired the Muscle Shoals Sound studio and catalogue – was a stable of songwriters old and new. From Larry Addison – former keyboard player with Jackson funksters Freedom – came the warmly consoling 'Members Only' and the mellow ballad 'After All'. Memphis legend George Jackson contributed the superb tearjerkers 'Second Hand Heart' and 'Heart Open Up Again'. And local boy Tommy Tate delivered the slinky, indignant funk of 'Get Your Money Where You Spend Your Time'.

In subsequent years, Bland tackled beauties like 'I Just Tripped On A Piece of Your Broken Heart' – a magnificent song by Frederick ('I've Been Lonely For So Long') Knight that summoned the haunted blues-rock mood of Bland's ABC-Dunhill period – and the Mosley & Johnson songs 'I Just Can't Be Your Fool Anymore' and 'The Truth Will Set You Free', blues ballad throwbacks to his vintage Duke years. Additionally, he covered such classics as Little Willie John's 'I Need Your Love So Bad', Bill Withers' 'Ain't No Sunshine' and Rod Stewart's 'Tonight's The Night', all but making them his own in the process. Together these tracks give us a towering vocal artist in the third wind of his career, an astounding singer resurrected by a sympathetic team that worshipped him and knew precisely where to find his fan base. Bland has never wanted for fans – Van Morrison has long championed him, and Simply Red's Mick Hucknall recorded a whole album of covers on 2008's *Tribute To Bobby* – but it took Malaco to give his career the traction it needed through the Eighties and Nineties.

"They knew about me before I ever got there," Bland told me as he sat on the bed, weary but contented, in his London hotel room. "Wolf and Tommy had started out as fans of mine as young boys. They were kind of waiting on me."

Malaco Records, 2010

4 In A Cold Sweat
James Brown

Album bought in London in 1974

JAMES BROWN'S road manager takes me to one side and places a friendly paw on my forearm. "Please," Charles Bobbitt says. "Can you make sure to ask Mr Brown about his turkey giveaway." His what? "Every Thanksgiving, Mr Brown gives away turkeys to raise money for kids. Be great if you could axe him about that." You want me to ask James Brown about turkeys. "Yessir. If that's okay." Let me see if I can work in a question on that crucial subject. "Be appreciated. And 30 minutes, please, if you don't mind." How many of those minutes should be spent talking turkey? "Many as you like."

Here I am in a suite at the swanky Mandarin Oriental Hotel in twinkling Christmassy Knightsbridge, thousands of miles from the red dirt and collard greens of James Brown's native Georgia. The room is full of what I'm tempted to call "lackeys" – the entourage that always accompanies the godfather of soul, the emperor of funk, the icon of processed hair and blindingly white teeth. Actually, the entourage consists of about four men, including the tall and droll owner of Entrée Music – Brown's new home – but it feels unnecessarily intimidating. Why do I feel like I'm being granted an audience with Saddam Hussein?

Encircled by the lackeys, Brown sits alone on the sofa. He retains the stocky, compact physique of a man half his 70 years. His body language suggests the steely impenetrability of a Third World dictator. His words pour forth in a chewy, consonant-free flow of rural dialect, often hard to decipher. Even deciphered, they don't always make sense. We've barely begun talking when he berates photographer Tom Sheehan. "There's only certain kinda pitchers you can shoot," he grunts. "You can shoot here… and here. You can't get round *here*, and you can't get round *here*. This way, and *this* way. Can't git on the side." Tom doesn't git on the side.

IN THE AGE of 50 Cent, it's difficult to imagine – or even recall – what Brown represented as an African-American entertainer from the mid-Fifties to the mid-Seventies. At the peak of his success in the late Sixties, he came as close to being an unofficial Black president as anyone ever has. The self-proclaimed "Hardest Working Man In Show Business", Brown dragged himself up by his bootstraps in juke-joint Georgia, willing himself to power like a Nietzschean *ubermensch*. Built like a pit bull, with a preacher's scream that seared the eardrums, JB was the generalissimo of soul, drilling his Famous Flames like paramilitaries. He wasn't sexy, but he was an astonishing showman, his live performances working audiences into states of hysteria. The form was urban R&B, but the feel was raw country gospel. 1962's *Live At The Apollo, Volume 1* is the most thrilling live album ever recorded.

In 1965, with the revolutionary 'Papa's Got A Brand New Bag', James Brown invented funk. Stumbling on THE ONE, with the first rhythmic accent hitting at the start of the bar, he spent the next ten years honing the greatest grooves ever laid down on tape: 'Cold Sweat', 'Mother Popcorn', 'Sex Machine', 'Get Up Offa That Thing' and more. A kind of regimented sensuality – a *sex machinery* – funk was the door through which everybody from George Clinton to Prince to Chuck D would subsequently stampede. "Gospel always had The One," Brown says, "but it became more dominant once I clarified it. You go to church now, you hear more James Brown than you do in the dance halls. Because it's a way of life. We put our foot down, we lead off with the left foot most times – that's what soldiers and everybody do – and go from left to right, left to right, and we try to put it down solid each time."

Isn't funk basically about sex? "Well, a church is not made on sex, but if you don't release that tension you *will* be a crazy person. 'Get up offa that thing and try to release that pressure!' Funk is a routine. Country is great for certain people, or opera is great for certain people, but everybody wants to hear 'Sex Machine' or 'I Feel Good', so thank God." Behind his beats and bull-headed machismo, though, lay deep childhood wounds he never properly acknowledged. Abandoned by his mother when he was four, and more or less ignored by his father thereafter, "Little Junior" became – by his own admission – a delinquent thug. At 16 years old he was banged up in Georgia's Alto Penitentiary. "It was survival," he bluntly states. "You try to stay on top. If you burn, you try to get out of the fire and move some other place. There is no laws against saving your life. First save your life. Justifiable homicide or whatever. You gotta save your life, and that's basically what it's been."

In recent years, Brown has battled further odds – addiction to angel dust, a second jail term, the death of his wife Adrienne after plastic surgery – and again come through the storm. "We've fought it for many years," he says in a dry rasp. "Just about the time we say, 'Hey, we've done all we can', then here come a group o' people that build you back up and you'll go again. And then, later on, another group comes. Right now we been dealt a good hand. We're with the past, which is not the future. We're with the future, which is now going back to the past – they wanna see they've missed. So it all makes one family, you know? We're going and coming."

Brown's survival hasn't come without a toll. Shut down emotionally, he virtually terrorised his musicians for decades. Bobby Byrd, his right-hand man for years, says Brown "*had* to be in control". Head horn man Fred Wesley notes that Brown could never lose an argument. And in the recent documentary *Soul Survivor*, singer Lynn Collins says of Brown that "there was an anger on that stage that was not understood". (Collins also recalls a telephone hotline to her home whose purpose was to monitor her every movement. The house, she claims, "was like a little prison".) "I always refer to him as a sergeant or something," Brown's personal hairdresser Henry Stallings told writer Gerri Hirshey. "He's a man who can't show weakness to a lot of people who work under him. I know he feels things, but he never shows it. Maybe he goes behind closed doors and breaks down, but I never seen it."

"I stand behind my regimen," Mr Brown tells me coldly. "We do everything we can to protect the musicians, but I'm a firm person and I will fire my daddy. My daddy was working for me one time, and he didn't show like he shoulda. I fired my father. When I finished I said, 'Daddy, is there anything I can give you?' I fired my first cousin, who raised with me like a brother. A family that don't listen to the dad and do the right thing, you got a little problem. When you start listening to mom *and* dad and not knowing who to follow and what decision to take, it becomes a problem." Brown doesn't notice the obvious contradiction here – he's just described how he fired his own father – but I let it slide. My sense is that he's spent his entire life using "discipline" to cover up his hurt. Former road manager Alan Leeds, one of the precious few JB insiders to tell it like it is, says in *Soul Survivor* that his old boss has never been able to trust another human being. When I ask if this is true, Brown answers with an emphatic and unhesitating yes. "In the Biblical words," he says, "our currency in America has got 'In God We Trust' on every bill. All the rest we check. And that's what it's about." He points at the president of Entrée Music. "This man and I work together, but he has to look at my papers and I have to look at his papers. We don't know what his people might have done, and or what *my* people might have done." Does James Brown even trust in *God*? "That's all I had, all along. As you get older, you know more why you should trust in him. When you're younger, you trust your parents. You don't call God, you call 'Momma!' and 'Daddy!'" But, I point out, you didn't have a mom or dad to call. "No… not all the time I didn't. But my daddy stayed as long as he could." An awkward pause follows.

I ask Brown if, despite his extrovert exterior as a performer, he's actually quite a shy and vulnerable man. "Uh, shy… yeah, shy. Because you can't say all the time what you know, and you can't *do* what you can do all the time. Sometime you have to hold back a little, like a horse on a trot. You turn him loose, he might give out, so you hold him back and let him maintain at a certain point." Is he a typical Taurean? "If God had made me a Pisces or Capricorn or Aries or whatever, I'd have wanted to get ahead and do better. But now, according to the thing, I *am* a Taurus. I'm a hard Taurus. And I made a mistake in marrying a Taurus woman. Half my age. And Leo is my rising sign."

Did white America demonise the Black energy he represented because it was too threatening? "Well, I defined what they were calling truth into a lie. Because I was looking at it every day. But I didn't *call* nobody a liar. I just kept raising the questions. And then when the country needed me, I was there. And I'm always there when it needs me, whether it's poor families or something I can do for the government or the schools."

Didn't the government in the Seventies, via the IRS, try to stop him in his tracks? "Oh, yes. I mean, why would you investigate a man like me? They sent me a letter one time for tax evasion, so I wrote a letter back to President Jimmy Carter, who I knew very well, and I said, 'Mr President, you've seen my work and you know what I do.' And I said, 'You cannot charge a man with tax evasion unless there's intent. Since I don't have an education beyond the seventh grade, there's not enough knowledge for there to be intent.'"

Does he think that the long-term legacy of slavery – which surely underpins the ongoing racial tensions in America – will ever heal? "Well, it has to be healed if you're religious. Those people that are not religious are not gonna heal. But the religious people gonna heal, because they even wanna turn the other cheek. They like to find a solution to where we go from here. And you're not going any place until you forget the past." Really? Aren't those who forget the past condemned, in Santayana's famous phrase, to repeat it? "Well, sometime I be out with my wife and I think about something I don't like that she did a long time ago, and I'll mention that. And that's *not* gonna heal up the future. You gotta leave the past behind. If we hadn't have been able to be in show business, we would've been hating the system and hating the people that run it. But when you get into it and you start to find out there *is* a way out… I just don't like to see big people blocking *little* people from using the bridge to get over. There *is* a bridge there."

THE NIGHT before the interview, I watched James Brown and band tape a live performance in a church on London's Old Street. I tell him I couldn't help notice there were maybe five Black faces in the whole joint. "Well, when you got a lot of musicians on the road and you gotta pay 'em all, the price gotta go up. And who can pay the price? The white kids. Blacks can't pay. We do a lotta things free now to make sure the Black kids can see it. We play the Apollo Theatre and we'll play in the middle of the street, in the wind and the rain." I don't tell Mr Brown what I really thought of his show, which was that it was a hackneyed, anachronistic ritual: horn men in cummerbunds, earth-mama backing singers, the inevitable dorky white guitarist. I do ask if he'd ever consider making a hip, stripped-down album like Johnny Cash's *American Recordings* or Solomon Burke's *Don't Give Up On Me*. "Well, I don't mind that, but I wouldn't imitate or emulate somebody. I wouldn't get no concept from nobody, unless God told me to go out and get the people, like with Paul Simon in South Africa. I have done my music and God's given me the insight. I think Solomon is preaching, I believe. He's a minister. There is one album that I intend to do. There's a couple of people I'd like to use. Bobby Byrd is one of the people. There's some other musicians I'd like to sit down with and cut an album entitled *In The Beginning*. That's an album that would be real – more real than what we're doin' now. I'm makin' sure the words come out kinda clear, but there is another voice of James Brown."

What did he think of P-Funk, to whom Famous Flames "Bootsy" and "Catfish" Collins defected in 1971? "Well, I took the invisible lift that God gave me. Other people take the elevator. God showed me something and I was almost in mid-air, levitating, because I had to find a way out. So P-Funk was good for Bootsy and George Clinton, like what Mick Jagger plays is good for him. But all those fellows learned from me, Bootsy and all of 'em. So we know what it is."

What does he think of fellow Georgia scions OutKast, arguably inheritors of the P-Funk mantle? "I admire 'em for trying to make it, and for their concepts. What they do and when they do it is not my concern, it's not my call. I do see the young Caucasian kids getting heavy into funk, and I see the Black people getting washed up because of the fact that they don't have the facilities and the right representation."

Is it still a man's, man's, man's world, or are relations between men and women very different today? "Oh, different. But it's still a man's world." *Should* it be? "God made man first. See, the thing is that man is indispensable right now, because you got a hundred women to one man. They gonna lock us up and use us when they need us, like we did to them."

Has he ever changed his son's diaper? "Haven't changed it yet but I will."

Oops. I never did ask about those turkeys.

Uncut, 2004

5 Music Of His Mind
Stevie Wonder

Album bought in Sudbury, Suffolk, in 1973

KOREATOWN IS hushed and still in the small hours of Saturday morning. The odd vehicle rattles along Western Avenue, but most of the Friday night clubbers have dispersed and headed home. "Little Seoul", if one can call it that, is slowing down. Unbeknownst to the few locals still awake, though, the legend once known as Little Stevie Wonder is hard at work in the studio that sits slap-bang in the midst of this improbable neighbourhood, where few signs or billboards are in English. The blind genius who recorded at least five of the most remarkable albums in the history of American music is rounding off another night behind the massive SSL console of Wonderland, putting finishing touches to a track from his forthcoming *A Time 2 Love*.

Stevie Wonder at work is everything you might imagine, or hope for. His head sways from side to side as he mumbles melodiously along to 'Please Don't Hurt My Baby', the track he's working on tonight. The famous gums of his open smiling mouth show above his upper teeth. His braided hair is bunched behind him, tiny seashells dangling at its ends. He's dressed entirely in black that matches his sunglasses. A TV monitor above the console displays a group of women wearing denim and cornrows, standing around a microphone lowered from the ceiling. The most senior of them, Shirley Brewer, has sung with Wonder since 1972's *Talking Book*; hers is the hollering voice that comes in halfway through 'Ordinary Pain', from his 1976 masterpiece *Songs In The Key Of Life*. Like the others, she is trying to master a tricky vocal line that involves compressing ten syllables into approximately two seconds. Wonder makes the women repeat the line again and again – not like some punishing tyrant, merely like a producer who hears each misplaced micro-nuance and needs to hear it done right. He demonstrates it to them once again, semi-scatting the line into their headphones. Eventually they get it down, sensuously purring the line *"Before you were usin' it like a toy"* in a way that makes all too plain what "it" is. Wonder is like a kid brother around these women. It's not difficult to imagine the 12-year-old Stevie on the buses that took the famed Motown Revue around America in the early Sixties – the pint-sized japester who'd steal up behind Diana Ross and pinch her petite *derriere*. He strolls over to one of the singers and extracts a packet of Frito-Lays from her pocket. Before inserting one into his mouth he lifts it to his nose. *"Oooh, smell like dirty feet,"* he says in the voice of a Mississippi cotton-picker. *"Smell like Uncle Charlie's feets…"* The ladies squeal with delighted displeasure. He repeats the phrase several more times and then gobbles down the Frito-Lay.

Wonderland is a hermetic haven of a studio. The family of employees he has created around him makes for an atmosphere that's insular but always friendly. Even the security guys are teddy bears. Laughs come thick and fast here, and one of the most infectious belongs to Nathan Watts, who's played with Wonder for 30 years. "I should be in *The Guinness Book Of Records* for longest-serving bass player," he says. It's Watts' birthday today, which is why he's hanging around long after his services were last required, putting off the long drive back to his home in Chino Hills. Stephanie Andrews, the president of Stevie's production company, is also sitting in tonight. A tiny woman with a pretty, light-skinned face, she has bought an ice-cream birthday cake for Watts, whose cuddly physique – squeezed into a pair of high-waisted denim shorts – suggests such treats aren't strangers to his diet. Wonder himself packs a fair paunch under his loose shirt as he emerges to join the impromptu party, which inevitably entails the rendition of 'Happy Birthday', his jubilant 1980 tribute to assassinated civil rights leader Martin

Luther King. When the cake has been devoured, Wonder challenges one of the singers to a game of air hockey on a table that sits in the studio's main recreation room. Despite not being able to see the plastic puck, he repeatedly wins the game, demonstrating what he would doubtless call his Taurean need to triumph at all costs. Then it's time to go back to work. "We're trying to stay in the realm of getting things happening at a reasonable time of day," he replies when asked if his sessions always run this late. "Sometimes we do work long hours, but very rarely do we work and sleep here for a whole week."

It turns out that music has reverberated inside these walls for several decades. Back in the Forties, Wonderland was McGregor's, a studio used by Benny Goodman, Nat "King" Cole and others. The interior of the building is like something out of Polanski's *Chinatown*, all wooden panels and intricate tiling. When you wander round the back of the studio, outside the bubble-like chamber of the control room, you stumble on relics from Wonder's own past. Standing alone and somewhat neglected is the original Moog he used on *Music Of My Mind*, *Talking Book* and *Innervisions*. Around the corner from that magnificent creature, and draped in black cloth, is the Yamaha "Dream Machine" he used on *Songs In The Key Of Life*. At the risk of fetishising technology, I feel a certain awe in beholding these outmoded dinosaurs. So significant was the role Moog and Yamaha played in the radical brilliance of Wonder's run of masterpieces from *Music* (1972) to *Songs* (1976) that one feels like prostrating oneself before such superannuated devices. "I'm always intrigued by his orchestral use of synthesisers," said jazz giant Herbie Hancock, who played on *Songs In The Key Of Life*'s impassioned track 'As'. "He lets them be what they are – something that's not acoustic." Listening to the almost classical arrangements of songs such as 'Pastime Paradise' and 'Village Ghetto Land', one knows what Hancock meant: it's as if Wonder is celebrating the very artifice of synthetic sound. "I think everything has its own character," he says. "Even in sampling strings, a keyboard player cannot really play like a string player. You can have various samples at various places on the keyboard to accentuate a feel and give you a sense of that, but the whole purpose of me using synthesisers was to make a statement and to express myself musically – to come as close as possible to what those instruments could do, but also to express how I would allow those things to sound."

His discovery of electronics was just part of the extraordinary burst of creativity that flowered when he came of age in 1971, ten years after signing as a pint-sized prodigy to Berry Gordy's emerging Motown label. In a frenetic four-year run, he left "Little Stevie" behind and became one of the towering artists of the new decade. Imagine Black American music without 'Superwoman', 'Superstition', 'Too High', 'Living for the City', 'Higher Ground', 'You Haven't Done Nothin'', 'I Wish', 'Sir Duke' or 'Pastime Paradise'. Or without 'Blame It On the Sun', 'He's Misstra Know-It-All', 'They Won't Go When I Go', 'Knocks Me Off My Feet', 'Joy Inside My Tears'. This is a concentrated body of work that stands alongside the best of the Beatles or Brian Wilson, and frequently eclipses even them. It's also a body of work in whose shadow Wonder has lived ever since. The question in 2005 is, will he ever emerge from it?

EVEN AS A KID, Wonder was hailed as a genius. Brought to Motown's Hitsville USA offices in Detroit by the Miracles' Ronnie White, he astonished not only Berry Gordy but everyone within hearing distance. "I think his mother was with him, and a couple of brothers," the Supremes' Mary Wilson told Gerri Hirshey. "He's just a typical ten-year-old, comes running in, so Berry says, 'Can you play this instrument?' So he played the piano. He played the organ. He played the drums, the congas. He played everything there. And Berry said, 'You are signed'."

The word "genius" had earlier been applied to Ray Charles, to whom Wonder's second album, released in 1962, was a tribute. Perhaps the blindness the two artists had in common made their talent seem all the more mysterious. Certainly it seemed to heighten their aural awareness, as well as their willingness to create musical hybrids out of supposedly incompatible genres. Incredibly, Wonder didn't know that Charles suffered from the same affliction. "It was only when I was 11 and I recorded *Tribute To Uncle Ray* that I found out he was blind," he confesses. "When I met him, it was a wonderful moment. I think it was at the Ford Auditorium, or maybe the Masonic Temple. He came out of his dressing room, and some people were leading him over to me. He was kind of laughing and jumping up and down a little bit. And I presented him with the album, and he said, 'Keep on doing what you're doing, young man'. And his drummer gave me a pair of drumsticks. I was so happy."

The spectacle of Little Stevie performing his 1963 No. 1 hit 'Fingertips – Pt. 2' – all grinning gums, glinting Ray-Bans and outsize harmonica – inevitably recalled the untrammelled spontaneity of Brother Ray. Uninhibited by visual awareness of their audiences, both singers communicated a kind of ingenuous joy, losing themselves in their grooves. If there was about him a touch of the circus-freak, or what Robert Christgau once termed the "sainted fool", the boy's talent was no sleight-of-hand. Much of his exuberant confidence stemmed from the self-belief instilled in him by his mother, Lula Mae Hardaway; unlike Charles, Stevie would never struggle with drug addiction. Born prematurely on May 13, 1950, in Saginaw, Michigan, Stevland Judkins' blindness was the result of being given an excess of oxygen in his incubator. At three, he moved with his half-sister and four half-brothers to east Detroit. His father he barely knew, not unusual in the 25th/26th Street neighbourhood where he was raised. Never having experienced sight, Wonder says he didn't know what he was missing. "I didn't really understand the severity of the circumstances," he says. "I think I was so in love with my mother and my brothers and my sister and my friends that my focus was not on those things." Cocooned by his family's love, Wonder didn't register issues such as racism until later in childhood. "I discovered the whole thing of colour when my grandmother passed away in Mobile, Alabama. There were some kids that lived nearby that shouted, 'Hey, nigger!' And I remember going, 'What?? I'm from Detroit!!' And I started throwing rocks, and I hit one of them and he ran and told his mother. The thing is, I have never accepted stupidity and ignorance in determining how good I was. If some kid taunted me by saying, 'Oh stinky blind boy, you're a stinky blind boy', I knew I was blind, but I knew I wasn't stinky."

A relationship with God was another constant from the earliest time he can remember, making up for the painful absence of his father. "I always felt God was next to me and had me in his arms," he says. "And so, whether it was a time when my mother and father weren't together anymore or whatever it was, I was really cool because I had my father who was greater than all fathers." Frowned-on at the local Whitestone Baptist Church for singing secular songs, Wonder knew he wasn't doing anything wrong. "I felt that if God didn't want me to sing that music, he wouldn't have given me the talent to do it. If he didn't want me to know the difference between right and wrong, he wouldn't have given me a mother and people that loved me and nurtured me." At nine, the boy had already mastered the harmonica given to him by a family friend. The instrument has remained a signature of his career, more akin to a saxophone in the jazzy, virtuoso use he's made of it than to a mere punctuating voice. But he could also play the little drum kit purchased for him by the local Lions businessman's association. Meanwhile his ears were wide open to music of every description: R&B, pop, jazz, even classical. "I listened to jazz stations, classical stations, even *Polish* stations. I was just curious. I didn't limit myself. It could be Motown or it could be

Neil Sedaka. It could be Charlie Parker or it could be John Coltrane." By 1964, when he made incongruous appearances in the inane teen movies *Bikini Beach* and *Muscle Beach Party*, Wonder's ears were open even wider. The sounds of Bob Dylan and the Beatles seeped in alongside Burt Bacharach's productions for Chuck Jackson and Dionne Warwick. Already melody was a source of almost hypnotic fascination. "Melodies are like angels from heaven," he says. "They express a place for the heart to follow."

It took almost three years to follow up the success of the live 'Fingertips – Pt. 2'. Certain Motown personnel had written him off as a child-star novelty, but not songwriter Sylvia Moy. Along with fellow staffers Hank Cosby and Clarence Paul – Wonder's personal musical director – Moy knew the well was far from dry. Late in 1965 she coaxed the stomping 'Uptight (Everything's Alright)' out of the 15-year-old. The song reached No. 3. A stream of minor Motown classics – 'A Place In The Sun', 'I Was Made To Love Her', 'Shoo-Be-Doo-Be-Doo-Da-Day', 'For Once In My Life', 'My Cherie Amour', 'Yester-Me, Yester-You, Yesterday' – gushed out of him in a four-year period, all Top 10 pop hits, most of them R&B No. 1s. For the most part, he took the success in his stride. Occasionally it was difficult to juggle his career with his ongoing education. "There was anxiety sometimes. Clarence made sure I stayed in line. Really, everyone was cool. Obviously they allowed me to discover certain things at the right age. I would not change anything about my life at that time. Every single one of those people played a significant part in wherever I am now." Yet he felt frustrated by the Motown conveyor-belt. While Gordy wanted to keep him forever young, frozen in a state of chirpy innocence, "Little Stevie" was growing up fast, discovering sex and tuning into the political tensions of the late Sixties. The discrepancy between Motown's Black-capitalist ethos and the turmoil on the streets of Detroit – in whose 1967 race riots 43 people died – was tough on the label's artists. In that year, Wonder got to shake the hand of Martin Luther King in Chicago's Comiskey Park. A year later, King was gunned down in Memphis.

On the radio, Wonder heard the new sounds of Black pride. Chicago's own Curtis Mayfield was just one of the songwriters taking soul to a higher political ground. "He was speaking from a sense of pride, a sense of self-respect," Wonder says. "He was one of those very special writers like Bob Marley and Bob Dylan and John Lennon and Smokey Robinson." (Wonder himself covered – and had a 1966 hit with – Dylan's civil-rights staple 'Blowin' In The Wind'.) If Clarence Paul's replacement Gene Kees saw Stevie as the new Sammy Davis, Jr., the sometime *wunderkind* had other ideas. Aware that at 21 he would come into the money that Motown had held in trust for him, he also knew he would be free to renegotiate the contract he'd signed in 1961. To his credit, Kees steered him the right direction. "I decided I didn't want to live my life in the fashion that was predictable to Motown at that time," Wonder says. "Gene went with me to New York and helped me to meet with different lawyers and record companies. He always encouraged me to do better and reach further." In New York, Wonder was introduced to lawyer Johanan Vigoda. "He was a prosecutor for a long time, and he had a very hard edge," says Stevie. "I said to him, 'Johanan, I'll do great music and you do great contracts, and we'll work it out.'"

The morning after Gordy threw a 21st birthday party for his prodigy, a brusque communication from Vigoda dropped on to Gordy's desk. It stated that Wonder's recording and publishing contracts were null and void. A new deal gave him a handsome advance, as well as unprecedented control of his musical future. "Berry and I have always had a very straight-to-the-point relationship," Wonder has said, perhaps explaining how he secured the favourable terms that eluded labelmates like Marvin Gaye. "I can't compare the relationship I had with Berry to the relationship Marvin had with him," he says. "As to what should have happened with some of those artists and some of those deals, we can go all day talking about, you know, 'They should have had better representation'. But that goes way back in the day. It's not just Motown. You can talk about Black artists, you can talk about some of the rockabilly people. They didn't have great representation either, and they ended up with little or nothing. At some point you have to take responsibility for yourself."

Wonder's willingness to take that responsibility was evident on 1971's *Where I'm Coming From,* an album entirely self-produced and co-written with his new wife Syreeta Wright. But he took things a significant step further with the decision to leave Detroit for New York, a city whose febrile energy electrified him. "I liked it a lot," he says. "It was not so far from Detroit, but it was not so close. It just felt right." Moving into the Holiday Inn on West 57th Street, he began planning an album unlike anything he or any other Motown act had recorded: a collection of songs written, arranged and performed almost entirely by the artist himself. *Music Of My Mind* would cement the legend of Wonder the autonomous genius, with the recording studio as an extension of his almost solipsistic mind. As the album sleeve put it, "the man is his own instrument/the instrument is an orchestra". Crucial to the brilliance of *Music Of My Mind* was his collaboration with Robert Margouleff and Malcolm Cecil of electronic group Tonto's Expanding Head

Band. An early devotee of Walter [Wendy] Carlos' 1968 album *Switched-On Bach*, he was already smitten with the potential of synths to create new textures for post-Sixties soul. Now he studied Tonto's 1971 album *Zero Time* and arranged to meet the duo. "The technology was happening," he says. "I'd seen a Moog, but I really didn't know how powerful it was until I met Bob and Malcolm."

Investing almost $250,000 in studio time at Manhattan's Electric Lady studios, he began the intensive bout of recording that produced his greatest music. With Margouleff and Cecil, he would regularly work 48-hour shifts, breaking for three or four hours' sleep when his body could take no more. And all this without drugs. Like Marvin Gaye with *What's Going On* – and Sly Stone with *There's A Riot Goin' On*, come to that – he had a new sense of what the standard "long-player" could be. Where Motown had always been primarily about singles, now the label's bolder artists were upping the creative ante. Significantly, *Music Of My Mind* did not include a hit single. "Obviously I was tremendously impressed by *Sgt. Pepper*," he says. "To me, that was an incredible work. I was also impressed by Sly & the Family Stone's albums. I felt, wow, they were having fun and it was a journey. It was an experience, and they were all good songs. Same with *Hot Buttered Soul* by Isaac Hayes." Wonder's new mature style was defined by the eight-minute 'Superwoman', its soft sensuality and melodic complexity a template for the intimate, intricate sound of both *Talking Book* and *Innervisions*. "A lot of it had to do with the engineering and the interpretation of what I was doing," he says. "My voice would be very close to the microphone. It was just the sound of me and the piano, starting off almost like a demo and then building on that." What really set him apart from soul's other singer-songwriters was the jazziness of his chords and vocal lines, a feel only enhanced by the fluid funk of his Moog and ARP fills. "I've always been a lover of jazz," he says. "Using chords that are considered abstract: raised ninths, flatted fifths, major sevenths, all those different chord structures. I learned to play [Coltrane's] 'Giant Steps', but for a long time I just couldn't get it. Finally I got it and I thought, 'I'm one o' the cats now, baby!' I always had that spirit of wanting to know and discover."

When *Talking Book* followed on *Music*'s heels, Wonder silenced any remaining disbelievers – at Motown or elsewhere. The album was simply a *tour de force* of clavinet-driven funk ('Superstition', 'Maybe Your Baby'), bittersweet balladry ('Blame It On The Sun'), and shimmering Latin inflections ('You've Got It Bad, Girl' and 'Lookin' For Another Pure Love', the latter boasting an exquisitely lyrical solo by a visiting Jeff Beck). "Different emotions happen at different times," he says of the album's emotional range. "You feel moments of passion in a tender way and moments of passion in a way that's like 'Let's hit it'. Some days are very mellow, some days are a little crazy, and that's the same with music." His new status as a self-contained auteur, with Motown's "Quality Control Panel" squarely behind him, was underscored when the Rolling Stones invited him to be the support act for their 1972 American tour. As uncomfortable as he was with the band's debauchery, he was happy to climax each show by joining them for encores of 'Uptight' and 'Satisfaction'. By the tour's end, he had officially crossed over to a white rock audience.

1973 brought the release of the album he believes to be his best. *Innervisions* was *Talking Book* through a socio-political lens, exemplified by the spacey narcosis of 'Too High', the urgent sermonising of 'Higher Ground' and the pounding, storyboarded 'Living For The City'. This was Wonder grappling with urban poverty, pushing hope through Jesus and TM, perceiving things only the blind could see. For those who found the Big Apple nightmare of 'Living For The City' too blaxploitative, the honeyed melodies of 'Golden Lady' and 'He's Misstra Know-It-All' were more than a sop. *Innervisions* was a sublime journey through his kaleidoscopic mind. "It was a snapshot of a certain part of the reality of life," he reflects. "'Living For The City' was very real for certain people, but 'Don't You Worry 'Bout A Thing' was fun. 'Higher Ground' was a place of hope." *Innervisions* was very nearly Wonder's last recorded testament. On August 6, 1973, while en route to a benefit show in Durham, North Carolina, a log detached itself from a truck and smashed through the windshield of the vehicle in which he was travelling. The log hit him in the head, putting him in a coma for a week and causing him to re-evaluate his entire existence when he came out of it. "The only thing I know is that I was unconscious," he recalled, "and that for a few days I was definitely in a much better spiritual place that made me aware of a lot of things that concern my life and my future and what I have to do to reach another higher ground." The seeds of his political and charitable work in the following decade were planted here.

1974's tongue-twistingly titled *Fulfillingness' First Finale* – unfairly disparaged as a disappointment after *Innervisions* – was the first of Wonder's albums to top *Billboard*'s pop chart. Its title made plain a sense of summation. '*Fulfillingness*' was just me working the word," he told *Billboard* last December. "The idea of fulfilling is like a female. The other part of that title, the 'First Finale', was sort of referencing an ending of the period after *Music Of My Mind* and these three albums." As Craig Werner wrote in

A Change Is Gonna Come: Music, Race And The Soul Of America, the album's Jackson-5-backed single 'You Haven't Done Nothin'' was arguably "the most explicit statement of Black anger ever to reach No. 1". If *Fulfillingness'* other highlights soft-peddled Wonder's politics, there were pleasures both slight ('Smile Please', the cod-Jamaican 'Boogie On Reggae Woman') and profound ('Creepin'', the mournful 'They Won't Go When I Go') on the album. "I think it was a good record," he says. "I don't know if it was equal to *Innervisions*, to be honest with you. It was just different."

For Wonder, *Songs In The Key Of Life* – two years in the making – was "like the beginning of another kind of place". The double-album set, released in the hot summer of 1976, was a banquet of ghetto funk, soulful pop and luscious Black MOR. Sly met Mozart, and Ellington met Bacharach as *Songs* ranged over not just four rollercoaster sides but a bonus EP to boot. From ebullient pop-funk (the nostalgic 'I Wish') to chamber-soul lamentation ('Village Ghetto Land', the Coolio-sampled 'Pastime Paradise'); from jazz ('Sir Duke') to jazz-rock ('Contusion'); from the stately, aching 'Joy Inside My Tears' to the righteous litany of minority American heroes that was 'Black Man'; few were the moods and forms Wonder didn't master on this sprawling epic. How does he explain it? "It happened simply because I had all those songs," he says. "I felt that all of them were, again, snapshots of a time and a place and an emotion that fit together very well. I'm very conscious of the flow of the music on an album and that whole deal, because I'm listening objectively as a person." The flow of the original vinyl Side 2 of *Songs* ('I Wish', 'Knocks Me Off My Feet', 'Pastime Paradise', 'Summer Soft', 'Ordinary Pain') may be the single greatest sequence in Seventies soul.

WHETHER WONDER will ever do anything as radical as recruiting a group of Hare Krishnas to shake their bells to the chilling 'Pastime Paradise' must be doubted by anyone who's followed his post-*Key Of Life* career. Perhaps it was because he took another three years to deliver the soporific, self-indulgent *Journey Through The Secret Life Of Plants* that he lost his own plot. The mainly instrumental soundtrack to a documentary film nobody bothered to watch, *Journey*'s savage reception by critics seems to have thrown him, causing him to settle for commercial compromise in the ensuing decade. But then the Eighties were a wretched time for soul giants beached by hip hop and house music. For Wonder, it was particularly difficult to write when so many younger artists had incorporated his influence into their sound. Michael Jackson, who'd lifted his "hee-hee" vocal signature from Stevie's 'Maybe Your Baby', made two blockbusting albums (*Off The Wall* and *Thriller*) that effectively took the crown from his mentors. "That vocal thing was mine for him to have," Wonder says generously. "They say that's the greatest form of flattery."

It's unfair but inevitable that we think of Wonder's Eighties in terms of 'Ebony And Ivory' – his saccharine racial-harmony duet with Paul McCartney – and 'I Just Called To Say I Love You', the sappy No. 1 hit from the soundtrack to the rotten *Woman In Red*. The uplifting *Hotter Than July* and new-agey *In Square Circle* weren't terrible albums – and did their admirable bit for both Martin Luther King ('Happy Birthday') and the fight against apartheid ('It's Wrong') – but they were formulaic where his great Seventies albums had been unpredictable. By the time the tired and over-programmed *Characters* appeared in 1987, Wonder was a beatific cliché in braids. Even when the superior *Conversation Peace* came out eight years later, its swingbeat grooves and ballads suggested he was now following the lead of Teddy Riley and Babyface rather than the other way round. Was the well now officially dry? Or was he simply too comfortable in his iconic role as the Pope of Black music?

It didn't help that, in the Eighties, a new superstar stole up on him, trouncing him at his own game. Like Wonder, Prince was a polymorphous jack-of-all-trades, playing every instrument himself. "I knew that was a form Prince took, but I didn't say, 'Oh, he's doing it like me'," Wonder says. "I liked the stuff that he did, and I felt it was daring. It reminded me of Marvin, though Marvin was maybe a little more abstract with how he said it. When Marvin talked about religion and making love, people said, 'Woah, this guy's gone crazy'. He had a song that was originally called 'Sanctified Pussy'." As it happens, Prince – whose music declined after his *own* double-album masterpiece, 1987's *Sign O The Times* – is one of several guests on *A Time 2 Love*, the album he is racing to finish on the night I meet him. The diminutive one had stopped by Wonderland to add funky guitar licks to 'So What The Fuss', the album's first single. "He is a very nice man, and I know him more personally now than some years ago," Wonder says of the artist formerly known as The Artist. "I always saw him being exactly where he is right now spiritually. I envisioned that that would happen at some point." Other guests on the album include such fundamentally unthreatening figures as Doug E. Fresh, India.Arie (who co-wrote the anodyne 'Positivity') and a female practitioner of the talking drum who came all the way to Wonderland from Nigeria. The likelihood of the albums changing the perception of Wonder as a creatively spent force seems remote. "*A Time 2 Love* is something that came out of different things," Wonder says. "Watching television, listening to radio, reading magazines, meeting people, traveling and then coming to my own conclusions. Or just having a place of *in*conclusiveness."

Though no light enters the inner sanctum of Wonderland's control room, it is now early morning in Los Angeles. Unsurprisingly, Wonder is fading. A black Range Rover purrs outside in the parking lot, ready to take him back to the San Fernando Valley – and to the wife who is expecting his seventh child. "We are hopefully days away from finishing," he says with a weary smile. "Obviously there are dates and numbers we are trying to respect, but creativity overrules punctuality. Otherwise you turn something in and spend the rest of your life kicking yourself in the ass… or *the arse*, as you say in England."

Uncut, 2005

6 Looking At The Devil
Sly Stone

Album bought in Palo Alto, California, in 1982

DICK CAVETT didn't know what had hit him. The mild-mannered and impeccably liberal TV host had welcomed some pretty far-out guests to his ABC talk show, but no one like Sylvester Stewart had ever plonked himself down in the guest armchair before. Certainly no one in Stewart's physical state, for which the term "wrecked" would have been a polite euphemism. Slurring his deep nasal words and rolling his tired eyes as he shuffled in the chair, the man known more familiarly as Sly Stone had Cavett somewhere between mystified and terrified. Supercool and pimpadelic in a black hat that resembled a tea-cosy-cum-turban, Stone had finished up a thrilling version of the brilliant 'Thank You (Falettinme Be Mice Elf Agin)' before sauntering over to chat with Cavett. He looked like some exotic street-corner warlord. "I look in the mirror when I write," he drawled when Cavett asked about his songwriting methods. "The reason why I do that is because I can somehow be a great critique [sic] for myself, and I can react spontaneously before I realise that I'm going along with what I'm doing, and dislike it or like it before I realise that I'm doing it…"

The bemused Cavett didn't know how close Stone had come to not making the show at all. The previous evening, after visiting Muhammad Ali in New Jersey, the singer suddenly announced he was flying back to his house in Los Angeles. Only the remonstrations of his friend Bobby Womack, and his right-hand-man Hamp "Bubba" Banks, stopped him in his tracks. "He just found every excuse to not go on that show," Womack told Joel Selvin, author of the chilling *Sly And The Family Stone: An Oral History* (1998). "He was petrified, now that I look back on it." Come show time at the ABC's Manhattan studios the next day, Stone was nowhere to be seen. He was still in his hotel, working his way through a stash of cocaine and deferring departure for as long as he could. Every time Banks or Womack got him downstairs to the lobby, Sly headed back to his room for another fat line. Eventually it became so late that Banks had to charter a two-passenger helicopter to pick Stone up and fly him into Manhattan. Breathing a sigh of relief, Bubba watched the chopper take off with Stone and Womack aboard. Even then the crisis wasn't over. Driving back to the airport terminal, Banks noticed the helicopter circling back to land where it had taken off. He raced to the launching pad to see what the problem was. Turned out Sly needed to swap seats with Womack. A draft on Sly's side of the chopper was blowing his cocaine away.

To anyone on the inside of the Family Stone circle, the incident was merely par for the hazardous course Sly was on in mid-1971. No-shows, crap outs, and last-minute helicopter rides were frequent features of life in and around the group that had done so much to bridge the worlds of Black soul and white freakdom. The previous year, Stone had failed to show up for 26 of the 80 live dates booked for the band; so far in 1971, he'd blown out 12 of the group's 40 shows. Those he *did* make, he was invariably late for. Far from feeling remorse for this, he revelled in the power it gave him. More hair-raising still was the twilit world within 783 Bel Air Road, the palatial mansion Stone was renting in LA's exclusive Coldwater Canyon from John and Michelle Phillips, the sometime Papa and Mama who themselves had turned the former home of actress Jeanette MacDonald into a den of rock debauchery. Here it was that Sly was working on a new album, one with the working title *The Incredible And Unpredictable Sly & The Family Stone*.

The most unpredictable thing about the fifth Family Stone LP was whether it would be finished at all. So long was it taking – with only 1970's *Greatest Hits* to placate impatient fans – that Stone's neurotic gay manager

David Kapralik had devised a marketing slogan for Epic Records that read "Two Years Is A Short Time To Wait for A Work of Genius". "Sly was simply not producing albums at all," wrote Clive Davis, who'd signed the group to Epic in 1967. "I heard stories that he was laying down hundreds of instrumental tracks in Southern California studios – without vocals. There was strong speculation that he would never sing again." For those involved with the album, the sessions at 783 Bel Air Road and at LA's Record Plant studio were very different from anything Sly and the Family Stone had done before. Where the group's groundbreaking anthems – exuberant bursts of polyrhythmic rock'n'soul such as 'Dance To The Music', 'Everyday People' and 'I Want To Take You Higher' – had been recorded with the emphasis on live feel and big-room ambience, now Sly was overdubbing instruments one at a time and plugging them directly into the board for a parched, almost claustrophobic sound. Family Stone members weren't even featured on some of the tracks. Instead, a rotating cast of cronies – Womack, Billy Preston and others – pitched in with musical cameos during sessions that rarely began before midnight but often flowed over the course of several days. Sleep only punctuated these recording marathons when the musicians' constitutions could stand no more cocaine. When Sly himself fell asleep it was literally impossible to wake him. "It was so spacey," Bobby Womack told me. "I remember sitting there in the dark in Sly's studio, coked to the brain, trying to sing, staying up four, five, six days. That's just the way he was."

Stone's new music was murky, restless, unpretty, a superfly nod to the spacey wah-wah meta-funk of Miles Davis' *Bitches' Brew*. It was *bad*, even evil, a radical break with the rainbow-coalition soul of 'Everyday People' and 'Everybody Is A Star'. "Sly said to me, 'Man, I'm comin' outta left field o' these motherfuckers'," Womack remembered. "He said, 'My music is like the devil's music, it's got a little of yours in there but you can't recognise it coz it's so loose and raw'."

Miles himself is known to have dropped in on the *Incredible Unpredictable* sessions. Other musical peers hanging out at Bel Air Road included Ike Turner and Johnny "Guitar" Watson, both West Coast R&B veterans with a taste for the white stuff. A more unlikely presence was that of white southerner Jim Ford, whose gritty country-soul album *Harlan County* had been released in 1969. "Sly wasn't the easiest guy to hang around, but he loved Jim Ford," says Bobby Womack. "I think for Jimmy to be that close to Sly, he had to be doing something that was very important to the situation."

Anyone who's taken cocaine will be familiar with the temporary illusion of omnipotence it affords. Sly's need to control the members of his entourage knew no bounds; nor did the paranoia that escalated as he kept tooting. Coke wasn't even the worst of it: things got *really* out of hand at Bel Air Road when the dreaded hypnotic sedative PCP, aka "angel dust", was added to the chemical mix. Factor in a pack of psychotic dogs and a virtual arsenal of guns and there was a pretty scary scene going down in the house. "[Sly's] goons were sullen, unfriendly and armed," John Phillips wrote in his autobiography *Papa John*. "These people were *rough*. They laughed at me. There were lots of guns, rifles, machine guns, big dogs."

"It all fell apart at Coldwater," Hamp Banks told Joel Selvin. "That is when Sly did the PCP and he was just out of it. He was all the way out. There wasn't anything happening no more. He was doing shit you would expect to see in some kind of institution for mentally retarded people."

"Sly would be dressed all in red leather, handing out the orders," Womack told me. "Like, 'Tiffany baby, I want you to take Bobby to your room, y'know, fix him up'. As time progressed, I became paranoid at everything, I was always thinking I was going to get killed, that the Feds was gonna bust in on Sly. Later, you give Sly one hit and he's looking around the room, very paranoid, you couldn't make no music with him. I got to the point where I said, 'I gotta get away from here'." Like Womack, Stone's loyal secretary Stephani Owens also made it out of Bel Air Road in the nick of time. She called the band's acting manager Ken Roberts, begging him to send a cab and 200 dollars, and fled for her life. "I had dissipated down to nothing, from no sleep, alcohol, and doing drugs," she said. "When I came home at the airport, my mother looked at me and started crying."

In the immortal and beautiful words of Sly himself, *"You can't cry 'cause you'll look broke down/But you're crying anyway 'cause you're all broke down..."*

THOSE WORDS hail from 'Family Affair', the biggest hit and the most famous song from *There's A Riot Goin' On* – the title the album bore when it finally appeared in the fall of 1971, after which Sly began a long disappearing act, only to resurface against all the odds at this year's Grammy awards in Los Angeles. The LP's least typical track, 'Family Affair' was sexy, touching, minimalist, cantering on a groove Sly had programmed on a very primitive drum machine. Released as a single against Sly's wishes, it shot to the top of the US charts in November 1971 and remained there for three weeks. *"One child grows up to be/Somebody that just loves to learn,"* Sly droned in a hollowed-out baritone like Lou Rawls on quaaludes. *"Another child grows up to be/Somebody you'd just love to burn…"*

For some insiders, this mini-meditation on nature vs nurture was ironic, to say the least. David Kapralik, as crippled by cocaine as his star client, told *Rolling Stone* the song was about the fissures within the Family Stone itself. "The family, to me, was one of the most hypocritical things that I had ever seen," said J. B. Brown, one of Stone's lackeys. "I thought it was a sad situation because you respected them, thinking they are church and their religious thing was valid. But you watched them allow all this crap to take place… just the weirdest stuff you ever want to see."

Just how did the Family Stone get so dysfunctional? How did this Bay Area troupe, so innovative in its racial/sexual shake-up, become such exemplars of Hollywood Babylon sleaze? They'd started out as a mid-Sixties bar band in the suburban towns of the San Francisco peninsula, pounding out soul and R&B covers in after-hours joints like Redwood City's Winchester Cathedral. Sly alternated between his role as bandleader and his day job as a fast-talking, wise-cracking DJ on KDIA in Oakland. Years before that, Sylvester Stewart and siblings Freddie and Rose had been part of a family gospel group, the Stewart Four, a crucible for their overlapping vocal arrangements.

Sly also had a foot in another important Bay Area camp: the acid-rock scene fomenting around San Francisco's Haight-Ashbury district. A meeting in 1964 with DJ and impresario Tom "Big Daddy" Donahue led to Sly becoming in-house producer for Donahue's Autumn label, for which he crafted pop hits by the Beau Brummels and Bobby Freeman. Sly was at the controls on early recordings for Haight-Ashbury legends the Charlatans and the Great Society, though his domineering approach rubbed both bands up the wrong way – especially when he put Great Society singer Grace Slick through 50 takes of 'Somebody To Love'. His exposure to the freaky goings-on in the Haight, like his readiness to mix up rock and soul on his radio shows, made it inevitable that his Family Stone would be no ordinary group. "We had all this input no one had ever thrown together before," recalled white drummer Gregg Errico. "You had R&B, you had white pop, you had the psychedelic thing and the English thing, mixing together for the first time."

When their debut album stiffed badly, David Kapralik – then an Epic A&R man overseeing their career – advised Sly to simplify the songs on the next record. Sly took his advice and came back with 1968's 'Dance To The Music', pulverising the polarities of Black and white, male and female, rock and funk. Built on the stomping grooves of Errico and bassist Larry Graham, and lifting the listener ever higher with its mix of horns (Jerry Martini and trumpeter Cynthia Robinson), churchy keyboards (Sly and Rose Stone), fuzzy rock guitar (Sly and Freddie Stone) and unisex vocals, this was superbad psychedelia – James Brown at the Human Be-In. The following year, 'Everyday People' sat at No. 1 for four straight weeks in the spring; the lovely and lilting 'Hot Fun In The Summertime' hit No. 2 in August. If Otis Redding had intro'd soul to "the love generation" at Monterey, Sly sanctified the hippies with a magnificent, middle-of-the-night set at Woodstock.

In late 1969, though, a new and darker note crept into Sly's music. Against the backdrop of the Manson murders and the militant Black Panthers – formed in Oakland – the Family Stone dispensed with the flower-power euphoria. The *Stand!* album featured the mordant 'Don't Call Me Nigger, Whitey (Don't Call Me Whitey, Nigger)' and the joyless jam that was 'Sex Machine'. Then in January 1970 came the real sucker-punch: the stunning 'Thank You (Falettin Me Be Mice Elf Agin)', with its evocation of Sly's teen years in the gangs of his hometown Vallejo and its startling Larry Graham bass line, birth of the thumb-plucked "popping" bass style that underpinned funk through the Seventies and Eighties. If the song's third verse expressed gratitude for survival, for the healing of wounds – *"Mama's so happy/Mama starts to cry/Papa's still singin'/You can make it if you try"* – what stayed with the listener was the wired terror of its opening line: *"Looking at the devil, grinning at his gun…"* That, as Papa Stewart himself could have attested after one of his periodic visits to the house, was closer to the reality of everyday life at 783 Bel Air Road.

Just as Motown was giving the Jackson 5 a Family Stone makeover with the exhilarating 'I Want You Back', Sly himself was retreating into a cocoon of cocaine and brooding introspection. *"Feel so good inside myself,"* he sang on the opening 'Luv'n'Haight'; *"Don't need to move."* The music on *Riot* was the antithesis of the joy and openness of 'Everyday People' or 'You Can Make It If You Try', spurning Sly's role as Lord of the Black Hippies. The group had certainly caused riots – of both the positive and negative kind – but this album was a solipsistic riot of the mind, not some Bacchic uprising. "The songs seem to wander," Greil Marcus wrote of *Riot* in his *Mystery Train*; "to show up and disappear, ghostly, with no highs or lows." Ghostly is right: there's precious little warmth on this album. Even tracks as implicitly tender as 'Just Like A Baby' and '(You Caught Me) Smilin'' sound diffuse, drifting. 'Poet' and 'Spaced Cowboy' (the latter complete with sardonic yodeling) flaunt Sly's self-absorption. *"Out and down/Ain't got a friend,"* he sang on

'Brave And Strong'; *"You don't know who turned you in."* 'Time' is formless, inchoate, the work of a man who forbade the presence of clocks at 783 Bel Air Road. "We used to call it the prison because we couldn't get off the hill," Family Stone production manager Robert Joyce said of the mansion. "Sly's thing was no time. He made time, that was his thing. *Now…* we are doing it right *now*. That was the mentality." Concluding the album was 'Thank You For Talkin' To Me Africa', a reworking of 'Thank You' that drained the song of all its groove and spirit, grinding remorselessly on for seven dead minutes. It sounded like the ultimate disavowal of funk as party music.

In fact, *Riot* as a whole is one of the definitive death-of-Sixties artefacts, an aural downer in the aftermath of the decade that was supposed to change the world. Charlie Gillett, reviewing it in January 1972, described the album as "the diary of a man going through a lot of pain in an attempt to identify and define himself". Others were more flummoxed, less charitable. *Creem*'s John Morthland bemoaned "the same plodding, lethargic beat that continues seemingly unabated for 45 minutes"; *Let It Rock*'s Pete Wingfield decried the album's "sniffing self-pity". On the back of 'Family Affair', *Riot* made the top of the US album chart for two weeks in November 1971, thus funding Sly's drug bill for another year. A new contract bought out David Kapralik, who'd been reduced to a snivelling, coked-out wreck. "David got very rich," the late Al Aronowitz wrote, "but playing Jewish mother to a Black pimp left him thinking about what every Jewish mother thinks about when her only son doesn't call her anymore. Suicide." On at least one occasion Kapralik attempted just that.

Sly took to cruising the freeways and boulevards of Los Angeles in a 36-foot Winnebago, a sealed chamber even more hermetic than the studio at 783 Bel Air Road. "We used to ride around, getting high and making music," Bobby Womack remembered. "We'd ride all up in the hills and he wouldn't never stand still. He'd say, 'Keep drivin'! I was already spaced out because I was losing my wife. He said, 'I ain't never gonna give no woman that much action'. He said, 'You're too nice. I'm nasty, I don't give a fuck'." He gave more of a fuck when the Winnebago was stopped and searched by police on Santa Monica Boulevard in July 1972. By then, though, the original Family Stone was no more. Larry Graham and Greg Errico were gone, to be replaced on 1973's *Fresh* by bassist Rustee Allen and drummer Andy Newmark. On the album's opener – the nervy, supertight 'In Time' – Sly sang *"there's a mickey in the tasting of disaster/in time you get faster…"* Disaster Sly had certainly tasted; remorse for his behaviour he was apparently incapable of feeling.

The enduring cult status of *Riot* says much about our ongoing fascination with the dark side of Black music. Long before crack devastated America's inner cities, cocaine turned more than a few pioneers of soul and funk into psychotic monsters. At least two of Sly Stone's most devoted disciples – George Clinton and Rick James – had their own draining battles with the demon flake. But Sly was just as much an influence on the teetotal Prince, whose Revolution were a transparent nod to the multi-race/gender collective that was the Family Stone. Sly and *Riot* haunt R&B and hip hop to this day, their menacing moods and grooves heard in the work of acts from D'Angelo to OutKast. "D'Angelo played *Riot* constantly in the studio while recording his masterpiece *Voodoo*," says writer Miles Marshall Lewis, whose study of *There's A Riot Goin' On* is published in Continuum's excellent 33⅓ series. "R&B and hip hop both owe a tremendous debt to the honesty of *Riot*'s lyrics in describing the darker side of the Black experience."

Sly never touched the genius of 'Thank You' or 'Family Affair' again. A grave decline was already clear by the release of *Small Talk* (1974), though that was nothing next to abject albums like *Heard Ya Missed Me, Well I'm Back* (1976) and *Back On The Right Track* (1979). Throughout the Eighties, he continued to struggle with drugs. In 1983, he was found semi-conscious in a Florida hotel room after a cocaine overdose. In November 1987, he told the *Los Angeles Times* that he was clean, only to be charged days later with cocaine possession. Declared a fugitive in 1989, he was arrested in Connecticut and extradited to Los Angeles, where he pleaded guilty to driving under the influence of cocaine and then guilty again to two counts of cocaine possession. Inducted into the Rock & Roll Hall of Fame in 1993, he kept both band and audience waiting as the Family Stone ran through a version of 'Thank You'. "As usual, it's just us," Rose Stone sighed onstage. Finally materialising in an electric-blue leather jumpsuit, Stone gave the most perfunctory of speeches, muttered "See ya soon", and disappeared into the night.

Since then, Stone sightings have been few and far between. No one is entirely sure where he even resides, other than that it's somewhere in California. George Clinton believes his old friend is in Malibu. Wherever it is, it's unlikely Sly is in fine fettle. His manager Jerry Goldstein has admitted the singer is "frail". When Stone attended his father's funeral four years ago, his back appeared to be hunched, the result possibly of the desperately poor nutrition that attends chronic cocaine use. "He's been in seclusion for so long, he's like J. D. Salinger," Greg Zola, director of a new documentary about Stone, told the *Washington Post*. "He was so famous for a period of time, but he's just not around anymore. A lot of people who you'd think are in the know actually think Sly Stone is dead."

THOSE WHO WERE involved with *There's A Riot Goin' On* – and who got burned by it – look back and shudder, all too aware that the album's creation was nothing less than a dance with the devil. "There were many nights that I didn't want to go home," Bobby Womack reflected. "I was just there and we just kept cutting. Sly would say, 'Bobby, you gotta sing on this, you gotta do this'. Well, to be into that you had to *live* it."

The Observer, 2006

7 Doing It His Way
Bobby Womack

Album bought in London in 1982

I'M NERVOUS setting out here. Nervous because I'd like to reach some "heart" of Bobby Womack where I don't have to tell you how he cut *this* album after *that* album; how *this* song is gospel and *that* one is blues; how *The Poet II* is part of the resurgence of *real soul music*. I'd like you to hear the Womack that's in my head, the sound that floods my brain suddenly as I'm standing in a bus queue, the feel of the specific shapes and inflections he presses into his words. I want to tell you that (for me, for some reason), his is almost the greatest music on earth. There are songs of his which have taken me over for hours, days, weeks, enveloped me because within them there is a hold on the dynamics and tensions of soul music which is fuller, more absolute, than the hold or emotional grip of others. A gut grit, a root pain which Bobby would say is his gospel base but for me just *is*, is this pure heart, the gnawing need to give out the pain as a joy. I can't touch this heart with critical language.

I suppose I want to say, in all seriousness, that his music moves and transforms me more than all the music of Marvin and Stevie put together. When I hear this voice at its best, I fall into its movement, its pace, more helplessly than into any other I know. I'll be walking home, and out of nowhere it'll grab me, fill me till I want to burst with it. It's as though my own voice strained with his, my own throat winding round his snarls and those long, burnt cries. Other singers have done this to me, pulled me apart with the fury of their desire or sorrow, but not many of them are still kicking. Womack seems to me the most original and longest-surviving of the classic, gospel-rooted school. Screw the soul boom: *The Poet II* album this year outshines everything. 'Love Wars', the SOS Band, the lot of them. The passion of *Poet II* is titanic, Womack & Womack's is merely local. Even the great opera duets take second seat to Bobby and Patti Labelle on 'Love Has Finally Come', the most towering love testament of the year. There's nothing fit even to grovel at their feet here. Every time Patti launches off on "But there's one side of love..." I die a small, ecstatic death. I've played this song, oh, close on 200 times since it came out. I've played the roaring Van McCoy-esque symphony of 'Tryin' To Get Over You' another hundred. I've jumped over and over to the super-sleek DMX hiss of 'Tell Me Why'. And I've almost wept alone to 'Wish I Had Someone To Go Home To' a few long nights now. I can pin nothing on Bobby Womack, other than to note that he is a certain kind of breath trapped between certain sorts of beat. He is the moment of emotional truth that *will* keep escaping. If one could write down, notate what Womack technically does when he turns a tiny phrase into a magical confession ringing in your ears for years... well, there'd be no need for him to do it, would there?

"I hear you knockin', love, but I'm afraid to let you in..."
"I could never be happy over here..."
"So afraid to face the time of day..."
"Tried my best to make you happy..."
"I wonder would you mind, would you mind if I just..."

Maybe these moments go under your skin too, convince you, like me, that Bobby Womack has simply the best timing in the business. The very best.

FROM BEHIND a pillar in a Belgravia hotel, the last great soul man is suddenly upon me. At his side are wife Regina and infant son Truth (sic), making for a tank-like Daimler limousine in the street. I feel grubby and excessively un-Black, un-American. "You doin' the interview?" he susses. I nod, knowing I don't belong in the limo but taking my place in its vast whale-belly, bound for tonight's show at the Oxford Apollo. Womack is looking good, but he's tired. His grey suit makes him seem edgily efficient. I can't connect the weary street growl with the gruff, lovable patter of his records. He's hungry, too, so we stop at what he assumes is a Hollywood-style deli – the Sloane Ranger's Greenblatt's, mayhap – on the bend of South Kensington tube station. He buys various meats, sausage, salami. Can't understand why they don't have no mayo or ketchup. "We're not a sandwich bar," whines the morose deb-thing behind the counter. "Lady, jes' gimme the meat," Womack despairs. We remove to a Mini-Mart where he locates some Heinz sandwich spread. Back in the car, he lays the food all over the seat and we head for the M40. Twenty minutes later he's asleep, exhausted from three days of gigging, vidding, and, well, jes' plain rapping.

Left with Regina, Truth and singer Altrina Grayson, I'm regaled with homesick descriptions of their favourite cars, soap operas, and shopping malls. Gina would like a Ferrari, her favourite soap opera is *As The World Turns*, and she shops at the Promenade in Woodland Hills. I'm enthralled. "Oh my, here's an English ghetto," she exclaims, spotting a collection of caravans beside the motorway. "And you have cows across the street from apartment buildings! 'Scrazy!" It's not long before I doze off, too, roused only when we hit a long tailback on the outskirts of Oxford and appear to be in imminent danger of late arrival. The traffic is due to a home game at Oxford United. Womack stirs too, except he's muttering something about Regina not watching the road, and hasn't she wrecked enough cars for one year. She shrieks with laughter. Womack rolls back into his unconscious.

A HALF-HOUR later, he's bounding onstage in a salmon-pink tunic looking for all the world like some Hollywood Fela Kuti. The band is 13-piece; four hornmen, three backing girls, no less. They're snappy, too, despite the comically regimented dance steps: more than can be said for the man himself, who plainly would rather not be here tonight. The set seems forbiddingly formal. The songs slip into each other in a pleasant medley-ised flow, but Womack ain't involved. "See if you remember this one," he announces weakly. Only big, belting Altrina fires the show with any spirit: her hard, pure voice is very close to Patti LaBelle when she tackles 'Takes A Lot Of Strength'. There's no encore.

Next morning, on the bus in Birmingham, I hear the man's post mortem: "I felt terrible. I felt like I was gonna die. I always feel like I would die if I over-exerted myself, always have had that vision. If you watched me on that stage, you'd have seen that I kept pushing the onus onto the others, the girls or Fernando [sax] or Courtney [guitar]. When they can see I ain't gettin' into it, they get in the way. I don't like it like that, but that's the way it is. There ain't other way when you been singing this long. I only know how to sing one way. I can sing pretty cool, stay pretty mellow for a while, but if I'm really singing, and I get physically and emotionally into it, then that works you, it ain't easy. I don't sing a lot of falsetto, I blow out, and when you blow out like that everything is hitting on the throat. Somebody say, 'All you got to do is work two hours a day', but them two hours, Jack, is strenuous." Womack's rested some, happy now to relax in conversation. His talking voice is irresistible, a grizzly-bear version of James Brown. It talks of itself, and of the way it was shaped back in church by two especially great gospel singers: Sam Cooke, and Archie Brownlee of the Five Blind Boys. "First time I saw Sam Cook[e], I had to be about six years old, and he was young, wild, different for the gospel field, more like a Muhammad Ali. He did things you don't normally do in church. He was such a good-looking guy. He was fast, and he would comb his hair in church, a real pretty boy." Womack primps his hair, warbling 'Wonderful', before an imaginary pocket mirror. "Sam could sing, and he knew he could. Before you knew it, young kids were coming to church to see him, and they'd go away saying this music is not as square as we thought it was." Womack was Cooke's touring guitarist in the secular Sixties. Three months after the singer died in 1964, he married Cooke's widow Barbara.

What about Archie Brownlee? "I played guitar for Archie. I left home to play for the Five Blind Boys when I was 13, and I didn't go back until my father tracked me down. I went around with these five blind guys, and I would take them to their hotel rooms, dress them, take their clothes and get them cleaned, and they'd let me get a little nookie on the side when their girlfriends would go for it! Archie was just a beautiful person, he was unique. I'll never forget how I felt for a year after he died. Matter of fact, he died onstage. I was always trying to learn how to scream like him, 'cause he had a scream that was a real note, it was a beautiful scream. When I asked him how to do it, he would just say, let nature take its course." One might almost see Womack's voice as a compromise between the wild, harsh ecstasy of Brownlee and the graceful, magnetic melancholy of Sam Cooke. Would he agree with Jerry Wexler's verdict that Cooke with the Soul Stirrers was the greatest soul singer of all time? "Up to this day, he was the greatest, yeah. But he couldn't put the rough with the smooth, and that's why I started putting more of a roughness into my voice, more of a Wilson Pickett, because when I started singing people said I was trying to copy Sam. I started screaming more, using an Archie thing. Another guy I liked was Clarence Fountain of the other set of Blind Boys [Alabama rather than Mississippi], though Clarence was more flashy, he would clown and wiggle onstage. Archie was more serious, he could really make you cry."

Through his teens, Womack sang with his brothers as the Womack Brothers, but in 1962 they signed to Cooke's SAR label and crossed into the secular market, eventually becoming the Valentinos of 'Lookin' For A Love' and 'It's All Over Now' fame. How long had he been writing songs at that time? "About four years. First song I wrote was called 'Give That Man Some Cover', on account of us five kids sleeping in the same bed sharing the same Salvation Army blanket. See, in the middle of the night, one of us would wake up cold and pull the blanket onto his side, then a bit later somebody else would wake up and so on... so I started the song, and we would sing it. I must've been about 12." And writing came naturally? "I really wanted some cover!"

How did he feel moving out of gospel? I noticed he'd gone back to songs like 'Yes, Jesus Loves Me' and 'Yield Not To Temptation'. "I felt very lost, and very afraid of everything I saw, 'cause that was just another world. I didn't feel protected spiritually. As time went on, things got more comfortable, because what fooled me was being able to pay my hotel bills and eat regular, and I said, 'Man, this is different'. But I always noticed that nobody invited you to their homes anymore, you never got a chance to meet people like you used to at the big cookouts after church. I used to always miss that, until I got so used to it and so many years passed by that when someone did invite us to their house, we didn't wanna go. We just said, 'We don't know what to expect. We'll go to their house and maybe we won't wanna be there... just maybe, maybe, maybe.' 'Yes, Jesus Loves Me' was a song Archie did, and I played guitar on it, and I loved that song, so I cut it, and I duplicated it the way he would've did it, I really tried to get close to him. It's funny, though, sometimes I wonder whether a song can take people somewhere they don't need to be. I mean, sometimes you can get a person so up but it's a *down*-up, it makes them think about people that's gone, people they lost, and I don't know if that's where you should leave 'em."

*

THE BUS ROLLS into a drizzled Warwickshire, through Stratford-upon-Avon to a tourist stop at medieval Warwick Castle. The jolly Englishness of turrets and dungeons is lapped and snapped up by one and all. "Bobby needed this trip," his wife confides in me. "He was getting bored to death at home. He was even planning to spend some time alone in New Orleans." We wander through the State Rooms, currently fitted out with Madame Tussaud waxworks of an Edwardian "Royal Weekend Party". Womack disappears in search of food. An hour later and we're back on the road, in 1965.

"I joined Chess a year after marrying Sam's wife. I had a very rough time over that period, because people were very uptight over the fact that I had married her, but she put up the money. She asked me, 'Are you really as good as my husband thought you were?' I said, 'Yeah, I think I'm better than him, I really do, I think I do more things than he did'. So she got his arranger and all the guys that played on his sessions." There's a new Chess compilation, misleadingly entitled *Bobby Womack And The Valentinos*. Half of it is solo material: it's the better half, too, displaying early signs of the classic Womack style, especially on 'See Me Through' and 'I've Come A Long Way'. "They were too deeply rooted, people didn't know where I was coming from. But that's what I wanted to do, I wanted to stay rooted, and that's why I'm still here, I'm still in the roots. Otherwise I would've moved on out, and you'd have heard a lotta strange things coming out of that. Thing is about me, I've tried a lot of things with other people, saying 'Let's try it this way, let's cut it like this', but I won't do it with me. There's always a thing holds me back, says don't go too far… left-field. You know it ain't you."

Womack left Chess and went to Jerry Wexler at Atlantic. By now he was enjoying some renown as a songwriter and session guitarist. Wexler promised a deal if he would just play on Aretha Franklin's 'Doctor Feelgood'. The result was one non-happening Atlantic single, 'Find Me Somebody To Love', produced by Bob Gallo. Was it exciting to be involved with soul music in so many capacities? "What the James Browns and Sam Cookes and Jackie Wilsons had started, these guys was carrying on. They added another dimension, but not too much of a dimension. They just stayed in there, in soul. Motown was kicking, but they didn't get that rooted, they didn't think that would grow. It helped my career hanging around the Tom Dowds, the Jerry Wexlers, to play out there as a musician and then go into the control room and work from that end. When I go into the studio now, I don't have to listen to the radio to know what's happening commercially. Reason why is because everybody's doing it, they all follow trends. One guy says it and

131

everybody else follows it, and if you miss this one, you'll catch the next one. Everything has got a lotta handclap on it, everything is synthetic drums cued real high. It's amazing you can hear the lyric with that drum sound. I tell you, I think pop music kept on going, I really do. I think Black music stopped, but pop music kept on going. Lyric-wise, some of these cats are still writing great songs, and the production is great – the Cars, Boy George, Billy Joel, and I like the guy who does the Pointer Sisters' stuff [Richard Perry]. I mean, he's *on* it!"

A first version of 'What Is This' on the Keymen label – "a bass drum and guitar and some guy off the street holding down a coupla piano chords" – preceded signing with Minit Records and a move to Memphis to work with Chips Moman at American Sound. Here he stayed for seven months, "learning the board" and sitting in on sessions by Joe Tex, King Curtis, even future country star Ronnie Milsap. When it came time to cut his own material, Womack had given most of it away to Wilson Pickett. The two Minit albums were thus a peculiar mixture of classic Womack deepies ('Thank You', 'Baby You Oughta Think It Over', 'Somebody Special') and covers of MOR staples such as 'Moonlight In Vermont', 'I Left My Heart In San Francisco' and 'California Dreamin'' (though even on the latter he manages to inject the giveaway phrase "somebody help me"!) "It's fascinating, coz later in disco, everybody started doing standards like that, messing with them. Now I figured I could arrange a song. I was always a good arranger, and I could make a song sound like you never heard it before."

Why was he so generous with his songs? "Well, I became very negative about myself after my marriage to Sam's wife. Everybody was down on me, saying I would never make it because I sounded too much like him, and I almost ruined my voice trying to sound different. People were very cruel at that time, so I just figured I'd have a better shot giving my songs to somebody else. Eventually people were saying, 'This cat's got hits in him, and he can't go waking Sam asking him what to do'."

Did the Stax sound affect him? "I wanted to be different from the Stax cats. It was like all of those acts was branded. It was the company that was famous, and I wanted my style to be so unique. I wanted to have a sound that wherever you took it, people would say, 'That's the Womack sound'. Once I'd accomplished that, I wasn't afraid of going anywhere and letting people dominate me. At that time, people were tryin' to figure out where Womack had come from. 'How come Detroit didn't get him?' So it became that his sound was unique, it ain't but one guy doing it. Now if I'd come into the Stax fold, I'm quite sure they'd have been using the same horn lines, turning 'em round backwards and putting them on everybody, and I would've been caught right into that."

The turning point was 1970's *The Womack Live*, recorded at LA's California Club. Recorded in 1968, the album included a sublime version of Sam Cooke's 'Laughing And Clowning' with a walk-on guest vocal by the great Percy Mayfield. "When I cut it, I knew what it meant, and how it felt, to be real. People had said to me, man, you are so live, if you could just capture some of that magic…" It was here that Bobby finally came out as "The Preacher", on an eight-minute monologue of the same name. "I thought the only way to get your message across was if you talked about a certain subject, in a low key, and you built into the song. Like, say: '*I remember a time in my life when I had nothing to live for, I remember laying in my room and nothing mattered anymore. All that mattered was me getting wasted, and that's why I'm gonna sing a song for you called 'I Don't Give A Fuck' and you'll understand why I didn't give a fuck when I say (breaks into song) darlin yoooooou…*" You know, you've talked 'em all the way up. Preaching still works. And I always wanted to be a preacher, because all the preachers had everything in the neighbourhood, they had all the money and the Cadillacs and they got the best part of the chicken!"

THEN CAME Sly Stone, who influenced much of the music that wound up on Womack's first two United Artists albums, *Understanding* and *Communication*. "I met him when I was divorcing my wife," Womack says. "I went up there with a suit and a tie, and Sly was shocked. He said, 'Is this the guy that make all the funky music?' He said, 'You too funky to look like that. Pull that shit off.' So we got to hanging. Sly said, 'Bobby, you're one of the last gospel singers, and anything you do gonna be gospel. That's what you know, that's what you *bleeed*'. And he says, 'Maaan, I'm coming outta left field o' these motherfuckers, my music is like the devil music, it's gotta little of yours in there, but you can't recognise it coz it's so loose and raw'. He told me I should open up more." It's strange to reflect that two Sam Cooke protégés, Womack and Billy Preston, should end up on Stone's *There's A Riot Goin' On*, the scariest cocaine soundtrack ever committed to vinyl.

We pull into the tangled, multi-levelled heart of Birmingham, and a few hours later find ourselves on either side of the stage of the city's Odeon theatre. The place is only just over half-full, strange considering the three consecutive sell-outs at Hammersmith. Tonight, the band's rigged out in black sub-Jacksons military outfits, gold tassles and all. Here it's only a handful of numbers before Bobby eases into the part. "It's hard to git started," he booms, "but once I git started, I jest can't quit!" 'Who's Foolin' Who' is the high-stepping handclapped opener, but it's an anguished 'Nobody Knows You When You're Down And Out' that slays me. *"If I ever git mah hands on a dollar again…"* he moans, doubling up like a jack-knife and tearing the words from his chest. There's a smoother clip through the mellower climes of 'Woman's Gotta Have It', 'Stop On By' and 'That's The Way I Feel About Cha', followed by his brother Fernando blowing and singing 'Inherit The Wind'. With a Brownlee-esque screech, 'Lookin' For A Love' slams to a halt. The pace drops. *"Is it alright for me to talk about this woman o' mine?"* prefaces 'If You Think You're Lonely Now'. The audience indicates its permission and Womack takes off, shouldering himself around the stage, jogging on the spot as the song builds to one of its semi-climaxes. *"Woo-oooo, baby!"* A swirling 'I Want To Take You Higher' is unleashed as tribute to the "cleaned-up" Sly Stone, with Womack coughing out rawly untreated guitar (sort of Neil Young crossed with David T. Walker), and 'It's All Over Now' is almost garage punk. New single 'Surprise Surprise' sounds like a contemporary 'Harry Hippie'. 'It Takes A Lot Of Strength' is the show's carefully staged highlight, however: a ten-minute-plus, *almost* riveting ritual of break-up and seduction, with Womack and Grayson falling about each other, coyly fumbling with their microphone chords and working themselves into almost comical simulations of agony. Part of soul's function, it seems, is to gesture at pain in an almost mock-operatic way, to represent it: the dangerous magic begins when the living, livid pain of the voices transcends the theatre of the "sketch". "Let's stay together, babe, Johnnie Taylor say it's cheaper to keep her…" Encores of 'So Many Sides To You', 'Games' and a divine country-blues version of 'Bring It On Home To Me' tie up the best of the four shows I saw on this tour.

WE DEPART Birmingham at a bright nine in the morning, the trip home giving us just enough time to skim over the Seventies. The basic message of the *Communication* and *Understanding* albums seemed to be: *Everybody wants love, but everybody's afraid of love.* "Yeah," Womack concurs. "Everyone wants attention, wants to be noticed, even those people that start a fight in clubs. But there's a lot you give up for love, too, if the word 'Love' really exists the way people use it. People use it to get over, they use it for security."

What made him go down to Muscle Shoals? "I heard Pickett do 'Hey Jude' and he said, 'Bobby, they got a bigger sound than Memphis, they got a bottom under it. You take your stuff down there and they'll wear it out."' Bottom is right: the thick heart of David Hood's bass, the glue of Barry Beckett's electric piano, the liquid horns. Has there ever been a soul sound to match it? Three more Womack albums were put down at the Alabama hotspot, and three of his absolute best. *Facts Of Life* (1973), *Lookin' For A Love Again* (1974), and *Home Is Where The Heart Is* (1976) contain some of his greatest performances: 'Doing It My Way', 'I Don't Wanna Be Hurt By Ya Love Again', 'Nobody Knows You When You're Down And Out', 'A Little Bit Salty', 'Something For My Head'. In between came the pretty decent *Don't Know What The World Is Coming To* (1975), the terrible *Safety Zone* (1976), and a splendid country album in *B.W. Goes C&W* (also 1976!). "I was very sincere about that, but people categorise you and say 'Wha–?!' But country is part of my roots, it's deeply rooted in the songs and the lyrics. My people came from the hills of Virginia. That's why Blacks always say country and western makes hits out of R&B. I mean, Charlie Rich, he's *baaad*. Now you ain't gonna tell me that ain't soulful, the way he bends the melody right there…"

The country album, which includes two classic Rich songs, was Womack's last for United Artists. A spate of soul legends – Tyrone Davis, Z.Z. Hill, Johnnie Taylor – signed to Columbia in 1976, and Womack was one of them. *Home Is Where The Heart Is* was the first album for the label. Two years elapsed before the second: "I didn't like *Pieces*. I didn't cut those songs, Don Davis did, and at that time he was so used to working with Johnnie Taylor that he couldn't find my pocket. I don't feel that album had Bobby Womack in there for real. With 'Caught Up In The Middle', that was a serious song, but I couldn't get serious with it, I was *enjoying* being caught up with two women. 'When Love Begins, Friendship Ends' was a good song, I just wasn't up to the part vocally. I hadn't been singing for a year. I was doing more of a performance for Don Davis, because he was a real admirer." Columbia dropped its golden voices as swiftly as they'd picked them up, leaving Womack to descend into a three-year narcotic hell, hardly helped by his brother Harry's murder in 1978.

When he returned with 1981's *The Poet*, loyal fans were thrilled to find that not only had he not declined, he'd improved. The album's second side, consisting of three long mid-tempo pieces that worked as a single sustained suite, was his finest music in years. Crack LA sessionmen Nathan East and James Gadson proved more than adequate substitutes for the Muscle Shoals crew, and the production was a model of relaxed but detailed sound. The only problem was that he wasn't paid any royalties, which is why it's taken three years for *The Poet II* to see the light of day. For most of that time he's been involved in a protracted lawsuit against Beverly Glen owner Otis Smith, a man he came to loathe so bitterly that last year he actually punched him out in court.

Thankfully, it's all over now. We have *The Poet II* on Motown, with Womack at last free of the Beverly Glen contract. We have a big American MCA deal in the offing. And finally, we have a Womack who presses on, perseveres with the heart-fever of his art, a last great soul man who can't stop pushing it out because it will always be in there, that compulsive disease of music. "Berry Gordy said, 'I love Bobby Womack, but he wouldn't fit our roster, it would be like giving credit to something we tried to change'," he says. "Now soul stayed in for a while, but when Stax fell, that was the end of it, and when you look, there's nobody else out there, all those guys is either shootin' up or whatever, but they ain't doing nothin'. There's myself, I seem to be the one, out of all that music that's the only guy I know who still does the same thing, but in a new world. And out of all the acts that went down fighting for the real music, the only one to reap the benefits was Michael Jackson. Two hundred years later, Black people will be saying, 'Hey, we're finally getting our dues'. I say, 'Michael's getting his dues, because of a lotta people that did, and now they're done'. And that includes the Slys and all the others who kept hitting on that door. They said that one day a guy's gonna come along that's got the right size nose, the right fine hair, you can't tell what he is, but he's gonna be a Black guy and all the kids are gonna be into him. It's a funny thing, man. I know a lotta people, but I don't have no friends. There's about two people I know. When I was off into drugs, the only people I knew was the drug dealers. I didn't wanna know anybody else. I been doing this for 20 years now, I'm fucking tired of it. It's lonely, though, it's real strange. There's not enough that my wife can do for me, to make me content. She be saying, 'Well, we can take the kids to Disneyland', but I don't want to stand in a queue five miles long waiting on a ride. I see enough monkeys and shit on the street. She says, 'You gotta live a regular life like other people do'. But I can't go into a club without the DJ putting on my record, and I know they wouldn't be playing my record if I wasn't there. Why they fuckin' playing it now? You know, it's like, 'Ladies and gennlemennn, over in the corner, Mistah Bobby Womack! Get your autographs right now, ladeez an' gennlemennn!'

"It's really a false life. I tell you what I need and that's a whole lotta money. Then I would just travel. I'd leave here and go to Paris, leave Paris and go to South America, cut an album down there. I would try and go behind the Iron Curtain and get some musicians over there, see what they do different. I think the reason my kinda music ain't crossing over is because there ain't no movement on it no more. Used to be a movement, when the Sam & Daves and everybody was doing it. But it ain't there no more. Nobody else doing it but me."

NME, 1984

8 Right Place, Right Time
Dr. John

Album sent by Demon Records in 1982

A QUARTER OF a century has passed since Malcolm Rebennack, trading under the sinisterly exotic stage name "Dr John The Night Tripper", first descended the steps of Soho's Trident Studios to begin work on his fourth album, *The Sun, Moon & Herbs*. When "Mac" opened the door of Trident's main room, the story goes, he couldn't quite believe his eyes. Not only was the room packed with a multitude of drummers and percussionists from several continents, he could also make out the faces of Mick Jagger and Eric Clapton among the throng – superstars who, in the haphazard spirit of the times, had simply dropped in to jam with him because they knew an intensely funky time would be had by all. Also present at the session were Clapton's fellow Dominos Carl Radle and Bobby Whitlock, soul siren Doris Troy, and Graham Bond, the black-magic-dabbling Brit for whom Rebennack had produced an album in Los Angeles two years earlier.

Much has happened since that group of revellers came together in the English capital. Radle and Bond are no longer with us. Jagger and Clapton are even bigger superstars than they were *then*. And Rebennack would appear to have given up the old night-tripping for good. Strangely, though, he is now signed to Blue Thumb, the same label to which his managers Charlie Greene and Brian Stone were attempting to sign him 25 years ago. Something has come full circle. "That trips somethin' in my brain cells," says Rebennack, who – back in London to promote his new album *Afterglow* – looks like a character sitting outside a French Quarter bar on a steamy summer's day. It's less the hat and the braces and the famous walking stick that you fix on; more the size of the man's huge moon face, and the history embedded in it. It's the eyes – stoical, sleepy – which have seen too much, the slow, gravelly voice, thick with the music of the town whose torch he continues to carry: the magical and crazy Crescent City of New Orleans.

ASK ANY of his peers in the business – or *"bidness"*, as he pronounces it – and they'll tell you Rebennack is the gen-u-wine musical article. Jerry Wexler, who produced *Dr John's Gumbo* (1972), calls him "the Blackest white man in the world", and everyone from The Band to the Stones has come knocking at his door, hoping a little of his hoodoo 88-key funk will rub off on their records. More recently – simply because there is no one else around to do the job – he's become an unofficial custodian of New Orleans R&B, so closely identified with the city's spirit that he was hired to play in a Southern Comfort ad. "Well, I wear that jacket now and then," says the man who now lives in New York City. "Somebody hung it on me yesterday, sayin' I should be the official musicologist of N'awlins music. But see, when you been workin' with musicians like [saxophonist] Red Tyler for, like, 40 years, it sounds like we're talkin' about history. But to us it's real personal things. Red doesn't remember anything about Little Richard sessions he cut 40 years ago, but he'll remember some little incident that only musicians would remember. Man, a lotta times we black out the memories, 'cause they wadn't all that great."

In last year's riveting autobiography *Under A Hoodoo Moon*, Rebennack lamented, *en passant*, "another little bit of vanishing New Orleans". Does he think all the great Crescent City traditions will eventually be eroded? "The saddest thing is the amount of New Orleans artists that only had one hit record. There was nobody ever there to look out for anybody's career, with the exception of Fats Domino, who had Dave Bartholomew. Some o' the younger cats is startin' clubs, 'cause they been so caught in the corner of havin' no gigs that they *had* to, but there's very little happenin'. New Orleans is a very poor place, and it doesn't attract a certain element of investment. Willie Tee just built a new studio, and Allen Toussaint's startin' to revamp his place. But, I mean, just compare it to Nashville."

Almost as central as New Orleans to the Rebennack legend is the heroin habit the man hauled around with him for the better part of four decades, and from which he only properly freed himself six years ago. Reading *Under A Hoodoo Moon*, you wonder how he found the energy to put one foot in front of the other, let alone make dates on the road and in the studio. "I look back to my life early on, way back in the Fifties, and I see somethin' was wrong even then," he says. "Somethin' should have said, 'This is not makin' things better'. I have no idea what I was thinkin'. Least I know what I'm thinkin' today. My life is so much nicer and pleasanter." What about the multitude of premature and/or violent deaths with which his book is strewn? Does it ever shock him? "It makes me real disgusted when I see the same stuff goin' on today. I mean, two weeks ago in New Orleans, one of the young kids in the Rebirth Brass Band got murdered. He was another one of the Lastie family. The number of people in that family who've died young is so phenomenally out of synch with any family I've ever met, and they were all so talented."

You could say it's a miracle Rebennack himself is still with us today, and clean and sober into the bargain. Vivid in his mind are the words of veteran Dixieland banjoist Danny Barker, who died after playing on Mac's superb *Goin' Back To New Orleans* (1992). "He said to me right before he passed, 'A lotta things that happened changed my life, but now I look back and it don't even seem like that *was* my life'."

LOOKING BACK, of course, certain uncharitable souls have suggested Rebennack's long journey from *Gris Gris* and *Babylon* (with their heebie-jee-bie lyrics and deranged time signatures) to *In A Sentimental Mood* and *Afterglow* (with their faultless big band arrangements of Tin Pan Alley standards) has effectively been a retreat – even a betrayal. He sees it less as a gradual move towards the Harry Connick Jr. market than as an inevitable process of decel-eration – and makes no apologies for either of his "standards" albums. "I really feel like it's all music. I'm just tryin' to learn how to sing in tune – little things like that. At some point I figured I better learn how to be a frontman and how to be a singer. I always felt comfortable playin', but I'm tryin' to learn how to do this stuff professionally. That's the only thing that's really at all different to me. And now I'm not panicked for chump change or immediate fixes and nervous breakdowns and all o' that. And I'm gettin' older, and all of that goes together with something and it's like, I can take time to enjoy things. As far as the journey I've made, it's like the song says: 'I have had my fun if I don't never get well no more'."

ONE OF the lesser-known facts about Rebennack is that he only became Dr. John because there was no one else around to play the part. (The original intention was for Ronnie Barron, sometime member of the Night Tripper's band and a great pianist in his own right, to assume the role of the root doctor from mid-19th century New Orleans.) It says a lot about the man's innate humility that for a long time he never saw himself as much more than a glorified sideman. From his earliest days hanging around the great musicians at Cosimo Matassa's studio on Governor Nicholls Street, he rarely strayed into the spotlight for more than the odd number. He penned songs like 'A Losing Battle' (for Johnny Adams) and 'Lights Out' (a hit for Jerry Byrne), but otherwise worked primarily as a bandleader and A&R man. A formidable guitarist, he rapidly became a pianist fit to choogle alongside the great keyboard masters of New Orleans: Archibald, Huey Smith, James Booker and of course Professor Longhair, purveyor – as he memorably puts it in his autobiography – of "deeply felt spirituals with a rhumba-boogie beat, incantations to the jollamallawalla gods".

He had no loftier ambitions when, in 1965, he followed the trail that had lured so many New Orleans greats to the gold-paved boulevards of Los Angeles. Not that he was exactly enamoured of what he found there. "Walking into a Phil Spector date with massive amounts of people makin' minimal amounts of music was a total culture shock," he says. "Just seein' the kind of money New Orleans guys like Earl Palmer was makin' blew my mind. When I first went to Earl's apartment, it was like walkin' into a cathedral." Mildly appalled by the way such homeboys as Palmer and Harold Battiste were squandering their talents on the likes of Sonny & Cher, he decided to carve out a little piece of New Orleans magic in Southern California. Using downtime during a session at the Gold Star studio where Spector had cut so many hits, he rounded up a band of exiles – Battiste, Jessie Hill, Dave Dixon, Ronnie Barron, Alvin "Shine" Robinson and others – and recorded the extraordinary tracks that became the 1968 debut by Dr. John The Night Tripper.

By pure coincidence, the exotic and darkly menacing *Gris Gris* album – featuring the original 'Walk On Gilded Splinters', as covered by everyone from Marsha Hunt to Paul Weller – was released into a world only too receptive to all things freaky and deaky. "Because nobody knew anything about New Orleans, everybody thought it was just some psychedelic thing," he remembers. "But it wasn't. We was so outta synch with what was happening, but people didn't realise. We thought *Gris Gris* was just keepin' a little of the New Orleans scene alive. It dint sound that freaky to me. Man, we didn't have a *clue* about hippies. We thought anyone who smoked a joint in public was outta they minds!" He says he only realised how out of step he was when "a little kid, literally" wandered up to him in San Francisco and said, "you guys are like dinosaurs… everybody's groovin' on acid and you're just a buncha junkies!" Actually, they were more than just a buncha junkies; members like the percussionist Richard "Didymus" Washington were pretty heavy customers, and most, like Rebennack himself, had done time.

He says that when he delivered 1969's *Babylon* – a thoroughly wacked-out response to post-psychedelic America replete with choice couplets like *"Donate the chef to the charcoal barbecue/transplanted heart sewed to the sole of my shoe"* ('The Patriotic Flag Waver') – he figured Atlantic would never release it and "it would end the whole Dr John thing so's I could get back to doin' some other things". Fortunately, the label stuck with him long enough for him to team up with Jerry Wexler and record the paean to N'awlins that was *Gumbo*, and for Allen Toussaint to produce the righteously funky *In The Right Place* (1973), his most successful album to date. Boasting the Top 10 single 'Right Place, Wrong Time' alongside the equally lubricious 'Such A Night', *In The Right Place* also featured Art Neville's Meters, then unquestionably the hottest band in New Orleans. "Everything I ever did with Allen is real special to me," he says. "Jest playin' on sessions with him from day one was special, and then it was double special when we did *In The Right Place*. The Meters was the funkiest little band you could ever find, and the combination of Allen and us was so hip. I felt real good about bein' on the road with them, but when Allen honed some of those tunes down in the studio, it was killer. He's a piece of work, man. I always look at him like he's a prince, like he's some mystical presence."

The Seventies success of Dr. John notwithstanding, Rebennack never completely gave up his side gig as a star sessionman. It is a mark of his pedigree and longevity that he can talk about playing on a record like *Exile On Main Street* and make the experience sound as if he'd been cutting demos with a bunch of mates. "When you do sessions all the time, every now and then one sticks out. And at the time, that session was somethin' similar to a lot of other Stones stuff. See, when I'm doin' a date, I'm waitin' to hear somebody do somethin' new." *Under A Hoodoo Moon* clears up one little mystery about *Exile*, which is the true identity of Amyl Nitrate, the marimba player on 'Sweet Black Angel': turns out it was none other than Didymus, the Night Tripper's fearsome percussionist. "And I'll tell you somethin'," Rebennack adds. "Didymus was real pissed about that credit. Those guys [Messrs. Jagger and Richards] don't know how close they came to gettin' hurt! I mean, Didymus hurt a lot of people over the years. It was probably good he couldn't get a passport to come to Britain." Rather more memorable, for different reasons, was the session Rebennack played with John Lennon in December 1973. Was he surprised by the mess the ex-Beatle was in when he showed up to play on *Rock 'n' Roll?* "At that time I was in a weird zone with John, and with Harry Nilsson and Phil Spector too. I was gettin' further and further away from John by the minute, and I blame a lot of it on that chick who was hangin' around [May Pang]. I always think things wouldna been so bad had she not been there. That situation was bad, and it led to some incidents with John where I had to just cut him loose. Last time I saw him was when he was doin' a record in New York and there was the same set of people all around him, and I had to get out of there. I told [guitarist] Hugh McCracken to tell John I said goodbye."

One gets the feeling Rebennack is not overly impressed by the egocentricity of his fellow rock'n'roll stars. Fair or unfair? "Well, you know what it's like. When we was in Paris recently and the Stones was playin', I felt like seeing some o' the people. But I said, 'Lets go see 'em *after* the gig, 'cause I don't wanna be around all that shit'. Even when I was in the middle of it in the Seventies, I couldn't handle it. It all started when they screamed for the Beatles, 'cause they wasn't even listening to the music. It's like a whole other thing is happenin'. I like it better if they're dancin' or something – at least connected in some way to the music." I ask if he feels any differently about Van Morrison, whose Rebennack-produced album *A Period Of Transition* was the recipient of some unwarranted flak when it came out in 1977. "Van is a deep cat," he says. "That poetry that comes out of him is like automatic writing or just spiritual flows. It's so hip, man. He's still got that thing and it's so powerful. I just got blew away the other night when I heard him doin' a thing on the radio and it just brought me to a place, man; it touched me real good. I still think if the original idea of me and [veteran R&B producer] Henry Glover doin' somethin' with Van had come off, it woulda been a whole other thing. I think maybe if I had been around Van a little longer, I would've started readin' him better."

IN *UNDER A HOODOO MOON*, Rebennack says his worst nightmare was always that he'd "end up a solo-piano lounge act, staring at Holiday Inns or bowling alleys for the rest of my natural life". It's ironic, therefore, that two of his best-loved albums are the solo-piano collections *Dr. John Plays Mac Rebennack* (1981) and *The Brightest Smile In Town* (1983), both recorded for the tiny Baltimore label Clean Cuts. Ironic, too, that one of his dearest friends and principal inspirations, James Booker, did a long stint in a Pennsylvania cocktail lounge in the early Seventies. Of all the musicians he namechecks, the mercurial Booker haunts Rebennack the most – the man who best embodies the tragicomic spirit of New Orleans' musical history.

"Booker and me was so close," he says, "and then toward the end we weren't tight any more, and I felt bad about it. It broke my heart. After he lost his eye, he lost all the people in his life that he was close to, and he flipped. He started writin' these newspaper articles that became stranger and stranger. And he'd go to this seminary in Mississippi and chill out, and there were so many weird things going on. I used to try to talk to him, because I felt like I owed him so much. But the more I would try to open him up, the worse it would get. He'd say things like, 'I'm gonna lose my other eye and then I'm gonna be like Ray Charles.' It got really scary, and when he started doin' these little solo gigs, it got even stranger. He was writin' songs that insulted people in the clubs and he was sabotaging everything he could." After Booker died of a cocaine overdose in November 1983, it transpired that he'd been left unattended in a wheelchair in New Orleans' Charity Hospital. "I heard he'd been dead for a while," Rebennack says grimly of the man who was a regular fixture of his band for several years. "That's a terrible thing, and he didn't deserve it. All of his life was really unnecessarily bad."

His tone as he says this almost suggests the guilt of the survivor: *How come I'm still around when so many of my junco partners is dead and buried?* But then he remembers his other great friend Doc Pomus, the New York songwriter who co-wrote most of Rebennack's *City Lights* and *Tango Palace* albums, and whose main concern while heroically battling cancer on his death bed in 1991 was that the song 'I'm On A Roll' be finished properly. "It was somethin' he was still writin' in the hospital," Rebennack says. "And the last words Doc ever said to me was, 'Make sure it sounds like one o' them Louis

Jordan songs!" Fittingly, Rebennack performs the song on the recently released Pomus tribute album *Till The Night Is Gone*.

One of the tunes Rebennack pulled out of the cupboard for *Afterglow* was 'There Must Be A Better World Somewhere', a mournful Pomus-Rebennack ballad that earned B. B. King a Grammy when he cut it back in 1981. By way of concluding our interview, I ask him if the song's sentiments still speak for him today.

"That song means somethin' different to me than maybe the way it looks on the surface," he says. "It came out of me tellin' Doc about this old hymn and him coming up with a little vignette. It really turned me out when I heard Irma Thomas doin' it on the tribute album. She did it almost like it was originally written – a little churchy, a little in the vibe of Percy Mayfield's 'Please Send Me Someone To Love'. See, it ain't about wallowin' in pain. To me, it really is like a hymn."

MOJO, 1995

9 Still Is Still Moving To Me
Willie Nelson

Album bought in London in 1984

A YEAR ago I was in Austin, Texas, watching Willie Nelson walk out onto a stage, flanked by his fellow country singers Lyle Lovett and Rodney Crowell. Though the three men were about to tape a special "songwriters' night" edition of the TV show *Austin City Limits*, it was more like seeing a weather-beaten warlord being escorted to his throne by his aides-de-camp. As Nelson took his place at the centre of the stage, you could have heard a pin drop. Without further ado, baring the most regal of smiles, Nelson launched into 'Pretty Paper', a song of his that Roy Orbison turned into a hit in 1964. Sitting all of 20 yards away, I felt the hairs rise on the back of my neck. Accompanied only by his own famously battered gut-string acoustic, Nelson sang the song with the quietly meditative intensity that distinguishes everything he performs: no theatrics, no excess emotion, every note delivered with a needle-sharp vibrato that tingled your spine.

The sense one had of being in the presence of majesty was mirrored in the reverential expressions on the faces of Lovett and Crowell. For them and for countless other contemporary country artists, Nelson is the Great Elder of the tribe they belong to, a man who commands a respect his peers have spent their lives forfeiting. He may ride with Johnny Cash and Waylon Jennings in the supergroup that is the Highwaymen, but as a redneck-hippie chieftain he stands alone, a figure of dignity and integrity in a world of drunks and degenerates. Dignity and integrity, I hear you snigger? Isn't Nelson the guy who diddled the IRS out of $16.7 million? The man whom a highway patrolman found asleep in his car with a huge bag of weed in the passenger seat? The singer, furthermore, who claimed his intake of pills during the Sixties would have "choked Johnny Cash when he was at his worst"? Well, yes and no. He's had his fair share of ups and downs – and full-on tragedies – during his 40 years in the country music business, but he's never turned into the kind of rhinestoned slob for which Nashville is only too renowned. "Jerry Jeff Walker had a great statement," he tells me. "He said the only difference between Hank and him was that Hank used to go backstage to throw up."

He relays this clearly oft-used quote in a tone of comradely solidarity, but it's a long time since anyone saw him throw up either on *or* offstage. It's true the fabled serenity which had his dear friend and fellow Highwayman Kris Kristofferson nicknaming him "the Buddha" may have something to do with the prodigious amounts of herb he has ingested over the decades. (He makes no great secret of his partiality to marijuana, though he's hardly up there with Cypress Hill or the Black Crowes in the proselytising stakes.) But no amount of illicit smokables could account for the sheer graciousness of the man when I finally manage to penetrate the inner sanctum of his tour bus outside the Cirkus in Stockholm, where he's just performed. You could say it's easy for a 61-year-old American legend to be patient when a couple of Swedish fans produce 35 of his albums from a large bag and ask him to sign them. But is it? How tired must he be after a string of European dates that have taken him through nine countries in almost as many days? And when there's a Swedish EMI rep standing by, telling them to pack their albums away, wouldn't it be easier just to have these guys gently removed from the bus? So what does he say? He says, "Wait a minute, everything's wonderful…" And maybe he doesn't sign all 35 albums, but he signs a good few of them. And he does it with courtesy and respect. A little touch of Zen in the frosty Scandinavian night…

Nelson tells me he is on the road "a coupla hundred days" a year, with the rest of them spent in or around the studio. When is he going to tire of this lifestyle? "I don't know. I still seem to enjoy it. It's still fun." I'm tempted to say the show I've just seen wasn't half as much fun as the *Austin City Limits* taping. With a budget-sized back-to-basics band, powered by the increasingly unsteady hands of long-time drummer Paul ("Me and Paul") English, the set sounded tired, for all its spanning of his greatest songs: 'Whiskey River', 'I Never Cared For You', 'Blue Eyes Crying In The Rain', 'Angel Flying Too Close To The Ground'. The truth, I suspect, is that he's been on the road so long, he wouldn't know what to do if he got *off* it.

Interestingly, his career has just come full circle with his departure from Columbia (on which he debuted with the mega-selling *Red Headed Stranger* in 1975) and a subsequent return to the Liberty label for whom he recorded way back in the early Sixties. Except, of course, that the Liberty of 1994 is a rather different place from the Liberty of 1962. "I guess it is – I don't even know if Garth Brooks was *born* in 1962! Back then, it was Al Bennett and Snuff Garrett – and Leon Russell, who played piano on the first album I ever did." (Russell, it may be recalled, hooked up with Nelson again for the 1979 album *One For The Road*.) Interestingly, too – or perhaps just strangely – he has followed up the star-studded, Don Was-produced, pretty damn great *Across The Borderline* album with a sumptuously orchestrated MOR affair called *Healing Hands Of Time*. Featuring schmaltzy versions of three of his most famous songs ('Crazy', 'Night Life' and 'Funny How Time Slips Away'), it was produced by Liberty supremo Jimmy Bowen, a country boy whose CV includes easy listening classics by the likes of Frank Sinatra and Dean Martin. "Jimmy and I were old golfing buddies," he says. "We'd talked about doing an album together for a long time. Charles Koppelman was also very interested in doing the whole 75-piece orchestra number. He does the Sinatra albums, so he knows how to market that kind of record. He wanted me to do some of *my* old standards in that style, too." Does he envisage doing a show with a 40-piece orchestra? "There are plans to do a Valentine's Day TV show in Los Angeles with these musicians. I don't think the network has been decided yet, but they're talking about it." So will we see him in a tuxedo? "Absolutely! No problem!" How will the album be marketed? "I think it'll be marketed in a similar way to albums by Sinatra. I would hope they'll service all the country stations, but I don't think they're going to depend entirely on that market."

Is it hard to get airplay on country radio these days? "Oh yeah, and not only me," he says. "A lot of people over 40 are finding it hard now. We're supposed to die at 40. Country radio doesn't realise that Johnny Cash and George Jones have many years left in 'em and still draw good crowds, regardless of whether they get played on the radio. All these things change over the years. Next thing you know, you'll be able to turn on the radio and hear Lefty Frizzell." Has the scale of country music's recent explosion surprised him? "Not really, because the things that happened back when Johnny and I and Kris were hot with the Outlaw thing, it was basically the same thing I see happening now with Garth and Billy Ray Cyrus. And we all benefit from their success. Garth doesn't tour much, so he doesn't get to Stockholm as often as I do!" Perhaps it's significant that rock producers such as Don Was and Rick Rubin are queueing up to work with Nelson and Cash, and making such rewarding records with them. What were the most memorable experiences from the sessions for *Across The Borderline*? "Oh, gettin' together with Bonnie Raitt, gettin' together with Mose Allison – that was a treat. Sinead O'Connor, Bob Dylan. There were just a lot of things happened there that were great. Very nice and very positive."

Cash's *American Recordings* reminded me slightly of Willie's own two-volume *Who'll Buy My Memories: The IRS Tapes*: 24 of Willie's greatest but lesser-known songs – 'Jimmy's Road', the aptly-titled 'Who'll Buy My Memories' itself, 'I Still Can't Believe You're Gone' – recorded with no backing other than the aforementioned gut-string, the idea being to generate funds with which to reimburse the Internal Revenue Service. "I like that kind of recording very much. I like Eddy Arnold and his guitar, Jimmie Rodgers and his guitar. *The Tapes* were such a novel, left-field idea that the material sometimes got overlooked, but I really enjoy recording that way." How do things stand now with the IRS? "We're all even now, which feels good after 14 short years." How much has the whole thing affected him? "Not much. Not a whole lot. It was pretty ridiculous to begin with. All of a sudden, here was this guitar player from Abbott, Texas, who owed the government $32 million!"

In his autobiography, Jerry Wexler says Nelson shares with Sinatra "a gift for incredible vocal rubato – prolonging one note, cutting short another, swinging with an elastic sense of time that only the finest jazz singers understand". How does Nelson remember his brief stint on Atlantic, the label for whom he recorded two unsung classics in *Shotgun Willie* and *Phases And Stages*? "I have very good memories of working with Jerry. It was sad for both of us when we had to stop making records. We've talked since about doing another album – maybe a Western Swing album. He has thousands of Western Swing songs." Why did the songs dry up after *Phases And Stages*? Even the classic *Red Headed Stranger* was mainly a collection of covers. "Well, I have a stockpile of songs I haven't released yet. See, it's a little discouraging to be working on songs that might take years to get out there, so at some point I realised I wasn't recording songs as fast as I was writing them. It was just sort of a showdown. I *still* have hundreds of songs out there that you haven't heard. I have a lot from the last four or five years that I intentionally didn't put out, because my records wasn't doin' that great and I didn't wanna throw away an album of ten good songs. I haven't written anything now in about six months, so it's about time. I usually write better when I'm off the road and don't have a lot of things to think about. I like to get in my car and take off down the freeway for two or three hundred miles and then turn around and come back. Somewhere in there I usually write something."

A by-product of this particular methodology was the wonderful last track on *Across The Borderline*. Bearing the Zen-like title 'Still Is Still Moving To Me', it comes as close as anything Nelson's written to explaining why Kris Kristofferson calls him the Buddha. Is the gentleness and serenity he exudes an accurate reflection of the man? "Oh, Kris is easy to fool." What about the people who said you should run for president? Nelson gives a sweet laugh. "I wasn't sure if they were serious or if they'd just been smokin' some bad stuff."

MOJO, 1995

10 The Ol' Sonofabitch
Lee Hazlewood

Album bought in Palo Alto, California, in 1982

ON A PERFECT Florida afternoon in late February, Lee Hazlewood wedges himself into a large grey couch and eyes a rather sad plate of sandwiches on a coffee table. "You better eat 'em soon," he says in the deep Texan drawl he's never quite shaken off, despite years of living in California and Europe. "They gon' curl up on yer." With that advice, the legendary producer of Duane Eddy and Nancy Sinatra leans back into a comfy mass of cushions and lifts a tumbler of Chivas Regal to his lips. It's his first day off painkillers after heavy-duty dental work, and he's making the most of it. "First day without dope, first day I can have some Scotch – which is dope too, I guess. Hell, it's five o'clock *somewhere* in the world."

Hazlewood and his young third wife Jeanie have been living in this house – one of a hundred thousand identikit boxes in the greater Orlando area – for less than a year. "Jeanie and I have lived in Spain, Las Vegas, Phoenix, and now here," he says. "I don't really like to stay in one place for too long. We get out when the rent's due!" Why Orlando, holiday destination of a trillion Disney zombies? Probably because Hazlewood's grown-up children Mark and Debbie live here. And because it's warm. Then again, it may just be because he has taken a shine to the alligator who lives in the lake behind his pool. "The Brit holidaymakers next door always try to feed him," he says of the eight-foot beast. "I'm always asking them not to." Sitting in his bath robe on this bright balmy day, Hazlewood is shorter and less forbidding than I'd anticipated. A notorious curmudgeon in his day, he grants interviews all too rarely; he's been known to scare off journalists. But four months shy of his 70th birthday, he looks in good shape; a wry smile plays constantly beneath the gruff exterior of his face. "I don't remember anything, and it's not because I'm losing my mind," he grins by way of prefacing our conversation. "I didn't even remember it when it happened."

A virtual recluse since he gave up the day-to-day business of making hit records years ago, he has deigned to talk for one simple reason. Not only does he have a new album out – a collection of Tin Pan Alley standards upon which he has bestowed the mystifying title *Farmisht, Flatulence, Origami, ARF!!! And Me* – but several of his ultra-obscure solo albums from the Sixties and Seventies are once again seeing the light of day, thanks to the efforts of Sonic Youth drummer and heavy-duty Lee-o-phile Steve Shelley. Sonic Youth? Surely not. But here's the rub: Hazlewood has long been a hit with the alt-rock crowd, or at least those alt-rockers who can be said to be in the know. Ever since post-punk high priestess Lydia Lunch and Birthday Party guitarist Rowland S. Howard covered the Nancy Sinatra/Lee Hazlewood classic 'Some Velvet Morning' back in 1982, he has become a totemic figure for musos who like their ballads doomy, lugubrious and MOR-ish, to the extent that he now occupies a place in the cult-singer-songwriter pantheon somewhere between Scott Walker and Serge Gainsbourg, rather than – as might be expected – between Johnny Cash and Kris Kristofferson, whose more offbeat compositions his songs sometimes resemble. It is Shelley's Hoboken-based Smells Like label that's issuing three batches of long-lost Hazlewood product, beginning this month with the 1970 LP *Cowboy In Sweden*, continuing in June with the way-ahead-of-its-time "concept" album *Trouble Is A Lonesome Town* (1963) and the darkly regretful *Requiem For An Almost Lady* (1971), and rounding out in the autumn with *The Cowboy And The Lady* (1969), a second "concept" work called *The N.S.V.I.P.'s* (1965), and a compilation of singles and miscellaneous items yet to be given a title. Further releases may follow should Hazlewood regain the rights to them.

Here's the even stranger twist to the story. Back in the early Nineties, Sub Pop employee Mark Pickerel had precisely the same idea of reissuing these Hazlewood rarities. Moreover, he obtained solid commitments from the likes of Kurt Cobain, Mark Lanegan, Mudhoney, Kim Deal, My Bloody Valentine and, yes, Sonic Youth to record Hazlewood songs for a Sub Pop tribute album. "A tape I'd given to [Sub Pop boss] Bruce Pavitt wound up in Kurt's hands," says Pickerel, who now runs Rodeo Records in Ellensberg, Washington. "When I approached him a couple of months later, he'd become a fully fledged Hazlewood fan and picked out the song he wanted to do." In the early Nineties, Hazlewood wasn't interested in any goddamn tribute albums, and told Pickerel as much. "When I finally managed to reach him, the amount he wanted for one song pretty much blew our entire budget," Pickerel recalls. "When I sent back a counter-proposal, I was just shot down in seconds. Lee faxed back some scribblings about how his attorney was going to be watching me if I tried to pursue this project. It was frustrating, because I was purely doing it out of love for his music and was immediately being looked at as some sort of industry slimeball who was trying to rip him off."

What on earth happened between then and now to make Hazlewood so receptive to the attention from the grunge generation? Why is he now so obviously pleased about the party Sonic Youth are hosting for him in Hoboken on April 20th? And why is the self-styled "Grey Haired Ol' Sonofabitch" sitting before me this afternoon in such a jovial mood? "I think maybe it has to do with Jeanie," reflects Suzi Jane Hokom, Hazlewood's girlfriend and musical partner back in the mid-to-late Sixties. "For a while there, Lee was just on a road to nowhere, and it was really sad. I mean, there were these phone conversations where he was really down in the dumps, and it was scary. I think maybe for a while he was very lonely. He just went into a deep hole. See, there's a real dark side to Lee, and you can hear that in some of his music." That Barton Lee Hazlewood is a dark and complicated figure will come as no great surprise to anyone who's heard such oddly disturbing songs as 'Some Velvet Morning' and 'Six Feet Of Chain'. Imagine Cash or Kristofferson crossed with Nick Cave or Leonard Cohen or Townes Van Zandt, and you'd still only have a partial idea of what his sleepy, fatalistic songs were like. Certainly one of the reasons for the Hazlewood cult is the fact that his hit productions – from Duane Eddy's 'Rebel Rouser' to Nancy Sinatra's 'These Boots Are Made For Walkin'' – seem to hail from an altogether different musical plane than out-there songs like 'My Autumn's Done Come' (1965). "He would have been 35 when he

153

wrote that," says Pickerel. "It's just a song about hanging out in a hammock, drinking as much Scotch as possible, and waiting to die. And that was pretty typical of a lot of his lyrics."

The way Hazlewood tells it, the eccentricity of his music is part explained by the fact that he hails from an unusual family. Born in minuscule Mannford, Oklahoma, on July 9, 1929, he was the son of a half-Indian mother and a wildcatter dad who'd rebelled against his middle-class family of judges and lawyers. A "lil, redneck Indian sonofabitch" is how he depicts his boyhood self – an "ornery little bastard" who grew up in and around Port Arthur, Texas, and was sometimes allowed to watch blues singers at the local juke joint. "I don't think there *were* any liberals in Texas except my mom and dad," he says. "I come from a bunch of super-educated people." His wasn't an especially musical family, aside from the fact that, when Gabe Hazlewood got a couple of beers down him, he'd start serenading his wife Eva with the kind of songs their son has now recorded on *Farmisht, Flatulence, Origami, ARF!!! And Me*. "He'd sing 'The Very Thought Of You' to my mom, and she'd say, 'Get away from me!' My dad, by the way, weighed about 220 and my mom was about 89 wet. It was a fun family to grow up in."

After junior college in Jacksonville, Texas, Hazlewood was preparing to go to medical school, but was instead drafted and sent to Korea – "a bunch of people in tennis shoes and tights that shot at you all the time" – for 18 months. On his discharge in 1953, he figured he'd seen enough wounded bodies to last a lifetime and junked the idea of a career in medicine. Instead, he headed for Los Angeles and "tried to get rid of *some* of my southern drawl" by studying at the Spears Broadcasting School. Eventually this led to his first job in radio, at the little KCKY station in Coolidge, Arizona. There he swiftly made a name for himself by creating various "characters" – the most celebrated being one Eb. X Preston – whom he would pre-record and then converse with on air. It was in Coolidge, too, that he first made the acquaintance of guitarist Duane Eddy, whose family had moved west from New York state in 1951. "Duane was just a 16-year-old kid that hung around," Hazlewood says. "He used to come by the station and pick up our overflow of country records."

By 1954 he had married his high school girlfriend, Naomi Shackleford, and become a father. He was also, without conspicuous success, trying his luck as a songwriter. "I would cut little demos and get on the bus from Phoenix to LA," he says. "It cost $9.90 to ride the Greyhound bus from Phoenix to LA and back, and I'd take my songs and play 'em to a few publishers. They never would tell me what was wrong with them, other than that they were some of the worst songs they had ever heard. But thank God they didn't like 'em. I don't know if it made me any better, but it made me think, 'Hell, I might as well produce my *own* records'." In late 1954, he took Eddy – then one half of duo Jimmy & Duane – to Phoenix to play a country date in an old wrestling arena called Madison Square Garden. That night he was introduced to 17-year-old Al Casey and his wife Corki, guitarists with house band the Arizona Hayriders. "I could tell right away that Lee was an ambitious guy," says Casey, who still lives in Phoenix. "I think he realised that producing records himself was the only chance he had."

Moving to KRUX in Phoenix in 1955, Hazlewood began recording local country and rockabilly singers (Jimmy Spellman, Loy Clingman) at Ramco, a toilet-sized commercial studio owned by local entrepreneur Floyd Ramsey. Perpetually on the lookout for teenage talent, he asked Casey – by now the principal lead guitarist on his sessions – to find him "a tall, good-looking kid who thinks he can sing". Casey scratched his head and remembered Sanford Clark, a high-school pal who sang Hank Williams songs. The result was 'The Fool', a single which accidentally crossed over from country to pop and, after being leased to Dot, broke into the *Billboard* Top 10. With a Casey riff adapted from Hubert Sumlin's immortal guitar line on 'Smokestack Lightning', and a droopy, mournful vocal by Clark, it signalled that Hazlewood the producer had arrived.

Few music-biz types in LA, or anywhere else, believed that such a great-sounding record could have been made in Arizona. From the start, Hazlewood used all his ingenuity to fashion classy sounds from primitive equipment – and primitive musicians, for that matter. He experimented for hours with echo and reverb devices, driving people hard. "He was pretty rough in those days," says Casey. "If somebody made a mistake, he would get frustrated, start yelling and screaming at us. But I think that's what made a lot of those records great, because we didn't have all the union restrictions. We'd take all day if that's what it took." The success of 'The Fool' was enough, early in 1957, to persuade Dot's Randy Wood to offer Hazlewood a job in LA, but it didn't persuade him that 'Movin' n' Groovin'', a guitar instrumental Hazlewood had cut in Phoenix with Eddy, was a hit. Hazlewood's brainwave had been to suggest that Eddy play very low, in the way Eddy Duchin played the piano, and to work that tremolo arm hard. To Wood's ears, however, 'Movin' n' Groovin'' sounded like "wires strung across the Grand Canyon", and he didn't mean that as a compliment. Hazlewood quit Dot to form Sill-Hazlewood Productions with seasoned Hollywood record man Lester Sill, then in the process of parting ways with songwriter-producers Jerry Leiber and Mike Stoller. After Sill cut a deal with Jamie Records in Philadelphia, the first of Eddy's many hits – 1958's 'Rebel Rouser' – jumped to No. 6 on the singles chart. The Eddy "twang" was born, assisted by squalling saxophones, whooping rebel yells, and a $200 grain elevator Hazlewood deployed as an echo chamber. "We had reverb, but I needed something to stretch it on out," he says. "As far as I remember, we went out and spent a very hot summer day in Phoenix yelling in grain elevators till I found one I liked. And then it all came together."

Over a four-year period, Eddy scored three Top 10 hits ('Rebel Rouser', 'Forty Miles Of Bad Road', 'Because They're Young') in America – and six in Britain, where he made thousands of kids dream of becoming guitar heroes. The records also caught the ears of such aspiring producers as Phil Spector, who badgered Sill to take him to Ramco so he could watch Hazlewood at work. History has long recounted that Hazlewood thought Spector an obnoxious git, and that Spector was the indirect cause of his eventual bust-up with Sill. Stan Ross, engineer at LA's Gold Star studio, remembered that when Spector produced the Paris Sisters' 1961 hit 'I Love How You Love Me' for the Sill-Hazlewood-owned Gregmark label, Hazlewood told Sill that he refused to "go in the same room with that little fart". Hazlewood declines to be drawn on any of this, though he remembers saving Spector's life when the diminutive *wunderkind* picked a fight with a giant redneck in a south Phoenix bar called Sarge's Cow Town. "It's bullshit that he pissed me off," he says. "I've seen that written a dozen times. I never said anything to anybody about Phil being a pain."

Whatever the truth of all this, Spector's rise as a producer spelled the end of Sill-Hazlewood Productions: shortly after 'I Love How You Love Me', Spector and Sill became partners in the new Philles label, and Hazlewood went back to producing Eddy. He also formed a folk group called the Shacklefords, recording two albums between 1963 and 1965. Out of this period came the remarkable *Trouble Is A Lonesome Town*, in its author's words "a sort of folk version of *Our Town*", written about his birthplace. "*Trouble* started at A and went to Z, it was one of those kinds of albums," he says. "They have other names for them, but that's what I call 'em. I'd tried to interest some people in the idea, but after a while I just gave up. Then I thought, 'Well, maybe if I just demo it, it'll make a good demo album'. And then I played it to Jack Tracy at Mercury – a jazz guy, but he liked the kind of garbage I did." In green-lighting *Trouble*, little did Tracy know that it was the start of one of the most oddly low-profile recording careers in pop history. A series of Cash-esque character sketches prefaced by hokey spoken introductions, the album sold unspectacularly but caught the attention of Mo Ostin, the accountant whom Frank Sinatra had recently installed at the helm of his new Reprise label. "Mo says to me, 'You got another album in you like that *Trouble* thing?' And I say, 'As a matter of fact I do. It's called *The Not So Very Important People* [aka *The N.S.V.I.P.'s*]'. So he says, 'Well, do *that* for us'." *The N.S.V.I.P.'s* (1965) was even more eccentric than *Trouble*, the daft southern humour of its spoken intros often at odds with Hazlewood's bleak tales of misfits and indigents. Exactly what Ostin made of the record isn't known: given Hazlewood had already written or produced several hits for him (e.g. Dean Martin's 'Houston', Dino, Desi & Billy's 'I'm A Fool'), he probably didn't care. "Mo thought I was a crazy little weird sonofabitch," says Hazlewood, "but he would protect me from the wiles of corporate bullshit."

"Lee looked at his solo albums as demos," says Suzi Jane Hokom. "A lot of things like 'Sand' and 'Summer Wine' we did together before Nancy Sinatra came on the scene. He was an amazing writer. He'd sit there with his Scotch, and these things would just come out of him. He was a very complex guy, a dichotomy unto himself. There's a part of Lee that's just out there, but there's still the guy from Oklahoma, the wildcatter's son." Late in 1965, Reprise staffer Jimmy Bowen asked Hazlewood to help jump-start the career of the boss' daughter. As it happens, it was Nancy herself who insisted on recording "a dirty old Texan tune" she heard Hazlewood running down one night. Lee told her 'These Boots Were Made For Walkin'' was a man's song, but she wasn't having it. And by the time she was in the vocal booth, Hazlewood was egging her on all the way. "I had the engineer turn off the mics so I could go out there and talk to my star," he says. "I said, 'Look, I want you to sing this like you're a 16-year-old girl who goes out with 45-year-old truck drivers. Now goddamn it, sing it like that'."

Sinatra *did* sing it like that. In January 1966, the record reached No. 1, Hazlewood's first chart-topper. Along with her performance in Roger Corman's *The Wild Angels*, 'Boots' established her as a female shitkicker – part country-pop vixen, part Jersey biker girl – and led to a string of hits and duets written and produced by Hazlewood. (The 1967 No. 1 Frank-and-Nancy duet 'Somethin' Stupid' was a Hazlewood/Bowen co-production.) Most of them, arranged by LA session supremo Billy Strange, were minor pop gems. Others – hybrids of psychedelic rock, Tex-Mex balladry and epic Spectorpop – stand as enigmatic classics to this day. "Few producers and songwriters have managed to combine such disparate elements *and* make the Top 40," writes Richie Unterberger in *Unknown Legends Of Rock'n'Roll*, a book which argues that 1968's 'Some Velvet Morning' may be "the strangest record" ever to enjoy major chart action in America. "Lee always had some kind of underlying message in his songs," says Sinatra, who was 11 years younger than her mentor. "I guess it's partly what he used to call 'beauty and the beast', the young girl and the older guy – that fantasy. We didn't have an affair, we didn't have a physical relationship, yet we created something that suggested we did. I guess people thought that was interesting because we were so different in age."

"If Nancy and I had ever had the Sonny and Cher thing going, I doubt it would have been as successful," Hazlewood says. "When she did her songs, she was a ballsy broad. When we did our songs together, we were some space-o unit, or an old man fooling with a young girl, or whatever it was. That would never have had the niceness of 'The Beat Goes On'. Sonny and Cher were very vanilla, whereas our songs were not necessarily very nice. Most of our duets are not double-meaning, they're kinda *triple*-meaning. If you're some Santa Monica doper sitting on the street, then it's a dope song. If you're some little innocent girl sitting in Nebraska, it's just a song. And then if you're really a Nancy and Lee fan, it means a lot of other things too. It's everything combined." So great was the success he enjoyed between 1965 and 1968 that it came as no surprise when MCA offered him a ton of money to launch his own label. Unfortunately, the demands of running a record company ill-suited Hazlewood, who failed to score a single hit during the label's existence.

"LHI seemed to be a glorious situation for him, but it turned out to be a lot of responsibility," says Hokom. "I think that was difficult, especially for an artist. I mean, Lee's an artist, he's a writer. He's not a businessman. There was no reason why he couldn't have kept on going – he'd already been through several different phases of music – but he burned a lot of bridges and pissed a lot of people off. I also think that having to deal with young bands that were coming up and had definite ideas of their own – who were less malleable than Nancy – wasn't conducive to the way he worked." Definitely less malleable than Sinatra were Gram Parsons' International Submarine Band, whose *Safe At Home* – the album that gave birth to country rock as we know it – was produced by Hokom herself. Long before he joined the Byrds, while still under contract to LHI, Parsons was rubbing Hazlewood up the wrong way. "Lee and Gram had such problems, though I think Lee looks back now and realises he blew it," says Hokom. "Lee was older and his ego just kinda got in the way. I think he was jealous – that's basically what it boiled down to, that he could not stand all this attention I was lavishing on these guys who were more of my generation."

In a sense, the squabbling over Parsons and the failure of LHI were symptomatic of the fact that Hazlewood was hopelessly out of sync with rock'n'roll. By the end of the Sixties, he was itching to move on, or at least get away. Though he kept his oar in, producing country sessions by Waylon Jennings and Eddy Arnold, his restlessness eventually took him to Europe – specifically Sweden, where, as the decade turned, he found a home away from home. "That was finally the end for me," Hokom remembers. "I took up with Doug Dillard and we went off into bluegrass heaven for several years. Next thing I knew, Lee sent me an album called *Requiem For An Almost Lady*, which was just brutally honest about our relationship. And he said, you know, 'This is the way I feel', and I went, 'Well, too bad! You blew it, and that's that'. So that's where his Swedish thing came in. He did have this amazing following there. He found a new life, a bunch of adoring people that would sit around and listen to his old jokes and stories."

The albums continued to appear – *Requiem, Cowboy In Sweden* and *13* all contain their share of fascinating songs – but Hazlewood channelled most of his energies into a series of films and documentaries made with director Torbjörn Axelman. Some won awards; one, interestingly, was about Leonard Cohen, whose 'Come Spend The Morning' Hazlewood covered on the 1973 album *Poet, Fool, Or Bum* (the one Charles Shaar Murray summarised so succinctly in the single-word *NME* review "Bum."). "I like Cohen, but I wouldn't wanna be in his ballpark," Hazlewood says of any mooted influence. "They're pussy songs, most of 'em. But I do like his melodies sometimes. He takes the same chords I use and gets better melodies than I do." Commuting back and forth between Europe and the States, he gradually faded from view. By the Eighties, he was living once again in Phoenix, watching ASCAP cheques roll in and raising his adopted daughter Samantha. (Samantha now has a daughter of her own, named – with a nod to 'Some Velvet Morning' – Phaedra.) "It was really a dead time," he admits. "Except for a few people doing my songs, not too much was going on. And by the way, it didn't bother me too much, because I had a daughter to raise and I was trying to be a very legitimate father."

When he finally re-emerged in the mid-Nineties, it was to accompany Nancy Sinatra on a successful comeback tour of the States. That was when he finally realised that all those alternative types who worshipped him were for real. "What is strange to me," he says, "is not that a 25-year-old knows some of the old hits I wrote, because they could've got it from their mom or dad or even grandma. What's surprising, and what still bothers me a lot, is they'll come up and ask me about some obscure song they shouldn't even know. And I go, 'How old are you?' And they go, '19, *sir*'. And they say they paid $60 for some old album of mine in Germany, and I say, 'You're outta your mind, I'd've *given* you one, for Chrissakes'. And then they say, 'Why didn't you sing 'After Six'?' And I go, 'How in the hell would you even *know* that song? *I* forgot I'd written it till two years ago'."

"We played the Limelight in New York, and Sonic Youth and the Breeders were there," Sinatra herself told *MOJO*. "I was just so shocked at the alternative bands that are interested in our music. I met Courtney Love at Lollapalooza – she's such a big fan. It's so touching, because you have daughters or sons who are that age, and you feel too old, you know it's their generation. But then when it's validated by those very people, you can imagine what it's like."

The evening sun sinks over the horizon. Hazlewood is on his fourth Scotch. "Any faxes come in?" he shouts to Jeanie, who is working upstairs. "Huh? Yeah? Well, I don't wanna see 'em!" [Pause for Jeanie's barely discernible reply.] "Oh, they're all *good* news?!" One, it turns out, is from Steve Shelley, its arrival prompting a moment of sincere gratitude. "I don't have any great visions of the albums selling," he says. "Steve thinks he'll sell a few copies, but Steve's weird. I care about them being played somewhere where we get performances on 'em, especially the obscure things. The strange part is, 'Why this late in life?' Because on July 9th of this year, I'll be seven decades old, and seven decades is a long time. And by the way, I enjoy it very much. I still wish I could run five miles like I used to, but other than that I'm comfy. I'm happy that Sonic Youth drag along a few other people who like obscure old fucks like myself. Steve has some obscure things on his label, but I think I'm the only obscure MOR person he has around there."

MOJO, 1999

11 Dark Angel
Laura Nyro

Album bought in London in 1974

IT'S A STONED soul picnic: the second night of the Monterey Pop festival, with the sun dipping into the ocean south of San Francisco. Everyone's here, all the beautiful movers and shakers of the blossoming rock sound. The Byrds have just played – uncomfortably, with David Crosby ranting about the Kennedy assassination – and the beatific crowd eagerly awaits Haight-Ashbury heroes the Jefferson Airplane. But what on earth's *this*? An all-but-unknown chanteuse from New York is gliding out on to the stage in a dark gown that suggests she got lost on the way to a cabaret engagement at San Francisco's Fairmont Hotel. The girl's got horns, vibraphones, Black backing singers in blue cocktail dresses, the whole Barbra Streisand caboodle: hasn't anyone told her this is the pinnacle moment of the summer of love, the nexus of the hippie rock revolution fomented in California?

"Everything I hoped she would bring to it, she didn't bring," Lou Adler, the festival's co-organiser, would remember of Laura Nyro's short performance that night. "She brought a nightclub act. She came in a long black gown. She brought background singers. It pretty much stood out as New York and not California." Talk about being out of step with your peers. Nyro is a 20-year-old singer-songwriter whose music, image and stage presentation are almost defiantly anachronistic in the setting of Monterey's emerging stars: Hendrix, the Who, the Airplane, and especially Janis Joplin, the unkempt Texan hellraiser whose ball'n'chain bawling tore the roof off the Monterey Fairgrounds stage this very afternoon – and who'll be back by popular demand after the Airplane's set later tonight. "The audience didn't get it at all," says producer Bones Howe, who engineered for Adler's acts at Monterey. "Nyro had this really high voice and she was floating around the stage and I don't think people understood what she was doing there. Here was Lou trying to give her a break, and she wasn't even primarily a performer."

True, Monterey Pop is also showcasing the unhip likes of Johnny Rivers and the Association – and, let's be honest, *de facto* hosts the Mamas & the Papas – but Nyro's East Coast art-diva act seems so out of tune with the zeitgeist that some spectators treat her as a traitor to the cause. "The curled lip, the clenched tooth, the uprolling eye, the slow head shake of opprobrium," one such Monterey patron wrote in a letter to the *New York Times* 30 years later. "That was me, I'm afraid, 30 rows back, suffering under the apparently mistaken impression that my seatmates and I were witnessing a dreadfully pretentious woman offering up exactly the sort of formulaic pop-music piffle we had expected to avoid by gathering in Monterey." In a report on the festival for *Newsweek*, writer Michael Lydon noted that among the "few disasters who can be written off from the start" was Nyro, "a melodramatic singer accompanied by two dancing girls who pranced absurdly." Watching Nyro from the wings of Monterey's stage is another young songwriter whose career will weirdly parallel hers. Jimmy Webb, who the previous day played keyboards with his mentor Johnny Rivers – and whose song 'Up-Up And Away' is just easing its way into the Top 10 singles chart courtesy of pop-soul quartet the Fifth Dimension – sees Nyro "in essence booed offstage, because in those days no one really knew what a singer-songwriter was". Neatly enough, Nyro's song 'Stoned Soul Picnic' will give the 5D their next smash hit exactly a year later, by which time she will be one of the most successful songwriters in America.

But did Nyro really tank that Saturday night? When *The Complete Monterey Pop Festival* DVD was released in 2002, it came with outtake footage of Nyro performing both 'Wedding Bell Blues', subsequently a No. 1 for the aforementioned Fifth Dimension, and 'Poverty Train', a harrowing song of drug abuse in the ghetto. Both appear to be received well, with effusive applause and cheers. If it is true that a mortified Nyro slunk offstage in tears, to be bundled into a limo by the Mamas & the Papas' Michelle Phillips, it seems conceivable that – in *Monterey Pop* director D. A. Pennebaker's words – "[Laura] just imagined the whole thing". "I don't remember booing so much as just a total lack of interest," says Bones Howe, who'd already flipped over Nyro's recorded version of 'Wedding Bell Blues'. "Let's just say she was *miscast* at Monterey. It was only in the context of everything else that happened there. It was really smoke-dope folk music and heavy rock music – people setting fire to their guitars – and she wasn't folk and she wasn't heavy rock." Whatever the truth really is, the legend of Laura Nyro's "disaster" at Monterey will dog every step of her way for the remaining 30 years of her life. She herself will refer to the trauma as a "crucifixion… the essence of failure". Furthermore, it will offer a possible explanation for the diffidence of her relationship with success and fame – and even for the relative obscurity in which her reputation now languishes. Or at least *did* languish until, once again, her name figured among the nominees for induction into the Rock & Roll Hall of Fame.

CERTAINLY IT'S fair to say that Nyro wasn't psychologically ready to play Monterey Pop on June 17, 1967. It was the first major live performance of her career, coming on the back of the Verve/Folkways release of her debut album *More Than A New Discovery*, and it was a gamble on the part of Lou Adler. Still, what he and others heard in those first songs – 'Wedding Bell Blues', 'Stoney End', and the extraordinary 'And When I Die', a song of mortality Nyro had penned at the tender age of 17 – was real enough. Hers was an awesome talent, a bridge between the best Brill Building writers of the early Sixties and the more adventurous female singer-songwriters who would dominate the early Seventies in America. New-York-rooted, the Bronx-born Nyro wrote rhapsodies of street life, complex pop that was equal parts doo wop and Stephen Sondheim (one of her more highbrow admirers). The great "trilogy" of albums for Columbia that followed her debut – *Eli And The Thirteenth Confession*, *New York Tendaberry*, *Christmas And The Beads Of Sweat* – remains breathtaking after all these years, easily the equal of anything Joni Mitchell produced in its wake. The late Ian Mac-Donald called Nyro's music "the most original, resourceful, and powerful composed by any woman in the field of popular music over the last 50 years".

"I don't know what it's like for others, but to describe what I feel when I hear her chords, her clusters of sound, it's like pure emotion," says Rickie Lee Jones, arguably her greatest disciple. "On settings of pure emotion, she put these lyrics that reflected true innocence and intellect. It was all so exciting and exotic to me, because it was written in that faraway land of New York City, where there were fire escapes and rough dark men and people wandered the streets late at night and rode trains under the ground." Jones' 1981 masterpiece *Pirates* sounds like a West Coast transposition of Nyro's sound, complete with the highwire soprano swoops that were one of the latter's vocal trademarks. Nor is it just the girls who hymn Nyro's genius. Philly *wunderkind* Todd Rundgren was happily fronting anglophile Who clones the Nazz when, in 1968, he fell under the spell of *Eli And The Thirteenth Confession* and ripped up his own rulebook. As the sometime Runt told *Uncut*, *Eli* was "an epiphany for me, altering my songwriting, and the direction it took me in wasn't really where the rest of the Nazz wanted to go." Nyro-steeped Nazz tracks like 'If That's The Way You Feel' and the 11-minute 'A Beautiful Song' were prototypes for all the great Rundgren piano ballads to come, precipitating the break-up of the band. (Todd would later work with and even enjoy a brief affair with her. His 1970 song 'Baby Let's Swing' explicitly namechecked her: *"Laura, I saw you in that magazine/ You looked like a gypsy queen..."*) It's hard not to assume, too, that Jimmy Webb copped more than a few Nyro tropes for his own pocket symphonies: time changes and harmonic clusters would be endemic to such epics as Richard Harris' 'MacArthur Park' and 'The Yard Went On Forever'. Like Nyro, moreover, Webb would experience major success as a songwriter to the stars while failing to convince the world of his greatness as a singer in his own right.

How should we categorise her music? We shouldn't, of course. But we might call it "orch-soul", or "avant-MOR". It's fearlessly flamboyant, emotionally explosive, the articulation of a giddy exultation in the sheer possibilities of life. It's a glorious hyper-pop hodgepodge of Broadway, holy-rolling gospel and street-corner soul; music that rides on impulse and switches time signatures compulsively, that grabs us by the scruff of the neck and carries us off into the sky. Next to the mellow pleasures of a *Tapestry*, Nyro at moments verges on the ridiculous and, yes, the pretentious. I'm not sure *I'd* have "got" Nyro if I'd been a 21-year-old hippie at Monterey. But the older you are, the more grateful you become for singer-songwriters who take emotional risks, whose rapture is about abandon and release. Perhaps it comes down to the particular nature of female yearning, of Woman's courage and vulnerability. It's what you hear in Nyro and Rickie Lee and Teena Marie, and what you hear in Kate Bush and Björk and Mary Margaret O'Hara too. It's thrilling and heart-stopping, and not everyone can handle it. It's significant, no doubt, that Nyro never nestled in the LA canyons, that she stayed put in gothic Gotham in her black clothes and black lipstick, a Jewish-Italian earth-witch singing of her city and its seething life. Taken up as his *cause célèbre* by the young and insatiably ambitious David Geffen, she nonetheless refused to defect to his LA-based Asylum label and stayed with Columbia, a quintessentially New York company.

Born Laura Nigro [pronounced *Neer-ro*] on October 18, 1947, she had several things going for her as a kid. Her father Lou was a trumpeter, her beloved mother Gilda a bookkeeper who urged her to read poets and novelists. Music of all kinds – jazz, opera, pop; John Coltrane and Miles Davis; Leontyne Price and Nina Simone – reverberated through the various Bronx apartments in which the family lived. Nyro soon gravitated to the Steinway grand her dad bought after he began moonlighting as a piano tuner. A melancholy introvert, Nyro was – so she said in 1969 – "always kind of alone" but always came out of herself at the piano keys. One summer in the Catskills, the upstate region where New York's middle-class Jewish community traditionally vacationed, she stunned everyone by organising and writing arrangements for a vocal group on "Sing Night". Her fascination with harmonies, a hallmark of her great "trilogy", grew still further when she sat in with a Puerto Rican street-corner quartet in the Bronx. Coupled with her classical studies at Harlem's High School of Music and Art, this asphalt education proved formative, the sound of East Coast doo wop, soul and girl-group pop a constant thread in her musical tapestry all the way through to her glorious 1971 covers album *Gonna Take A Miracle*. She was already writing feverishly by the time she graduated from Music and Art in June 1965. She saw herself as a backroom writer, a new Carole King, possibly even a female Bacharach (whose intricately subtle chords and inflections wowed her). When the comically monikered publisher Artie Mogull agreed to hear her in 1966, she played him a handful of the songs that would appear on *More Than A New Discovery*. He was impressed but perplexed by her rhythmic idiosyncrasies and stream-of-consciousness poetry, and unsurprisingly unsure of her bottom-line commercial prospects.

It was through him, though, that Nyro snagged her deal with Verve, an MGM subsidiary that was already home to Tim Hardin and Richie Havens.

"All I ask of livin' is to have to no chains on me," she sang on the almost Pentecostal 'And When I Die' – *More Than A New Discovery*'s last track – and the line might be heard as a credo for all her music. "I'm from the school that there are no limitations with a song," she told *SongTalk*'s Paul Zollo in 1994. "You can write the simplest song, or you can just write a song that is abstract art." The album, though, was flattened into conventional cabaret-pop by hack producer Herb Bernstein, something that may have helped Mogull – and subsequently Geffen, who acquired her catalogue from him – pitch her songs to other artists. 'And When I Die', 'Stoney End' and 'Wedding Bell Blues' would be covered by dozens of artists, bringing Geffen his first millions in the process. "When David started out, he was nothing but a music man and dealt almost completely from the heart," says Jimmy Webb, who himself wound up on Asylum. "Anyone who could take poor pitiful Laura under his arm after Monterey and say, 'Don't worry, darling, we'll make them eat this crow they've heaped on you' and then stand by her…. to me it proved he was all music and all heart." Awed by her talent, Geffen wanted to make Nyro "the biggest star in the world" – or at least make the recording of the second album a happier experience. Milking the relationship he had with Columbia's Clive Davis, then busy signing up everyone from Janis Joplin to Santana, he arranged for Nyro to audition at the label's "Black Rock" building in midtown Manhattan. Listening to her in the semi-darkness of his office, Davis was rapt and agreed to sign her on the spot. "I'd met David when I went east with the Association," says Bones Howe. "He told me he was going to make a deal with Clive, and he said Laura had made a demo of the album just at the piano. He came to LA and I asked if I could keep the demo overnight. And on that album were 'Stoned Soul Picnic' and 'Sweet Blindness'. I played 'Picnic' to the Fifth Dimension and told them it was going to be their first R&B No. 1 record." (Actually it reached No. 2.)

Geffen, whose role with Nyro lay somewhere between brother and lover, installed her in a penthouse apartment, with a terrace, on West 79th Street. At times they were inseparable; they even dropped acid together. More importantly he teamed her with Columbia arranger Charlie Calello, whose work included hits by the Toys and the Four Seasons. Calello instinctively grasped that orthodox production approaches would not serve Nyro well; backing singers, for example, were out, replaced by her own multi-tracked overdubs. The breathless energy of 'Lu' and 'Eli's Comin'' and 'The

Confession', with Nyro backed by such ace New York session players as bassist Chuck Rainey and guitarist Hugh McCracken, proclaimed a new kind of art-pop – like Carole King's legendary demos fused with the MOR symphonics of a Jimmy Webb. "I thought the record would make history because it came from a special place," Calello told *The Guardian*'s Richard Williams, himself a long-time Nyro evangelist. "I knew it was the best music I had ever done." 1969's *New York Tendaberry* was, if anything, even more satisfying than *Eli*. The sheer bravura of her singing and playing on *Tendaberry*'s title track, an ode to the metropolis she described as "a religion", and the brooding, intermittently explosive 'Gibsom Street' – a song about abortion – was intoxicating. Producer Roy Halee recorded Nyro's voice and piano live, overdubbing everything else afterwards: something of a challenge for players such as peerless drummer Gary Chester, given her often wayward timing. To Nyro's biographer Michelle Kort, Halee called the album "American classical pop". For him, the harmonic complexity of tracks like 'Captain For Dark Mornings' and 'Captain St. Lucifer' – as with Judee Sill, the Devil makes frequent appearances in Nyro's early work – was worthy of Gershwin himself.

By now, she was enjoying the fruits of the royalties she was receiving from hit covers by not only the Fifth Dimension but Three Dog Night ('Eli's Comin'") and Blood, Sweat & Tears ('And When I Die'); she was also happily in love with BS&T's bass player Jim Fielder. "Almost all her songs were about guys," says Bones Howe. "There were a lot of failed romances, and she would talk openly about them. Emotionally she was very vulnerable, and she would retreat to the sanctuary of her apartment. 'The Captain' was a recurring figure in her songs. She wasn't a particularly attractive gal, but she wasn't unattractive, and she was the sweetest woman. She was enchanting one-on-one." Howe became friendly enough with her for Clive Davis to request that he produce a new, Fifth-Dimension-style arrangement of *New York Tendaberry*'s pleadingly political 'Save The Country'. "Clive was furious that the Fifth had a smash with one of her songs when his A&R guys didn't even pick it as one of her singles," Howe recalls. "She came out to the Coast and we did it in the Columbia studio, just the one song." He believes there's a simple explanation for why other artists had hits with Nyro's songs when her own versions were commercial stiffs. "She didn't have a pop voice," he says. "She wrote great songs, and songs that could be recorded many different ways, but her voice was a bit shrill." ("Shrill" is an epithet frequently applied by critics to Nyro's pipes, and I contend that it's unjust – or at least a slightly sexist euphemism for "too nakedly emotional for comfort". Spend time with the voice and it penetrates to the core of human feeling.)

The third and final part of the Columbia "trilogy", if that's what it is, was arguably the best. Ian MacDonald wrote in 1974 that if he could have rigged the vote and snuck 1970's *Christmas And The Beads Of Sweat* into *NME*'s Best 100 Albums of All Time, he would have. But then, as he pointed out, male critics had long been quick to dismiss Nyro's ecstatic emotionalism as a sort of hysteria. "I hate Laura Nyro and her blackboard-and-fingernails voice and daintily soulful pretensions," Ed Ward wrote intemperately in *Rolling Stone*. Interestingly, the passion of her music didn't phase the great Duane Allman. Brought in by co-producers Arif Mardin and Felix Cavaliere to sear the magnificent 'Beads Of Sweat', the mutton-chopped Macon guitarist acknowledged Nyro as "a real outasight chick and a fantastic artist and composer". The peak moments of *Christmas* – the frisky soul of 'Blackpatch', the haunting exotica of 'Upstairs By A Chinese Lamp', the blithely beautiful and almost Joni-esque 'When I Was A Freeport And You Were The Main Drag' – rank with Nyro's greatest creations. I've spent much of the last year revisiting these songs and find myself constantly humming passages from them, hearing their vocal swoops and horn fills in my head as I pad about the house or surrey down the street. (It's well worth hearing them, too, on *Spread Your Wings And Fly*, a belatedly released live album of Nyro solo at the piano from New York's Fillmore East in May 1971.) She is one of those artists who completely takes you over, whose chords and grooves propel you through the world. Listen even more closely and you realise she was also one of the greatest poets pop ever produced.

Some might say that the musical fire in Laura Nyro died down after *Christmas*. No doubt it's significant that, as more than a few groundbreaking Sixties innovators would, she retreated to the comfort zone of a covers album. 1971's *Gonna Take A Miracle* was Nyro's homage to oldies, to the vocal/girl-group classics she'd loved as an adolescent, the affection underscored by the participation of Patti LaBelle, Nona Hendryx and Sarah Dash. Still, as "retreats" go it's a splendid collection, equal parts NYC, Chicago, Motown and Philly (where it was produced by Kenny Gamble and Leon Huff), with Nyro's piercing soprano coiled around the sharp harmonies of LaBelle and her soul sisters. The album presaged a still deeper retreat: the five-year silence that ensued before the serene return that was *Smile*. "The life of an artist stretches over a whole lifetime," Nyro told long-time fan Rob Steen in 1993. "It just takes its course. I do have a little more freedom these days, but I don't want to give the impression that I... just stopped working altogether. It's just... things kinda mellowed."

"She reminded me more of a writer or a painter – someone who spent a lot of time in a small room with a canvas or a typewriter," Bones Howe says of Nyro. "These are not out-front people. She stayed in her own environment most of the time. You'd have thought that in the Seventies – the era of Carole King and Joni Mitchell – Laura would have re-emerged, but maybe she wasn't driven enough. And she probably had enough money coming in from songwriting royalties." She had never cared greatly for fame, and wasn't unduly bothered about not being in the public arena. "[She] made a choice that has tempted me on many occasions," said Mitchell, who cited her as one of her few peers. "And that was to lead an ordinary life... which is brave and tough in its own way." After a succession of semi-famous but low-profile beaux – Jim Fielder, Dallas Taylor, a young Jackson Browne – Nyro married handsome Vietnam veteran David Bianchini, moved to the sleepy fishing town of Gloucester, Mass., and recharged her creative batteries. When *Smile* – an album that reunited her with Charlie Calello – finally appeared in 1976, it was noticeably simpler and mellower, though it did include 'Money', a funky side-swipe at David Geffen, with whom Nyro had fallen out after his sale of her catalogue to Columbia. *"I feel like a pawn in my own world,"* she sang on it; *"I found the system and I lost the world."* Her lack of interest in material reward is one of the more remarkable examples of an artist staying true to her muse. Ending her marriage and moving to Connecticut, she became explicitly feminist in her outlook, though in 1978 she did have a son, Gil, by one Harindra Singh. By 1982 Nyro was living with Maria Desiderio, a painter she had met in California and who remained her partner for the rest of her life. Rumours of bisexuality had followed Nyro ever since *Eli*'s 'Emmie', a track often hailed as the first lesbian love song. (Its author denied it was any such thing.)

If she never quite matched the dizzying heights of the "trilogy", it's hardly as though Nyro's genius deserted her. "There was no winning for Nyro with certain critics," Michelle Kort noted in *Soul Picnic*, a fine 2002 biography. "If she was passionate and unbridled, she was called undisciplined and shrill. If she simplified, softened, or showed more emotional detachment, she was deemed bland and was considered to have lost her wizardry." Albums such as *Smile, Nested* (1978), *Mother's Spiritual* (1984), and *Walk The Dog And Light The Light* (1994) were replete with marvels: 'I Am The Blues', 'To A Child', 'Woman Of The World'. Meanwhile the live *Season Of Lights* (1977) – belatedly released in its full double-length splendour in Japan in 1993 –

set her greatest songs to new jazz-rock arrangements played by a stellar band that included *Astral Weeks* bassist Richard Davis and former Sly & the Family Stone drummer Andy Newmark. The opening version of 'Money' was one of the most exhilarating performances of her life. A decade later, she re-explored her back catalogue with another live album, recorded at New York's Bottom Line with the usual grand piano surprisingly replaced by an electric keyboard. Alongside new pieces like the coolly funky 'Roll Of The Ocean' and the Native-American-themed 'Broken Rainbow', she reworked 'Emmie', 'The Confession', 'Stoned Soul Picnic' and 'And When I Die', though she stated, for the record, that "my show is not about nostalgia". A tiny but fanatical tribe of followers kept her legend alive on the club circuit. "I just think it's a very soulful connection," she said of her predominantly female followers. "Maybe the cult of the mother, the call of the wild…" Many of them shared her feminism and her commitment to the peace and animal rights movements. "No one was citing her," says Rickie Lee Jones, who occasionally spoke to Nyro on the phone. "She was playing to tiny audiences and her work was too esoteric to translate, singing about dogs and stuff at that moment. I saw her only once and she was sad, a barely attended colosseum show, things I now endure. How humble life makes us."

Nyro began feeling unwell in early 1995. By that summer, she'd been diagnosed with ovarian cancer, which had killed her mother 20 years before. At least she was able to bring things full circle when Columbia requested her input in the compilation of *Stoned Soul Picnic*, a two-CD anthology of her best work. Looking back on her Sixties albums in the process, she characterised the songs of *New York Tendaberry* as the sound of "a teenage wild banshee". "When you're very young you're just more emotional in certain ways," she told Paul Zollo. "Some of that stuff I was concerned about when I was 19, I just would not be concerned about now…" Thank heaven for youth, if that's the case. By early 1997, she knew she was dying; she passed away just before dawn on April 8th. *"And when I die, and when I'm gone,"* she'd sung 30 years earlier, *"There'll be one child born, and a world to carry on…"* It was a mark of how far she'd backed away from the limelight that news of her illness – let alone of her death – came as a shock to many of her rock peers. Fittingly, her funeral was not star-studded but made up of friends and family members who'd been close to her in her physical decline.

WATCHING HIGHLIGHTS of the Mercury Music Prize awards in September 2008, I couldn't help thinking of Nyro while Adele and Laura

Marling warbled their tepid offerings: Adele's ersatz soul, Marling's polite introspections. How bland, how *obvious* most modern-day songstresses sound. "[Nyro] does some fairly complex harmonic things, which is why her stuff is probably not popular now," jazz pianist Billy Childs told Paul Zollo. "I mean, what is popular now is beyond being simple; it's nonexistent, you know. Like, harmony doesn't exist."

Hear her while you still have time: she won't disappoint. As Rickie Lee Jones says, "Laura gave me the courage to say, 'Here I am like I am – I am Girl, and I am strong like the sun.'" She pauses, then adds: "Too bad everyone waits till people are dead. She could have used that glory while she was here."

Uncut, 2009

12 My Life Is Good
Randy Newman

Album bought in London in 1975

RANDY NEWMAN reclines in a well-padded chair in London's Savoy Hotel and sighs. He tends to sigh at some point in the interviews he gives, and the sigh is generally about the same thing – the fact that most people don't "get" Randy Newman. Arguably the greatest satirist Los Angeles has ever produced – as great as Billy Wilder and Preston Sturges, Frank Zappa and Albert Brooks, Garry Shandling and Steely Dan – he has just spent three days in London being filmed for a Channel 4 TV special with Jon Ronson. But what sticks with him most naggingly about the experience is how well he was getting along with the make-up artist until he started singing 'My Life Is Good', perhaps his most acerbic piece of satire. "We'd talk and we'd go at the same speed, 'cause she was smart," Newman says of the girl in question. "But then I started singing 'My Life Is Good', and I could see she was going, 'What the hell? *This* is what he does??' It's like you've got to be there at the beginning with me, and you've got to be listening to get what I'm doing. It's not the ideal thing for a medium that takes place in cars or at parties where people are eating olives."

On one level this is a damning indictment of pop culture, as well as an opportunity for all Newman fans to feel superior to people who like Sting and Elton John. But on another it points up the fact that no one else has ever written songs like 'My Life Is Good', the bellicose boast of a man who's just been told – by an "old bag" of a teacher – that his kid is misbehaving at private school; nor written songs like 'Rednecks', an ambiguous apologia for the American South with its forever-shocking line about *"keepin' the n*****s down"*. (I can't be alone in having wound the windows up while driving around with the track on the car stereo.) Well, *almost* no one. One of the rare exceptions – though it's hard to connect the two across their different genres and generations – is that Marshall Mathers kid. "There's some similarity and some influence there," Newman says. "Eminem didn't influence me exactly, but I have an affinity for what he does because it's vaguely in the same ballpark as what I do. And almost no one else has chosen to do that kind of stuff – songs in character, with bad guys most of the time."

Did it make Newman any more nervous to revisit 'Rednecks' on his new album *The Randy Newman Songbook Vol 1* than when he first recorded it for 1974's *Good Old Boys*? "It always bothered me when that word went by," he replies. "But I needed it in that song. There was no other way to do it. And I do the song everywhere, and people get it. It's kind of complicated, in that when you've got a big word like that, you've got to be careful it doesn't blast out the next minute and a half. And what that song is talking about is the Southerner complaining that the North pretends to moral superiority in its racial behaviour. And 30 years later the North is still segregated. LA is segregated. I don't see Black people in LA."

THE RANDY *Newman Songbook* came about when its namesake split from DreamWorks Records after one poorly promoted 1999 album, *Bad Love*. Disgusted that the company had done so little to inform the world of *Bad Love*'s existence, Newman signed with Nonesuch and agreed to re-record a bunch of old songs in the one-man-and-his-piano manner of his live shows. "One of the reasons I agreed to do it was that this was the way I wrote the songs and the way I most often perform them, and maybe there should be a record of that before I die," he says. "You reach a point where your style crystallises or ossifies, and what I did notice was that there was a consistency from at least *12 Songs* [1970] on, and maybe even from the first album. It wasn't like I did *Songs In The Key Of Life* and then dropped off."

Up to a point, I'll go along with that. From his 1968 debut *Randy Newman Creates Something New Under The Sun* to *Land Of Dreams* 20 years later, Newman put together one flawless collection after another (the absolute best being *Good Old Boys* and 1977's *Little Criminals*, the latter featuring the woefully misunderstood 'Short People'.) If *Bad Love* and *Randy Newman's Faust* (1995) aren't quite as great as he believes, *Bad Love* nonetheless contains 'Shame' – the only song I'm aware of in which the protagonist starts arguing with his backing singers. "The guy in 'Shame' is a character you're familiar with in literature, like somebody in Faulkner or Eudora Welty," says Newman. "He's a Southern guy who's old and sort of smooth but not smart enough to be *really* smooth, and he has a temper. He's got a Lexus, and he's got money and lives in the French Quarter, but this girl's killing him. No matter how powerful you are, if you fall for a 22-year-old it can destroy you. And I love that that exists."

One of the keys to understanding Newman is to realise how out of step he's always been with rock's prevailing ethos. For starters, he was the nephew of illustrious Hollywood composers Alfred and Lionel Newman. After studying composition and arrangement at UCLA, he started out as a backroom hack at Metric Music, the West Coast's very own Sixties Brill Building. His songs were recorded by everyone from P. J. Proby to Dusty Springfield before his breakthrough came: a song called 'Simon Smith And His Amazing Dancing Bear', about a boy and his improbable pet. "I had a different lyric – 'Susie, Susie', or some girl's name like that, and I couldn't stand it," he told me in 1995. "And whatever happened in my mind, something clicked, snapped, broke, and I wrote 'Simon Smith'." The template for many of his future songs, it was a hit for the Alan Price Set in 1967 and paved the way for a contract with his boyhood chum Lenny Waronker, then a mentor to the swelling stable of singer-songwriters at super-hip Warner-Reprise. Though he had little affinity with the CSNY-Joni-Jackson canyon-cowboy community, he benefited greatly from the new wave of interest in artists who did it all themselves. "Dylan and others like him made it all right for your voice not to be *bel canto*," he says, though for him the modus operandi didn't alter: most of his life has been spent sitting at his piano, waiting for inspiration to strike. "Things didn't change too much for me," he says. "There was marijuana, but I never liked it that much. I'd see Nilsson [who cut an album of Newman songs in 1970], but I wasn't part of anything. If they had a club, I wasn't in it. I also had a family real early – 22, 23 – so I was different in that sense. I wasn't free of drugs or ending up in places I shouldn't have been at three in the morning, but I did luckily have a solid wife and kids. I don't look on it as fun, the big drug days. There were more downs than ups, I thought."

Newman used to say that the depressives' favourite 'I Think It's Going To Rain Today' – a highlight of his debut album – was mopey and jejune. How did it feel going back to it for *Songbook*? "You know, I changed my mind a little about that song. I used to think it was just sophomore college boy romantic misery, sort of generalised young-man depression. I mean, I was 21, 22. But it's not bad. You know, *'Scarecrows dressed in the latest styles...'* Just the fact that the song uses the word 'implore' – it's almost outside the vocabulary you use for pop music nowadays. So I have a higher opinion of the song than I used to." Despite Ian MacDonald's verdict in *The People's Music* that *Randy Newman Creates Something New Under The Sun* is actually his best album, the debut was a stiff, prompting Waronker to suggest they dispense with maverick co-producer Van Dyke Parks – and the Mahler-esque orchestrations – and go straight for the rock jugular. The result was the sinewy, sensual *12 Songs*, which came within a whisker of featuring a Jimi Hendrix cameo. "I wrote 'Suzanne' with him in mind, and I talked to him on the phone about it. He said, 'You're a Sagittarius too, huh?' He was so lacking in confidence. So many people that are really good don't have a hell of a lot of confidence. It's unbelievable." (It's weird enough hearing Byrds guitarist Clarence White applying languid country licks to one of the creepiest items in Newman's catalogue – *"I'm gonna wait in the shadows, baby/ For you to come by/And then I'll jump from the shadows/And try and catch your eye..."*.)

If *Songbook* has any precedent in his work, it's *Randy Newman/Live* (1971), just Newman plus piano at New York's Bitter End club. Did he listen to it again? "No. The last time I really listened to my old stuff was when they put together that Rhino box set [1998's *Guilty: 30 Years Of Randy Newman*] and I had to." *Sail Away* (1972) is probably his best-known record, despite the fact its title song is an outrageous sales pitch for slaves to come to America: *"Climb aboard, little wog/Sail away with me..."* The withering black-heartedness of 'God's Song (That's Why I Love Mankind)' is matched only by the brazen jingoism of 'Political Science', a song that, with its famous lines *"They all hate us anyway/So let's drop the big one now"*, has never sounded more pertinent than it does today. "I never thought the song would remotely speak for anyone," Newman claims. "The Bush administration has gotten closer to it than anyone before, saying Europe's too old, just like I said in the song.

Old Europe! Who would ever dream anyone would be so ignorant? And the clumsiness of doing it out loud. Who knows what we've done or said in diplomatic channels, but you don't let it out. It's their ineptitude that's a little disturbing."

Could he write another song like 'Lines In The Sand', inspired by the Gulf War? "I could, if I gave myself that assignment. You could write a song about Paul Wolfowitz, who went on a talk show and said something like, 'Once democracy spreads to Iraq...' That's a song right there. You know, 'The Easter bunny will come...' It was just so bizarre that an intelligent fellow like that would believe this doctrine to the point of forgetting the weather and the rocks and the sand and the schools teaching people to hate the West, and what the steps would be for 20-year-old American soldiers on police duty. Put it like this, I don't have much hope that Iraq will be better off in two years." Two years after *Sail Away*, *Good Old Boys* was, more or less, a concept album about the South, where Newman had spent time with relatives as a boy. (The piano-based New Orleans R&B of Fats Domino and others is the foundation of what Randy calls his "shuffle" style.) 'Rednecks' and 'Louisiana 1927' notwithstanding, the soused love song 'Marie' is probably held in higher affection than any other Newman song. "The guy means what he's saying," he says of it. "He *does* love her. But he can't say it unless he's drunk. It's more interesting to me when it's something like that, I gotta admit. There's just more going on. There *is* all that extra stuff you know about the guy."

The sole selection from 1977's *Little Criminals* on *Songbook*, 'In Germany Before The War', was based on Fritz Lang's *M*, a film about a child murderer. It remains one of Newman's most chillingly beautiful ballads: the line *"I'm looking at the river, but I'm thinking of the sea"* has haunted me for years. "That line is the point of the song," he elucidates. "With a guy like that, you can't know what he's thinking about. It's just possibly incredibly stupid, or nuts, or it's just sort of a spooky picture. A lot of people in my songs, you always know what they mean, as bizarre or wrong-headed as they may be. But not that one."

Punctuating the 15 songs on *Songbook Vol 1* are three of Newman's movie themes (from *Ragtime*, *Avalon* and *Toy Story 2*) – the work that's provided him with his considerable bread-and-butter income for the past two decades. Does he ever think, "Gee, I must stop doing this fabulously paid hackwork and make another poor-selling Randy Newman album"? Is it harder writing for himself than for movies? "Well, I don't know how much harder it is," he says. "Getting started on a movie is very hard, and writing for orchestra is hard. The thing is, it's such a thrill when you get those four or five days with the orchestra, hearing what you wrote. But it can be a heartbreaking experience when a director starts taking it apart and making you do things you think are wrong. It happened recently on this movie *Seabiscuit*. Really I wanted to kill the guy for messing with what I'd done, because it was so clearly bad for the movie. In some of the reviews I've been attacked for things that weren't my fault. In terms of the music industry, I think they've become more intrusive with young bands, but in my career – because of people like Lenny at Warners and Bob Hurwitz at Nonesuch – I've been left alone."

Was it a relief to finally get an Oscar – for 'If I Didn't Have You' from *Monsters, Inc.* – after being nominated 16 times? "Well, it moved me more than I'd thought it would, because the orchestra stood up. The people I'd always wanted to respect me, it was clear they did. Or maybe it was just because I hired them. You know the award's not based on merit, so it wasn't like I was angry, ever, that I hadn't won it. There were times I thought, 'I could've won that.' 'Should've' has nothing to do with it."

Does he still mistrust sincerity? "I hope not, but I think I probably do, yeah. Almost every love song I've written – which is the meat and potatoes of pop songs back to Schubert – is somehow fudged. It'll be a love song to my first wife when I'm married to my second – like 'I Miss You' on *Bad Love*. That song says 'I'd sell my soul and your soul for a song'. And possibly I would."

Uncut, 2003

13 Curb Your Enthusiasm
Steely Dan

Album bought in London in 1974

THIS IS TOO perfect: Steely Dan strolling into a sleek hotel suite, the Pacific Ocean sparkling through the window behind them. For Los Angeles is still the city of *Gaucho*'s 'Babylon Sisters' and 'Glamour Profession', of *driving west on Sunset to the sea... jogging with the show folk on the sand*; still the endless, centre-less sprawl that Walter Becker and Donald Fagen so coolly dissected on that meta-funk masterpiece of an album. "I guess I see LA as, like, a theme park," Becker says with an owlish look. He turns to Fagen. "Don't you feel that way? Like, don't you feel like maybe it's just sort of here for our amusement?"

"It always *did* seem like a theme park," Fagen says in his slumped, mumbly way.

"Yeah, I guess I just didn't *get* it in the Seventies. It's like LA-land."

"La-la land. I don't know, y'know? I don't know the insides of it anymore, so I don't know."

The two men look quizzically at each other, middle-aged professors moonlighting as Borscht Belt comedians: the Walter Matthau and Jack Lemmon of Intellectual Jazz Lite. "Actually, I think of us more in terms of Walter Matthau and George Burns in *The Sunshine Boys*," says Becker.

"Or Gracie Allen and Molly Goldberg," interposes Fagen.

The duo's withering wit hasn't aged a jot since the days of *Gaucho*. As they skewered the vanities and pretensions of Tinseltown's showbiz kids in the Seventies, so on their new album *Everything Must Go* Becker and Fagen eviscerate America's New Yuppie-ism with microscopic precision. 'Things I Miss The Most', for instance, is merciless, worthy of Larry Sanders or Larry David – a catalogue of deluxe possessions gone with the recession. "As the whole house of cards starts to come down," Fagen says with a certain relish, "people at the top are beginning to feel it as well as the other economic classes."

"It's satisfying when the mighty are laid low, and it's satisfying to make fun of the Yuppies with their copper pans and Eames chairs—"

"*Comfy* Eames chairs," interjects Fagen. "And we had a lot of other stuff that we didn't have room to include in the song... Hummers, for instance..."

"That was the most fun part about writing it. Plus it's funnier to think of a guy like this laying around in his underwear and reading the *New York Post* than it is to think of somebody who was essentially doing that before."

Arguably the most remarkable thing about *Everything Must Go* is how (comparatively) swiftly it has followed on the heels of 2000's Grammy-grabbing *Two Against Nature*, the first album of new Steely Dan songs in the 20 years since *Gaucho*. At this rate we'll be getting a new Dan album every year. "There's gonna be a real acceleration," grins Becker. "A kind of Fibonacci progression, counting backwards down from the beginning of our career." And what a singular career it has been. When you think about it, could there really have been two less likely rock stars than Don 'n' Walt, spoddy jazz buffs bonding against pop mainstream as mid-Sixties students at Bard College in upstate New York? Growing up in the suburbs of Gotham, dreaming of halcyon days on 52nd Street, they thought they'd make a go of it as latecomers to the Brill Building scene – the missing link 'twixt Leiber & Stoller and Lou Reed, perhaps. Or Bacharach & David and Bill Burroughs. It didn't quite work. "We admired Leiber & Stoller and Bacharach & David very much," Fagen told me a decade ago, "but we knew our sensibility was very different. And because of that, we weren't very good at writing pop songs. Our idea of pop music was a song called 'Proud To Be Your Slave'!" Yet the pair felt equally out of whack with the new rock revolution, too smart and too cynical to join the free-festival tribes. "There was a rock aesthetic that existed that we weren't connected to," says Becker. "It was definitely isolating, because in some ways we were trying to do something that was so different musically and that was considered antithetical to rock."

About the only bands smart and cynical enough for our dastardly duo were the Velvet Underground and the Mothers of Invention. "We used to see the Mothers at the Garrick in New York, when they played there for most of the summer of '68," Fagen remembers. "I saw many of those shows because that summer I was just kind of lolling around the Village, and they were so funny and would do all kinds of audience *shtick*. We also liked the Velvets, and even went through a number of female singers whom we felt might assume some sort of Nico role. But we felt like idiots doing that." A stint with mob-backed pop group Jay & the Americans only further convinced the pair that they needed to establish their own vehicle for the quirky songs they were writing. (Kenny Vance of the Americans described them as "librarians on acid".) When ABC staff producer Gary Katz dangled the chance to work in Los Angeles, they jumped at it. "New York in the early Seventies was very depressing," says Fagen. "There was nothing happening, so we were at least glad to get out of town and not be taking the subway home to Brooklyn on freezing cold nights." Not that Becker and Fagen – limbering up to start work on Steely Dan's timelessly tuneful and wonderfully witty *Can't Buy A Thrill* (1972) – connected in any meaningful way with the ladies and gentlemen of the LA canyons. "Our world," says Fagen, "was confined to the ABC-Dunhill building on Beverly Boulevard, at least for the first few years. We had a little office with a piano there, where we were supposedly writing our canon of pop hits. There were a lot of transplanted New York Jews and blonde secretaries there. It still had that kind of Lenny Bruce-esque Yiddish dirtiness about it."

"There was one A&R guy," adds Becker, "who, so far as I know, never actually made a single record or had any interest in making a record. He wrote pornographic novels in his spare time and was making some sort of extended, detailed exploration of what kind of sex you could pay for in Los Angeles."

Fagen: "Sex, marijuana and betting on sports were the main things that went on at ABC."

Becker: "In other words it was an idyllic world."

Fagen: "It was a utopia."

Becker: "It was our own little private rolling bubble of *schlock* that sort of protected us and insulated us from the canyon cowboy thing."

Ironically, Steely Dan are now on Reprise, the canyon-cowboy-and-sensitive-singer-songwriter-friendly label they should probably have been on all those years ago. Didn't they feel any affinity at the time with Reprise artists like Randy Newman and Joni Mitchell?

Becker: "I had Randy Newman records and I certainly had Joni Mitchell records, but at the time I didn't—"

Fagen: "They were part of a Warner Bros. thing, they were in a higher social class than we were. ABC was, like, kind of a shit label, really. Like, I met Randy Newman a couple of times during that period, but I didn't really know him."

Becker: "We were shut-ins, it's just that instead of being shut in our homes with meals on wheels, we were in recording studios with takeout food."

Fagen: "After a while we lived at the beach in Malibu, both of us renting houses, and recording in Santa Monica or West LA, so we very rarely got into Burbank or that whole scene. I remember Don Henley came to a couple of sessions just to hang, but socially speaking we were pretty isolated."

This isolation was, of course, a part of what made Steely Dan so intriguing. Inscrutable intellectuals at one remove from the world of denim and cheesecloth, Becker and Fagen wrote elliptical and allusive songs about drugs, power, sleaze, gambling and the interstices of American culture – songs such as 'Do It Again', 'Reelin' In The Years' (*Can't Buy A Thrill*, 1972), 'Razor Boy', 'My Old School' (*Countdown To Ecstasy*, 1973), 'Rikki Don't Lose That Number' and 'Night By Night' (*Pretzel Logic*, 1974). *Creem*'s Joe Goldberg called it "hippie muzak"; 'Take It Easy' and 'Long Train Runnin'' it wasn't. Like Randy Newman, they liked to write in character, putting odious or politically suspect sentiments into mouths other than their own. Like Newman, too, they set sinister notions to bewitching hooks and grooves, sung in a voice – Fagen's – that was more Stephen Sondheim than Steven Tyler. Along with *Seinfeld* and *The Simpsons*, they remain one of the great rebuttals to the snooty European charge that Americans are constitutionally deficient in irony.

For a few years, they appeared to be a proper rock group, Becker playing bass alongside guitarists Denny Dias and Jeff "Skunk" Baxter, and Jim Hodder on drums. But *Katy Lied* (1975) and *The Royal Scam* (1976) found Becker and Fagen turning instead to the *crème* of LA sessionmen. 1977's *Aja*, cut at five different studios and utilising six drummers and *seven* guitarists, was the high-watermark of Seventies West Coast slickness. It sold millions, making Steely Dan one of the top-grossing acts of the era – all the more remarkable given Becker and Fagen had stopped touring live, and considering the shield of enigma they'd erected around themselves. "We were more self-punishing back then," says Fagen. "Plus you have to remember that the rock press in those days was made up of—"

"Idiots?" Becker interjects. "Either that or, you know, I think it was also that we were kids and we were having fun and trying to establish ourselves."

"And living in total chaos," adds Fagen.

"Anything that seemed weaker than us, we would pretty much pounce upon," says Becker. "It seemed the logical thing to do."

"Anything that wasn't actually inside the tornado."

Talking to him in 2003, it's difficult to imagine the boffin-like Becker grappling with a major drug problem. But the countless allusions to Class A abuse in Steely Dan songs ('Doctor Wu', 'Kid Charlemagne', 'Time Out Of Mind') were not mere reportage, and when Becker's publicist girlfriend Karen Stanley od'd and died in 1980 it proved to be the end of the road for the dynamic duo. Following *Gaucho*, a defiantly ironic celebration of airbrushed LA released at the height of punk and new wave, the pair called it a day.

As they were for many of the great Seventies acts, the Eighties proved to be difficult for Don 'n' Walt – notwithstanding their influence on the likes of Prefab Sprout and Danny Wilson. Fagen made a sublime solo album, *The Nightfly*, then effectively disappeared from view. Becker pieced his life back together and produced albums for China Crisis and Rickie Lee Jones. With the early Nineties came a gradual stirring of Dan activity. Becker produced Fagen's second solo effort, the cyberfunk suite *Kamakiriad*, while Fagen reciprocated by overseeing Becker's *11 Tracks Of Whack*. The next thing we knew, Steely Dan were *Alive In America* (1995), touring and playing classic songs that had never been heard live. Finally they decided to have a stab at writing new material again. Against the odds, the resulting (and rather good) *Two Against Nature* won four Grammies. Just how surreal was that? "Just going to the event itself was so bizarre," says Becker. "The programme had already been organised around the idea that Eminem was gonna win everything, and so for us to win the awards kinda left everybody going, 'WHAT?!'"

"It kind of pissed everybody off," Fagen agrees.

Becker: "You win an award and they drag you around the guts of the Staples Center being interviewed and having your picture taken, and, like, all these people were going, 'Not these guys *again*!'"

"It was perceived as some kind of weird dinosaur vote," says Fagen. "Which it probably was."

"It *absolutely* was," says Becker. "I mean, it was pointless to give us the Grammies."

"It would have meant so much more to Eminem than it meant to us."

"Maybe we should send him our Grammies."

Like *Two Against Nature*, *Everything Must Go* isn't immediately engaging – at least not in the hip melodic way that early ('Dirty Work', 'My Old School', 'Barrytown') or even late ('Black Cow', 'Home At Last', 'Hey Nineteen') Steely Dan was engaging. But just as 'Almost Gothic' and the droll 'Cousin Dupree' slowly grew on the average Danhead, so *Everything Must Go* turns out to be another winning Becker/Fagen sortie into the 21st century. As its title hints, it is Steely Dan's look at the foibles and failures of American capitalism, bookended by songs of economic crisis. The almost apocalyptic 'The Last Mall' sits at one end (the beginning), the title song at the other. The album could almost be 1976's *The Royal Scam* redux.

"In a way," says Becker.

"Just on a more global level," mumbles Fagen.

"Whatever was under way then is more or less being mopped up now. So we wanna throw in our two cents' worth before it's too late."

'The Last Mall' brings to mind George Romero's classic film *Zombies*, with its hideous visions of the undead still frenziedly shopping. What's your view of these soulless faux-communities? "When my kids got to a certain age, they wanted to go to the mall every day," reflects Becker. "And I realised malls were their cities. They were certainly emblematic of the swapping of these fake mercantile villages for real organic communities."

Fagen goes further back in time. "Without getting into what happened to America after World War II," he explains, "I lived in New Jersey, one of the first states to really start that kind of development – cars and malls. I was conscious, as I grew older, of the way my mother dressed and looked, and how her whole image became more and more plasticised as the Fifties wore on – the way her hair looked, and the change from cotton into various polymers. The way she stopped cooking and started buying frozen dinners. My parents essentially bought the whole trip." On one level, the album's title track is about a small business going belly-up, but on another it could be a swansong for Enron and Worldcom. "Originally the phrase '*Everything Must Go*' was associated with stores that were not in fact going out of business but were permanently pretending to go out of business as a come-on," says Becker. "So on one level the song is about the simulated death-throes that are so attractive to the feeding fish. And at the same time, when we were writing about this, the economy was going into a down-cycle again and people were telling themselves stories about what it meant that their businesses were going belly-up. Was it liberating? Was it the end? Was it the beginning? And all this is in the context of 9/11, when Bush kept telling the American people, 'Whatever you do, just keep shopping!'"

"It had that sort of *Fall Of The Roman Empire* feel to it," adds Fagen. "And then adding nuclear power to the whole mess gives it a real finality – some real commercial impact."

What is the duo's view of current polarisation of the US against the World? "I consider it a personal imposition on my future travel plans," says Becker. "That townhouse in Antwerp I wanted to buy is now outta the fucking question."

The clipped, super-funky 'Godwhacker' is not, it turns out, about George W. Bush. "Somebody else asked us that," says Becker. "But no, we didn't think of it."

"We were just thinking of the Western deity—"

"Mr Big."

'Blues Beach' is an infectious, futuristic fingerpopper that could be an outtake from *Kamakiriad*. 'Lunch With Gina' is another nerve-racking brush with a highly strung female, a sequel to *Nature*'s 'Negative Girl'. And 'Green Book' may be the most urbane song ever penned about online pornography. "Well, we imagine a pornography *beyond* online pornography," retorts Becker. "A pornography involving some sort of magical remote viewing, that flirts somewhere on the borderline between jealousy and intense arousal."

"With things like virtual sex," notes Fagen, "you get this sense that reality itself has become kind of fugitive. Which is part of what's created the problem we have now, because commercial reality is really a kind of virtual reality."

In that light, might it be fair to say that many Steely Dan songs are really about a kind of benign alienation?

Becker: "Depends on what you mean by 'benign'. But yeah, I think that's right – it's more or less harmless."

Fagen: "At least the hope that it's benign is there."

It's no coincidence that you come right out of 'Green Book' into 'Pixileen', an ode to a "soulful cyberqueen" straight out of William Gibson.

"Well, pretty much any sequence of our songs is gonna give you a lot of examples of that sort of thing," says Becker.

"You can shuffle them around if you want," Fagen concurs.

"But as I think about it, the idea of benign alienation seems right. Donald and I have been moderately successful at reconciling our sense of alienation with the actual need for survival – it's been more or less accommodated by the world, and by our wives and partners and by the physical realities of our bodies and so on, so that we can still sort of live in these fantasy bubbles of art. We spend most of the day planning our revenge without actually walking out into the middle of the traffic."

Is it ironic that some people think Steely Dan are old farts when they're actually writing more trenchantly about this fucked-up virtual world we live in than almost anyone?

Becker: "I think part of the reason we were able to slip through the cracks or get in the door in the first place was because you could see what we did at that level and it was mildly humorous yet palatable, and it wasn't necessary to know or be troubled by anything beyond that level."

"I think it was also lucky that we had these populist tastes," adds Fagen. "Kind of bad taste in a way."

Becker: "We've been able to combine, you know, high vulgarian stuff with low highbrow stuff—"

Fagen [*in fey English accent*]: "Or whatever…"

Uncut, 2003

185

14 Heart Food And Dark Peace
Judee Sill

CD picked up from Rhino Records in Burbank, California, in 2003

"OUT OF THE mud a lotus grows..." Judee Sill liked to talk in flowery meta-phors, often with a veiled religious tinge to them. Visiting England in the spring of 1972, she offered the mud/lotus image to a *New Musical Express* reporter as a way of explaining how beauty could stem from deep squalor. Squalor she certainly knew about. Presented by David Geffen's Asylum label as the archetypal singer-songstress of the period – all flaxen hair and acoustic guitar – Sill's background differed markedly from those of her navel-gazing peers.

While Joni Mitchell and her willowy sisters worked their way round the folk circuits of Greenwich Village, Judee was in reform school in Ventura, California. While Joni was warbling of Chelsea mornings in New York City, Judee was being arrested for stickup jobs in the corner stores of LA's San Fernando Valley, driven to such desperate measures by a $150-a-day heroin habit. "I did [heroin] with gusto because I wanted to escape my torment and misery," Sill told *Rolling Stone* of her three-year addiction. "But then I figured if I could maintain that kind of habit that long, the willpower I'd need to kick it would be a cinch."

Sill did manage to kick heroin. When her mystical, intricate songs started to attract admirers in the LA of the late Sixties, she was clean and keenly focused on her career. "She was troubled, but there were a lot of people then that were troubled," says music business lawyer Bill Straw, who met her in the fall of 1969. "She had been a junkie, and she contrasted *the white peace* – her term for LSD – with *the dark peace*, which was heroin. But she was not using heroin when I knew her." Straw did legal work for Judee throughout the short span of her career on Asylum Records, when she briefly threatened to join Jackson Browne, J. D. Souther, Joni Mitchell, the Eagles and Linda Ronstadt in the pantheon of West Coast talent established by David Geffen.

When Rhino Records last year reissued the Asylum albums *Judee Sill* (1972) and *Heart Food* (1973) as part of their limited-edition Handmade series, the rediscovery of Sill's talent prompted a few people to ask *why* Sill was never elevated to the heights her labelmates enjoyed. On the sleeve of her first album Judee gushed "David Geffen I Love You", the innocuous gratitude belying a genuine crush she had on him – a little ironic given that both of them were bisexual. But by the release of *Heart Food* her feelings towards the diminutive mogul-in-the-making had changed. The disappointment that neither album had made her a star slowly edged her back into the shadow-world of smack. When she died in November 1979, she was so far off the rock'n'roll map that Bill Straw didn't even learn of her passing for almost a year.

My own contention is this had she been male, and as pretty as Nick Drake, Sill would now be as big a cult figure as St. Nick himself. Songs such as 'The Pearl', 'The Phoenix', and 'Soldier Of The Heart' are as beautiful as Drake's but far more schooled and complex. Classically trained, she combined her love of Bach and other composers with her taste for the mellow, countrified sound of Seventies California, melding them into a unique style she termed "country-cult-baroque". If her songs share a complex delicacy with Joni Mitchell, the two women really sound nothing like each other. In fact, Sill sounds nothing like anybody except Judee Sill, though her vocal timbre and precise diction call Karen Carpenter to mind, and echoes of her unique melodicism can be heard in the songs of Liz Phair. "She was so different from everybody," says Bill Straw. "Everybody was writing oblique lyrics back then, but her oblique lyrics had a character of their own." Sill's songs suggest a hippie update of the cosmic epiphanies of William Blake or the metaphysical ecstasies of Henry Vaughan. Tracks such as 'The Lamb Ran Away With The Crown' and 'When The Bridegroom Comes' are explicitly religious, though one could hardly describe them as Christian Rock. She wouldn't have. For her, Christ was a symbol of the elusive, yearned-for lover – "my vision of my animus", as she put it.

Sill has touched many souls over the years. Recently, disciples have been coming out of the woodwork in ever greater numbers, from XTC oddball Andy Partridge to American singer-songwriter Shawn Colvin, who included 'There's A Rugged Road' on her 1994 album *Cover Girl*. "She didn't sound like anybody else," says Colvin, "but it was sort of like Brian Wilson or somebody, what with all the double-tracking and the fact that it was this great blend of blues and R&B and yet she was so folky and white. It was streetwise and yet it was religious music, ultimately. Those records just killed me." Reflects Graham Nash, who produced her debut single (and most famous song) 'Jesus Was A Cross Maker': "I knew very little about her. But I do know she was a very bright, talented, funny lady. She kept to herself a great deal… a *great* deal." For J. D. Souther, who broke Sill's heart and inspired her song 'Jesus Was A Cross Maker', there was nobody more important in his musical career. "She was light years ahead of most of us," he says. "Jackson Browne was the furthest along as far as having learned songwriting, but then I met Judee and I thought, 'Fuck, man, she's school for *all* of us'."

LIKE MORE than a few prematurely deceased cult heroes, Judee Sill was the unhappy product of privileged dysfunction. The bare biographical details of her early life make her problems almost inevitable. Bursting with talent, she was as insecure as musicians come. Born in Oakland, California, on October 7, 1944, Judith Lynne Sill was a typical middle-class California girl but came of English-Irish stock from the American south. Her father, a raffish type who owned a bar, imported and sold rare animals, a passion that Sill herself shared in her adulthood. When she was eight, her father died quite suddenly of pneumonia, a loss that shattered her. To make matters worse, her older brother had only just taken control of the business when he himself was killed in a car crash. Her alcoholic mother Oneta upped sticks for Southern California, where she met and married *Tom And Jerry* animator Ken Muse. Feeling betrayed and rejected, Sill declared war on Oneta and Ken and began acting out with the bad kids at high school. At Muse's

Encino home, she defiantly refused to show him respect. "He was an alcoholic," she told *Rolling Stone*. "Mean, dumb, narrow-minded. He used to beat dogs and stuff like that."

At 15, fleeing the violence and abuse at home, Sill succumbed to the charms of an older man who happened to be an armed robber. "I saw a lot of terrible injustice all around me," she told *Record Mirror*, "so I fell in with a bunch of hoodlums to express myself poetically." Together, this Bonnie and Clyde of the San Fernando Valley held up gas stations and liquor stores, stickups that got him a jail sentence – and Sill nine months in a girls' reform school, where she learned to play the church organ. Enrolling in the fall of 1963 at San Fernando Valley Junior College, where she majored in Art, she played piano in the orchestra. "I always wanted to harmonise with somebody, but I couldn't find anyone," she told *NME*'s James Johnson. "So I learned to play the piano so I could harmonise with that." After driving across America with two girlfriends in the summer of 1964, she flunked out of college. Orphaned when Oneta Muse died of cancer in the early winter of 1965, she was now alone in the world, with only a modest income from her mother's shares in a Texan oil company. Soon she was dabbling with heroin in the company of keyboard player Bob Harris, whom she married. Arrested for forging checks, she was thrown in jail, where she was "put into a dirty cell to puke my guts out" as she withdrew from smack. In this period her home was briefly a 1955 Cadillac she shared with three other junkies. In "the grungy central Hollywood flatlands" she regularly turned tricks for money. "As a hooker," she told *Rolling Stone*, "my heart wasn't in it… all I really cared about was getting that needle in my vein, squeezing off."

In interviews, Sill said the spiritual hunger which drove her to seek the "dark peace" also pushed her to express her pain in song. Her discovery of religious and Theosophical literature, as well as magick, gave her new subjects to sing about, too. "Musically, probably the turning point was when I became interested in alchemy and spiritual things like that," she told James Johnson. With amusing pomposity, she informed him that her three principal influences were Pythagoras, Bach and Ray Charles. Yet there *is* something almost mathematically perfect about her best songs, which she invariably arranged – and even conducted – herself. "My music is really magnified four-part choral style," Sill told the *Los Angeles Herald-Examiner*. "It gets to people's emotional centres quickly. That's why all church music is in four-part choral style."

Off drugs and out of prison, Judee decided she was going to become "the greatest songwriter in the world". Late in 1966, Bob Harris introduced her to John Beck of LA band the Leaves. 'Dead Time Bummer Blues', a song she had written while awaiting trial, so impressed Beck that he persuaded the Leaves to record it. "Although I remember being very impressed with Judee's song construction," Beck's fellow Leaf Jim Pons admits that "I didn't think she had much commercial potential". Through Beck, Pons slowly learned of her torrid past. But the stories of addiction and prostitution didn't gel with the personable, curious woman he befriended. "By the time I got to know her, she was an intensely spiritual, devout disciple of self-awareness," he says. "I lived with her one summer and never saw any sign of serious personal problems." When the Leaves fell from pop's tree, Pons became the new bass player for the Turtles, a more successful LA act whose star was nonetheless starting to wane. In emulation of the Beatles, the group's Mark Volman and Howard Kaylan decided to launch their own music publishing company, Blimp Productions. "Judee had been in Hollywood sort of poking around," Volman recalls. "Our hope at the time was that giving her a place to make music and write songs might help her through her problems." He and Kaylan, believing Sill might turn out to be their very own Mary Hopkin, were enamoured enough of the beautiful 'Lady-O' to record it as a Turtles single in 1969. "I remember one night sitting at her place, calling the local pop radio station and requesting 'Lady-O'," remembers Bill Straw. "That was her first real brush with fame, and she was loving it." 'Lady-O' was not a hit, but it got Judee attention in the mushrooming singer-songwriter milieu of Los Angeles. At the hub of this scene was super-ambitious agent David Geffen. He caught wind of her sets at little Hollywood dives like Arty Fatbuckle's, where she performed regularly for a devoted coterie of female followers. "I remember her coming home one night swooning over Geffen and telling me he was the man for her," says Jim Pons. "She also thought he was going to help her get to the top, which by now she'd decided was her destiny." Geffen, who'd made the first of his fortunes on the back of another bisexual songstress, Laura Nyro, landed Sill a lucrative publishing deal with a handsome advance. The money enabled her to make a down payment on a house on the Valley side of Stone Canyon.

"There was a lot of hanging out at her house," says Bill Straw. "She was surrounded by her adoring female fans. I remember going round there one morning and there were maybe four or five other women, all sunbathing in the nude." According to an old school friend, Sill ploughed through a series of female lovers whom she treated with mild contempt. "I just have her around to clean my house," she would say of some besotted creature when friends visited the house. "At that point Judee said and did a lot of things for effect," says Straw. "She was a typical self-centred artist who treated everybody around her like they were servants. But underneath everything she was a very, very sweet person."

Although Atlantic Records were interested in her, Sill opted to wait until Geffen's own Asylum label was up and running. To kill time, she went on the road as a support act, sometimes in sympathetic circumstances, often in uncongenial ones that made her seethe. "I saw her play once," says J. D. Souther. "Some woman asked her to sing a Judy Collins song. She said, 'I don't know that fuckin' song, and if I did I wouldn't play it. I'm playing my *own* songs, okay?' And I just thought, 'Right on.'" Jim Pons says "she couldn't tolerate crowds that weren't appropriately respectful... I heard her stop a song once at the Troubadour because several people at a table were talking". On her one trip to the UK – when she appeared on *The Old Grey Whistle Test* – she bitched about having to open for "snotty rock groups".

In 1971, Sill met and fell in love with Souther, a Texan-born singer-songwriter who was at the heart of the hip Laurel Canyon clique. A man of impeccable musical taste but an inveterate womaniser, Souther tore Sill's heart to shreds. "He went into the chambers of my heart and left it in disarray," she told *Rolling Stone*. "I felt devastated." The pain stirred up all the agony and abandonment of her past. "I remember going to a birthday party for her," Bill Straw says. "There was a large group of people there, including Linda Ronstadt. Judee was interested in J. D. Souther, and basically he then got interested in Linda Ronstadt. That really pissed Judee off." A bereft Sill finally went into the studio, with Geffen okaying John Beck and Jim Pons as producers but insisting that veteran Henry Lewy – producer of Joni Mitchell's seminal *Blue* – oversee the sessions. When *Judee Sill* appeared in early 1972, it was the first album on Asylum. Along with 'Jesus Was A Cross Maker', her song about Souther, the record featured such priceless examples of Sill's "baroque-country" style as 'Ridge Rider' and 'The Phantom Cowboy', together with her own version of 'Lady-O'. A masterpiece, the album had the misfortune to be followed swiftly on the Asylum release schedule by the debuts of Jackson Browne and the Eagles. It wasn't long before she was lost in Geffen's shuffle. By the time Grover Lewis' *Rolling Stone* interview appeared in April 1972, she was already expressing misgivings about the miniature mogul. "When I first met him, I thought he was some kind of knight in shining armour, you know," she said. "But I didn't understand the other things, the things that made him such a ruthless businessman."

"I thought it was only a matter of time until she wrote a hit song in the vein of, say, Joni Mitchell," says Jim Pons. "But I don't think Asylum knew what they had with her. She was hurt and disappointed, as much for the people who hadn't heard her as she was for herself." Pons and John Beck were gone when Sill recorded 1973's *Heart Food*, for which she received a co-production credit with Henry Lewy. It's another magnificent record, with the same distinctive blend of country, gospel and classical influences and the same intense imagery in her lyrics: *"I've been lookin' for someone who sells truth by the pound,"* she sang on 'The Pearl'. *"Then I saw the dealer and his friend arrive, but their gifts looked grim."* To be fair, the presence on *Heart Food* of such stellar session musicians as Jim Gordon and Bobbye Hall Porter suggests Asylum were not stinting on the budget. The album sounds as lustrous and lovely as the music Jimmy Webb was making in the early Seventies – not least on his own Asylum LP *Land's End* (1974). From the gossamer reverie of 'The Kiss' through the peppy 'Soldier Of The Heart' to the celestial shimmer of 'The Phoenix', *Heart Food* is one of the great LA singer-songwriter albums of the era. The closing track, 'The Donor', is an extraordinary requiem of a song that employs the Greek mantra 'Kyrie Eleison' in a web-like, multi-tracked chorus worthy of Arvo Part.

IT'S STRANGE how few people from that era appear to have any recall of Judee Sill. When I interviewed rock manager Ron Stone, who worked for David Geffen throughout the formation of Asylum, the name apparently meant nothing to him. It made me wonder if there was some lingering guilt about her fate – a conspiracy of silence around the fact that she had more talent than many of the Asylum artists who *did* make it. "She did have a falling out with Geffen just after the release of *Heart Food*," says Sill expert Bob Claster, who has made the demos for her unreleased third album available on the web. "She made a remark in a radio interview which sorely displeased him, and he never gave her the opportunity to explain or apologise. This not only ended her relationship with him and Asylum, but some feel it ended her entire recording career."

What exactly happened to Judee Sill for the remainder of the Seventies until her death is shrouded in vagueness. It's likely that she went back and forth between Los Angeles and Mill Valley, where she had a second home. "I knew her through the Seventies, slightly," says Bill Straw. "I would run into her here and there. I remember seeing her at an Al Jarreau show after he got his Warners deal in 1975." At some point, it appears, a car accident reduced Sill to such pain that she returned to "the dark peace". "I heard many years later that she despaired of her relationship with David Geffen and went back to drugs," says Jim Pons. Because of her criminal record, doctors would not prescribe her legal opiates. It was only a matter of time before she was scoring again on the street. Scotsman Brendan Mullen, who later made his mark on the LA scene by opening the legendary Masque club, experienced a peculiar encounter with Sill, not long after arriving in California in 1975. Picked up by her in a restaurant on Melrose Avenue, he visited her the next afternoon. "A beautiful mural-sized black and white photo portrait of Bela Lugosi hung above the fireplace," Mullen writes. "There was a large ebony cross behind her bed. The room glowed with racks of candles, the air reeked of incense and burning wax. All the curtains were drawn in the middle of the afternoon." Only slowly did Mullen realise that Sill was smacked out of her skull. Between bouts of sex with the naive Scot, Sill read to him from Rosicrucian manuscripts, and from Aleister Crowley's *Snowdrops From A Curate's Garden*. Later, she seemed to "morph into a serpentine cadaver", appearing to him as "a huge, grey reptile, stretched out and curling around on top of the comforter". Understandably Mullen freaked out and fled.

Years later, Sill fan Gus Dudgeon found himself on a panel with a man who'd once published her songs. He told the producer that Sill ended her life in "a trailer home in a typical American low-rent trailer park, had been raped by some guy, definitely had a very serious drug problem, and that she'd been in serious pain from her back injuries." Hearing she'd wound up in "such desperate circumstances", Dudgeon said, "just added even more sadness to her story. She was a really tragic figure, and like so many of us, was obviously affected throughout her life by her hopeless relationship with her parents."

The last person to have kept up with Sill was one of the school friends whom she accompanied on her 1964 drive across America. The friend, who calls herself simply "D", says Sill visited her in Santa Barbara in 1978. "In the last conversation I had with her, we discussed her oil income and how she might get more money out of it," D notes on the "Remembering Judee" website. "I suggested saving something to make interest. She scorned such a boring notion. I never heard from her again."

On November 23, 1979, Sill was found dead at her house in the unglamorous North Hollywood area where she'd spent most of her life. Cause of death was given as "acute cocaine and codeine intoxication". Her old Asylum friends did not find out till the following year. "It was so sad to hear of her death," says Graham Nash. "I personally had no idea she was taking drugs on that scale."

"As the death was at her own hand, it's officially a suicide," says Bob Claster. "There was no note left, and all who knew her were absolutely certain that she did not intend to die. She was flamboyant and egotistical enough that if that had been her intent, she'd have gone out with more of a bang and certainly left a note."

Unlamented and all but forgotten until Rhino's sterling work in reviving her reputation, the tragic Sill is well overdue for (re)discovery. "I can barely speak about her without crying," says J. D. Souther. "There's no one more important in my musical life: she was certainly as important as Linda or Jackson or the Eagles, whatever our twisted brotherhood is. But it was too esoteric. Judee just didn't get *out*."

The Observer, 2004

15 Sky Writer
Jimmy Webb

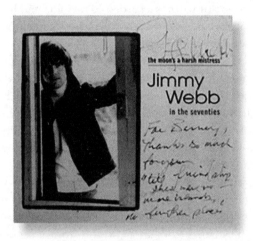

Box set sent by Rhino in 2004; signed in New York City in 2005

JIMMY WEBB seems sad. He looks around him at the world we inhabit and sees culture nose-diving everywhere. Subtlety is squeezed, ambiguity flattened. People don't read books anymore; songwriters don't care about chords. In 1998 he published a book, *Tunesmith*, in an effort to educate budding young melodists. "I find myself in a difficult position," he says as he sits in the corner of a café in the snow-flecked shadow of Manhattan's 59th Street Bridge. "My ideal of writing a score for a Broadway show involves complex chords such as Leonard Bernstein wrote, but when I put that material forward it's just not heard. It wasn't always so, because the Beatles' music was rich in dissonance and beautifully organised progressions. Joni Mitchell's music was an absolute *garden* of dissonance. But it's just not appreciated now."

A kind smile offsets the angst of Webb's hand-wringing. His frame has inevitably filled out in the years since he was a lanky Oklahoma farmboy struggling to make it in California, but a warm empathy remains in his

195

rough-hewn features. For a musician knocking on 60, he looks good. "We could take the whole afternoon and do Jimmy's Top 100 bitches," he grins. "Pretty near the top would be that nobody pays any attention to chords anymore." For anybody who *has* paid attention in the last 40 years, Jimmy Layne Webb remains one of American pop's pre-eminent composers. So much more than the cult kitschmeister of MOR renown (the Fifth Dimension's 'Up-Up And Away', Richard Harris' 'MacArthur Park'), Webb's body of work is a garden of melodic and harmonic delights – of pain and sorrow and occasional exhilaration, sometimes bombastically over-the-top, sometimes delicate as lace.

The Moon's A Harsh Mistress, the limited-edition 4-CD set released recently by Rhino Handmade, brings together all the gorgeous work from his Seventies solo albums: exquisite but little-known gems such as 'P. F. Sloan', 'One Lady', 'Met Her On A Plane', 'When Can Brown Begin', 'Crying In My Sleep' and 'Christiaan, No'. Like 'By The Time I Get To Phoenix', 'Wichita Lineman' and 'Galveston' – the geography-specific trilogy cut in the late Sixties by Glen Campbell – these are examples of singer-songwriter piano pop as richly satisfying as anything by Burt Bacharach, Brian Wilson, Paul McCartney, Joni Mitchell, Randy Newman or any other of Webb's personal pantheon of musical heroes. Not that he himself concurs with such an estimation. "I'm satisfied from an archival-historical sense of tidiness that it's all organised and put away on a shelf," he says of *The Moon's A Harsh Mistress*. "But from a strictly personal standpoint I wouldn't listen to it if you were holding a gun to my head. I've heard every thin quavery note escape from my throat, however unwillingly, and I would say that I probably didn't *begin* to become a singer until all of that was done. There's a kind of naivety, an awkward youth, that's difficult for me to listen to."

The fact that few of Webb's albums – from 1970's *Words And Music* to 1996's *Ten Easy Pieces* – have shifted a fraction of the songs he's had covered by other singers is something to which he's now resigned. He knows that the latest, *Twilight Of The Renegades*, is unlikely to buck a 35-year trend, despite furnishing us with further evidence of his greatness in haunting, urgent songs like 'Gauguin', 'Skywriter' and 'Time Flies' – the latter a Broadway-style ballad that would be beyond Andrew Lloyd Webber if he lived for the rest of eternity. The album's title is more than a melodramatic flourish. Webb genuinely perceives an extinction of the renegade spirit, not simply in American music but in Western culture generally. "The renegades are that breed of artist who are not the pawns of multi-corporate America," he says. "They're men and women who aren't afraid to write something offensive or political or just to be themselves. I'm thinking most poignantly of Warren Zevon, Richard Harris and Waylon Jennings."

The 19th-century painter Paul Gauguin, Webb says, was one of the first artists to turn his back on commercialised art. "He could already see this coming, this dreadful concretion of culture," he says of the man who left France for Polynesia and obscurity. "At the end of his life, he'd already abandoned painting and was just trying to help these native peoples keep their little towns alive. To have the solidarity of spirit to pursue your art with no fame and become a great artist in isolation – that's what the album is about." Webb glugs his coffee and proffers another weary grin. "I wish I wasn't so sentimental and nostalgic about the expiration of grace from our way of life," he sighs. "But it feels like there's a mighty pendulum swinging towards we know not what. It may be so cold and heartless that we wouldn't want to be there anyway."

Sentimentality and nostalgia have always featured deliciously in Webb's work, though both are rooted in the personal losses of his life. When he was just 16 his mother died suddenly, "a tragedy of Hindenberg proportions" for the insular Baptist family she left behind. "In our own highly concentric ways we all imploded," he reflects. "My father, who had not been a drinker, was suddenly borderline if not full-on alcoholic. My little sisters, four and six years old, were in complete shock and are not unscarred by it to this day. There's a mystery that always beckons and must be resolved. I myself realised, once she was gone, that I hadn't paid very much attention to my mother. And I had tremendous guilt because I would try to recall her face and couldn't." Only when he worked on the overlooked 1993 album *Suspending Disbelief* with producer Linda Ronstadt did he begin to recall his mother's features. Later she came to him in a dream and suggested he call his next album *Ten Easy Pieces*.

The loss of another woman also took its toll on Webb. After he'd come offstage at London's Royal Albert Hall on April 8, 1972 – a performance captured on a bonus disc in the Rhino box – a beautiful but troubled English girl entered his dressing room and told him she liked his songs. He was hit by lightning: for years she wreaked havoc with his heart, inspiring the 1974 album *Land's End* and altering the course of his life as a natural disaster re-routes a river. "I loved her for many, many, many, many, many, many, many years," he says. "Human beings can become involved in emotional attachments that are too overpowering and too debilitating, and I began a rather rigorous campaign to kill myself. But I sort of grew tired of that, and once I was over 30, I needed another plan. Part of it was learning to live with the fact that she was still in the world but that I would no longer allow it to be life-threatening. So that's really what *Land's End* was about." He is close to tears as he describes "the tragedy of an incredibly beautiful woman with nothing else to fall back on". Two years ago, she killed herself. He says he inevitably wonders sometimes what might have happened if she'd never walked into his life.

A decade before *Land's End*, reeling from his mother's death, Webb dropped out of San Bernadino Valley College and headed for the Los Angeles he'd heard hymned in the songs of Brian Wilson. Other decisive influences on him were Bacharach, Spector, and Teddy Randazzo's streetcorner-symphonic productions for Little Anthony & the Imperials. Signed up by the West Coast office of Motown's publishing arm Jobete Music, the shy young Oklahoman penned songs for Brenda Holloway and the Supremes but only made his mark when LA singer-guitarist Johnny Rivers recorded 'By The Time I Get To Phoenix' on his 1967 album *Changes*. For Rivers' own Soul City label, he wrote and produced hits for Black MOR quartet the Fifth Dimension, most notably the Top 10 'Up-Up And Away', theme music for a much-loved Martini commercial. Actor Richard Harris reached No. 2 with the absurd but magnificent 'MacArthur Park' (though check out the even more *outré* 'The Yard Went On Forever', with its unforgettable line about "the housewives of Nagasaki"). By the end of the Sixties he was a boy wonder, sought out by everyone from Sinatra to Streisand and offered small fortunes to play Vegas. "After the Beatles I realised that you could novelise," he says of his great songs from the period. "When you hear 'By The Time I Get To Phoenix' there's enough details included – the way a very clever liar will tell a lie – that it becomes believable. When the guy says, 'She'll find the note I left hanging on her door', that's something that would never have occurred to me before John and Paul."

But Webb chose not to throw in his lot with the MOR crowd. Smitten with the new sensibility of singer-songwriters like Joni Mitchell, Randy Newman and Jackson Browne, he schemed to join their gang instead. "What they were doing was almost conversational," he reflects. "People like Joni were fishing beneath the thermal clime, and so I began to reach very deep into the soul for my songs, to the point where the 'Phoenix' thing wasn't so important anymore." Carole King's crossover notwithstanding, entry into the hallowed sanctum of Laurel Canyon was not automatic. Though Mitchell accepted Webb, singing on both *Letters* (1972) and *Land's End*, others were snootier. "I wasn't welcomed with open arms everywhere I went," Webb says. "I came into a Joni session one night and Eric Andersen was lying under the piano having had a bit too much to drink. He raised up on one elbow and said, 'Oh, it's Mr Balloons'. I mean, you had to prove that you were a dyed-in-the-wool left-winger and that you had been to the barricades, whereas I'd achieved fame with very outspoken middle-of-the-roaders like Glen Campbell, who'd had John Wayne on his television show. I came into this world of exquisite artists having to explain that I used drugs and was really very hip."

He certainly proved himself on the drugs front. Acquiring the Encino estate of former screen goddess Alice Faye, he blew his considerable wealth on cocaine and cars, crashing a Shelby 427 Cobra five times and raising hell with the likes of Harry Nilsson. Unlike the latter, however, he tended to put work first and partying second: "I would go up to the edge and stop, whereas Harry would jump off. As he sailed down, he would shout, 'Come on, it's great!!' On the outside he could be gregariously charming, but when he went over the edge it wasn't something you would want to encounter." When Nilsson died in 1994, Webb says he "literally thought my heart was going to break".

His last Seventies album was *El Mirage*, produced in LA by George Martin. Despite its cascading orch-pop epics ('The Highwayman', 'Where The Universes Are', 'The Moon Is A Harsh Mistress'), its commercial failure was a crushing blow to Webb, who didn't release another record for five years. Come the mid-Eighties, California began to lose its charm. He swapped coasts and moved with his wife and five children into an old castle in Tuxedo Park, New York. "There's a terrible mantra of *mañana* that permeates all of life in Los Angeles," he says. "All of a sudden you realise you've been working on some proposed project for five years, and meanwhile nothing's really being done except in a very few intense rooms where decisions are actually being made. For the most part the city resides in this kind of languorous twilight of frustrated ambition." Now divorced and living in Long Island's Oyster Bay, Webb continues to dream of writing a successful Broadway show, but acknowledges the challenges of making it happen. "I watched *Oklahoma* the other day and I was thinking, 'Was it really three hours long?'" he says. "Nobody in this day and age would sit through *anything* for three hours unless it was a public execution."

The melancholy descends again, but just as Webb sinks into gloom he reminds himself of the extraordinary career he has enjoyed. "I'm always disturbed by my lack of focus, and by the fact that I can't get myself defined," he says. "But it's who I am and it's what I do. I became a sort of Zelig of Seventies songwriters because I moved in such variegated circles.

I'd be working with Sinatra in Vegas one minute and the next I'd be with Joni talking about some new songs of Jackson's. I had an all-access pass. I could go anywhere I wanted and do anything I wanted to do. Just the experience of having known Richard Harris and worked with that crazy, maniacal bastard was worth being born for. To have walked through all these different rooms is something I wouldn't have traded for anything in the world."

Uncut, 2005

16 Nothing Can Stop Him
Robert Wyatt

Album bought in London in 1974

THE DAY before I drive to Lincolnshire to interview Robert Wyatt, there is a march through the streets of Santiago: a procession of relatives of men and women "disappeared" years ago by the regime of General Augusto Pinochet. On this march, every wife, mother and brother carries a placard bearing a picture of a disappeared beloved and the simple, stark question "¿DONDE ESTAN?" I bring a newspaper photograph of the march to show Wyatt, who in 1991 released a quietly militant masterpiece called *Dondestan* – and who, as might be expected, is following the Pinochet affair with keen interest. "There you are!" he exclaims as he peruses the photograph. "And people think I make these words up! When I told them it meant Spanish for 'Where are they?', they would say, 'Well, maybe it is, maybe it isn't'. They didn't believe me."

Although the song 'Dondestan' itself concerns Palestine rather than Chile, the new five-CD collection *EPs By Robert Wyatt* does feature Wyatt's version

201

of a heartbreaking song by one of Pinochet's most sainted victims. Victor Jara's 'Te Recuerdo Amanda', its lyric translated in the box set's booklet, is an exquisite sketch of a woman, radiant with love, rushing to meet her lover on his five-minute factory break – except that her lover turns out to be a man who *"left for the hills/Who never did any harm/And in five minutes/Was destroyed…"* "Talk about brave protest singers," Wyatt almost shudders. "I think that's about as brave as it gets, really. And there's great pathos in singing about a disappeared person, and then becoming one yourself. So it's pretty timely."

I ask Wyatt and his wife Alfreda Benge – the "Alfie" who has long been his caretaker, collaborator and muse – if they think Jack Straw, the foreign secretary, will cop out and let Pinochet go home. "I was gonna bet with Alfie that he'd want to stay on the right side of Spain," Wyatt says. "But now the White House has spoken and said send him back to Chile, I think that's what he'll do. There's no question in my mind now." To his credit, Straw will prove the Wyatts wrong, but one can forgive these former card-carrying Communists for an ingrained cynicism about the overly cosy relationship between Blighty and Uncle Sam. I never do get to ask them about the blitzing of Iraq that follows two weeks later.

The release of *EPs By Robert Wyatt* is the final chapter in the reissuing of almost all the recorded work by this English master, a paraplegic with a Marxian thicket of beard and the sweet, doleful voice of a chorister. Comprising such Wyatt projects as the 1983 EP *Work In Progress* and an edited version of his 1981 soundtrack to *The Animals' Film*, the box ties up all the loose ends of the man's mercurial career, including his Top 30 hit version of the Monkees' 'I'm A Believer' and the Top 40 hit version of Elvis Costello's 'Shipbuilding'. It also features remixes of tracks from 1997's acclaimed "comeback" album *Shleep*, a serene and playful collection that chose the personal over the political in a way that returned Wyatt to the murky dream-states of his post-Soft Machine classics *Rock Bottom* (1974) and *Ruth Is Stranger Than Richard* (1975). As a fan of the spartan, one-man-and-his-Casio loveliness of *Old Rottenhat* (1985) and *Dondestan* – and of the wonderful Rough Trade Eighties singles collected on *Nothing Can Stop Us* (1982) – I was initially thrown by the collaborativeness that brought people like Paul Weller into the Wyatt frame. But in time I came round to *Shleep* as one comes round to everything this big-hearted man has done.

When I finally locate the house in the unspoilt Georgian town where the Wyatts live, I find them poring over a dictionary of Esperanto in their dining room. He is trying to find a title for his next proper album, and Alfie is suggesting musical terms to look up. "What's 'strum'?" she asks as she disappears into the adjoining kitchen.

"It's *ludate*," he says. "Which is rather nice."

"Look up 'sing'," says Alfie, out of view.

"I did. That's *kanti*."

"'Hum'."

A pause of several seconds. "Hum itself is *zumi*. That's *very* nice. That's good, isn't it? I was going to call the record *Humdrum*, so if I now look up drum… *Timburo? Tamburi?* That's alright, I suppose."

The Wyatts have been in Lincolnshire for a decade. Prior to that, they'd been wedged into a flat in Twickenham where Robert never had any space to work, and into which friends would drop at all hours. One day, Alfie set forth and drove as far north as it took to find a house for the price that the Twickenham flat was worth. "This house just simply, totally worked," she says. "It was somewhere we could go out and get everything with the wheelchair. It's quite hard to find a place like that in a place where you're not kind of cut off and imprisoned. It's totally practical."

Does she miss the bustling metropolis? "I feel resentful about the fact that I go to London and I haven't got a home there," she says with a smile. "I think it's disgusting." Muffled cackling in the background from Mr Wyatt. "Of course, you miss culture," she continues. "This is a total culture-free zone. There are no films, there's no art. Once a year, there's some jazz in Grimsby. If we hadn't got a Tardis full of entertainment we've gathered along the way – books and videos and things like that – it would be a desert island, really." She says the worst was when the Gulf War broke out, and she was on her own here. (Wyatt had just started work on *Dondestan*.) "I was watching it all happen, and it was so frustrating not being able to express your disgust and anger in any way. Because the town went on as it was before, and nobody talked about it. In London, you could have gone out and sort of stood somewhere with other people. On the other hand, we're at the right age where we know what we need. We've had our stimulation and our adventures. God help any child that's brought up here without access to the Science Museum or anything else."

"The ones that worry you," Wyatt chips in, "are the ones brought up in Lincolnshire as children and then go on to become Prime Minister. Then you really see what the payoff of that deprivation is." Since the Thatcher years coincided with his most trenchant musical statements about exploitation and imperialism, this seems as suitable a moment as any to ask if he is in any way dismayed by pop's almost wholesale retreat from political commitment. "Ooh, that's difficult," he says, wincing slightly. "I'm not a sociologist, for a start. And I don't think it's up to me what people sing about. I mean, everybody sings what comes up through their gut and out of their mouth. I never felt anybody *ought* to do anything at all in that regard. I mean, I was always pleased when people – whether it was Jerry Dammers or Paul Weller – got stuck into an issue. Because they spoke in that understandable language, they didn't talk obscurely. But it's none of my business. I mean, I'd have to be some kind of... *paedophile* to be that interested in youth culture."

Still, there's a fair amount of political/protest music on this *EPs* box, from Peter Gabriel's 'Biko' to *The Animals' Film*. "I'd like some of my stuff to be more anachronistic than it is," he says. "Sadly it's not an anachronism to be singing a song like 'Te Recuerdo Amanda', written by someone who was tortured to death by Pinochet's people. And the version of *The Animals' Film* is also timely for me, because there are arguments going on from vivisectionists saying that you can't equate the suffering of animals with the suffering of humans. And there is actually an organisation called DAARE, Disabled Against Animal Research, so it adds more moral clout if disabled people themselves say the whole purpose of doing good is to reduce the amount of suffering in the world. There's a central contradiction in the vivisectionists' argument: they say it helps to experiment on animals because they're so like us, but at the same time they're saying animals are so unlike us that they don't suffer like we do. You can't really have it both ways."

Going back to the start of his story, would it be fair to say he was blessed with unusually hip parents? "They were great," he says. "I've only just been orphaned, in fact: my mother died about a month ago. But a lot of the business about what went on in Kent was sort of a very creative interpretation by journalists imagining what they thought it might have been like. I've actually very rarely been directly questioned about it. I don't remember it being as breezy and glamorous and easy-going as people describe it. My dad contracted multiple sclerosis when I was about ten, and my parents moved out near Dover. So the backdrop was my dad retiring early and fading away fairly fast, and my mother struggling as a freelance journalist to make ends meet. They put their last money into a falling-down old house, and we were there, what, six, seven years. I went to school an hour bus drive away to Canterbury, and I have to say I was very unhappy there and did very badly. And though it's true I became interested in music and started playing with other people who were interested in music, this idea of some swinging scene is simply not how I remember it. It was grimmer, and I found Canterbury a rather po-faced town. I mean, I can remember going into Canterbury Cathedral and signing 'Jesus Christ' in the Visitor's Book, and a school prefect came up behind me and I was caned for that. And I couldn't keep up with schoolwork at all, so I left when I was about 16 and spent about six years or so floating about, really."

Floating about *where*? "What *I* remember is that it was a rather lonely time, in the sense that often in late teens people might be going to college or university, whereas I was having to earn a living. My parents went to live in Italy, and then I worked in a forest, and then as a life model at Canterbury Art College. And then I worked in London in a large kitchen, funnily enough at the LSE, though I'd only ever see the students through the hatch. There was a staff of about 80 people there, and I was about the only bloke and about the only non-Caribbean. They were such a laugh, and they made me so welcome. I didn't really know London very well, and they used to take me back to their places and their parties. They sort of mothered me around and sat me in dark rooms with cans of beer, blasting me with what was, I suppose, a proto-bluebeat type of music."

Does he retain good memories of making music in the Sixties? "I've been quite shocked to see bits of old film where I'm drumming. I watch it and think, 'Well, I did obviously used to get stuck in on the old drum kit'. But it all sort of collapsed in such an unhappy way that, to be honest, I don't dwell on it, no. Of course I worked with some great musicians, but in the end I never really found a home as a drummer. So that my period of stimulus and excitement sort of goes from having a really good time until I was about 10 or 11, until school started to get hard. Then it's sort of blank, really, till about 1971/2. What I do remember enjoying was just that little bit later on: working with people like Henry Cow, all that kind of thing."

Could Soft Machine have ever been as big as Pink Floyd? "No, it was too different. The Floyd had hit singles from the start, and terrific ones too. And they had a whole grandeur and presence that wasn't anything to do with us. The only thing we had in common was that some of the audiences were the same, in the sense that they were prepared to listen to tunes they hadn't heard before. I don't remember thinking in those terms. I was too much of a jazz fan. I like to travel light, with a little drum kit. I honestly don't need a lot of the other stuff. I do like eating fried-egg sandwiches. But anyway, I don't think Soft Machine had enough vision or coherence to get a loyal public. I would go so far as to say we didn't really know what we were doing."

When he played with Jimi Hendrix, did he think, "This guy is light years beyond what the rest of us are doing"? "It was a shock, yeah. A lurch. Just how far he'd got, not having seen the roots of it. Always underestimated, I think, was his group, and Mitch Mitchell particularly. There are very few drummers who could have ridden the storm and clocked for where the beat was, what the time was, and dealt with that funky beat, but at the same time flying like the wind and following Hendrix all over the place. Then again, Hendrix has to be given credit for it being such a loose group. You listen to it, and it's far looser than anyone else was at the time. To me, as someone who'd spent much longer listening to the glorious disintegration of bebop into Sun Ra and Charlie Haden and Don Cherry, this felt more comfortable to me than the strict time and neat and tidy blocks of sound that rock was locked into. The music breathed, it had air in it. Of course, bits floated off and got lost, but that suited me fine. They were a great encouragement to us, particularly Mitch, who at the end of the tour gave me his kit. Which I've still got upstairs. I've never used another. Everything you hear of me on a drum kit is on that Maplewood kit."

If he hadn't had his accident in 1973, would he have made the music he's made? "No. But one thing I'm really grateful for is not being a drummer anymore, as a primary thing. That forces me basically to make my own music. Not necessarily *write* my own music, but simply to take charge of my own music. It was high time to do that, and I should have done it before. In that sense it was a good career move… as everyone said when Elvis Presley died. I just carried on with what I do, which is basically just sort of slightly out-of-tune nursery rhymes. Up to that point, as a drummer and arranger, I'd been trying to sort of be part of a way of taking on everything there was to take on, in terms of music-making – all the harmonic and rhythmic ideas that were available. Which is a great apprenticeship in music, but then you end up saying: What actually *is* your voice? What is it you yourself have to offer? And the accident made me have to work that out."

Would it be accurate to say his voice is a countertenor? "I don't know quite what it is. I've lost some top notes recently. It sounds sometimes higher than it is. I've got a thing in my voice which is exactly that kind of falsetto that a lot of people use and that comes from Black music. My dad sang in a sort of light tenor. I've had to work out what notes I can do now, because I am losing a semitone every year just about. I can get comfortably up to about a G above middle C. It's partly because I used to listen to a lot of women singers like Dionne Warwick. I could sing along to Dionne Warwick easier than I could to Ray Charles."

I've always been curious to know how the sound of 1973's *Rock Bottom* – that wonderfully dreamy, murky minimalism – was born in his head.

Where did the keyboard sound originate? "The keyboard itself suggested it. Alfie got this thing called a Riviera in Venice, and what I liked was that you were able to slow the vibrato right down, and normally with things like the Hammond organ the vibrato is quite fast and it's set. So with this Riviera I was able to tune in with the kind of vibrato I wanted, and I was able to play rather like I would sing if I could be a little choir. I could set my voice right into it, and it was like stepping into a warm bath of sound. And I felt really at home once I'd got that. But where it comes from, I don't know." Would it be fair to say he is one of the godfathers of lo-fi? I'm thinking, for instance, of the very primitive drum machines on 'East Timor', on *Old Rottenhat*. "Absolutely right. And it goes back to when I used to like Paul Klee's drawings: those spidery pen-and-ink drawings with splodgy bits on and rather feeble colouring-in. I used to think that was so great. I remember someone shouting at me once and saying, No, I want a painter who stands up and strides in front of the canvas with big arm strokes and the whole macho thing. And I can see that, but I really like precarious, rickety things and always have done."

The last thing I ask Wyatt is if he can ever see himself giving a live performance again. "No," he says without hesitation. "I dream about it sometimes, and they're always nightmares. I can't remember the words, the band doesn't know what key the songs are in, and I've forgotten what order we're doing them in."

We wind down with tea and doughnuts: outside, a damp grey sky unfolds across Lincolnshire. When Wyatt briefly leaves the room, Alfie tells me conspiratorially about a new keyboard – a Yamaha "dance keyboard", she calls it – that he acquired after *Shleep*. "I'm always trying to get him to buy something new," she says. "And he does buy something. But then of course he can't make any of it work. He's just not made for machines. He doesn't even know how to turn them on. He still has the Riviera, but some of the notes started to break up. The next thing he was really fond of was this Wasp, a little small computer thing that made a very good bass sound – he did a lot of *Old Rottenhat* with that. There are all these sort of dead things upstairs. Like this old trumpet I got him in a car boot sale."

When Wyatt re-enters the room, he plays me the nine-minute 'Cancion de Julieta' that he contributed to the Lorca album. It's a huge, mournful thing, with groaning keyboards and horn sounds like baleful whale noises, reminiscent of something from Charlie Haden's *Liberation Music Orchestra*... "*Un mer de sueno/Un mer de tierra blanca...*" (*Oceans of dreaminess/A sea of white earth...*)

"This one was obviously meant for me," he says as we listen. "Sometimes I react against that kind of typecasting, but in this case they were absolutely right. It's serendipity, I think... though I never quite know what that means."

Alfie smiles across the table at him. "I think it's the future, myself," she says.

MOJO, 1999

17 A Little Knowledge
Scritti Politti

Single bought in London in 1981

GREEN STROHMEYER-GARTSIDE, to give him his full and slightly fantastical name, is feeling decidedly below-par on this muggy Manhattan afternoon. Clasping a Rolling Rock beer in a favoured nook in the NoHo neighbourhood of his favourite city, he is recovering from the previous day's video shoot for 'Tinseltown To The Boogietown', first single from *Anomie And Bonhomie*, the first Scritti Politti album in 11 years. "I was up at 5 a.m. ... and then ending up getting very drunk last night," he groans as he scans the menu for something inoffensive to his intestines. "I woke up with dreadful heartburn in the middle of the night, though the food on the shoot was very good." Turns out that the catering on said shoot was done by Lee Majors, one of the young hip hop guns Green hired to rhyme on *Anomie*.

Would that we could all look so good with a hangover at 42. It's been a decade since I last clapped eyes on the man, and he's barely aged a day: if anything, with his fine suede-head of hair, he looks younger than he did when *Provision* appeared in 1988. There aren't many fortysomethings, it must be said, who could get away with wearing a silver stud on a goatee'd chin. Then again, there aren't many who get to take the better part of a decade off from the arduous business of making pop music. Where has he *been* all this time? And how did he come to resurface in New York with a bunch of MCs for company? Ask him what connection there is between the hip-hopping elder statesman of 1999 and the lanky Marxist art student who caught the Anarchy tour in Leeds in 1976, and he will tell you: Not a lot. Ask how he looks back on the youthful Gartside of two decades ago, and he'll say simply that he forgives him: that when his boyhood hero Robert Wyatt came to play keyboards on Scritti's 'The "Sweetest Girl"', he told Gartside he "forgave himself for who he was back then and what he'd done previously in his life" – words the Scritti singer has clearly taken to heart.

So what's to forgive? Oh, you know, talking a lot of verbose collectivist twaddle instead of actually painting; disappearing up his own theoretical backside with the aid of Jacques Derrida… all par for the course for the period. If he winces at these memories more than some of us ("I do have problems with the past, though I say I discount it"), it may be because Scritti Mark II were such a radical revision of Scritti Mark I. Certainly it's no secret that he quickly tired of the strictures and limitations of the post-punk "indie" scene. Where the group's early singles and EPs on St Pancras/Rough Trade were all of a piece with the effete, scratchy, deconstructed funk of the period, the release of two superb Rough Trade singles – 1981's 'The "Sweetest Girl"' and 1982's 'Faithless' – showed Gartside had outgrown the worthy low-budget mentality and were halfway to embracing the new decade's shiny pop aesthetic. "An indie market had been identified, and certain features were required in the music that didn't really interest me anymore," he remembers. "I mean, I still loved Pere Ubu and people like that, but the memory for me is of the old Rough Trade shop where all the groups put up their Top 10s. Because it was always indie stuff. And I finally heard Michael Jackson's *Off The Wall* and thought, 'This is the fucking bomb!' When the power of that funk and syncopation really hits you and gets you, there's no turning back." Symbolically, the crunch came one night when Scritti supported Gang Of Four in Brighton. After the show, a sensation of paralysis overcame him and he was never quite the same again. "I thought I'd had a heart attack," he says. "It was very, very frightening, and I had subsequent panic attacks – I'm sure now they *were* panic attacks. And that was pretty much decisively what made me stop trying to play live."

"Green is self-aware to the point of it being paralysing," says David Gamson, the electro wizard who became one third of a new Scritti triumvirate after being introduced to Gartside by Rough Trade's Geoff Travis. "He is a little too clever for his own good. Performers can lose themselves, whereas he's just so analytical. Even his lyrics are self-referential. That's just the way he is." When *Songs To Remember* appeared in the summer of 1982, Gartside was already clear in his mind that he wanted to abandon Indieworld and record in – of all the ideologically unsound places – America. The contrast between a clunky early version of 'Wood Beez', originally slated for *Songs To Remember*, and the version recorded in New York with a phalanx of super-sessionmen spoke volumes about the transatlantic quantum leap he proceeded to make. Trading original Scrittites Nial Jinks (bass) and Tom Morley (drum programming) for the likes of Marcus Miller, Steve Ferrone and Paul Jackson Jr., all working under the supervision of Atlantic legend Arif Mardin, Gartside emerged on the other side of the pond as a sort of missing link between George Michael and Roland Barthes. And rather like ABC and Heaven 17, Scritti Mk. II – Gartside in tandem with yanks Gamson and Fred Maher – became a pop-group-as-syndicate: part pretty-boy techies, part ironic venture capitalists, part video-age Steely Dan. "There was definitely an ironical distance in what we did," he says. "There was an authorial intent that had a great deal of both seriousness and irony about it – neither of which were easily accessible to a listener, I don't think. I occasionally read things that talk about music in the Eighties, and Thatcher's name invariably comes into the first or second paragraph. I think simply to conflate Thatcherism with the type of pop music that a bunch of us from various places got into making then is just ludicrous, but I dare say it'll become the sort of idiot's history of pop. It was all meant as ironic commentary in a way, and that for me had started back in the Rough Trade days when we lifted slick packaging off cigarette companies and whatever else."

Cupid And Psyche 85 only served to refine the swooning electro-soul that 'Wood Beez' had blueprinted: the album stands to this day as a shining beacon in a sea of vapid Eighties synth-pop. Yes, it was slick; yes, it was all about dazzling surfaces. But how good it still sounds in 1999. Like Kraftwerk, Scritti used machines with a rare delicacy and sensuousness. Inspired by such underrated twiddlers as the System, as well as by what Green calls "the masters of early Eighties R&B production and arrangement" (Leon Sylvers, Quincy Jones *et al.*), Gartside, Gamson and Maher fashioned a minor masterpiece. "I could hear the difference myself, to be honest,"

Gartside says. "A lot of people used that technology in a very clodhoppish way. The Synclavier gave you enormous scope for articulating syncopation and timbre and colour, whereas a lot of people were just happy to have this horrible blaring Oberheim synth pad on an ugly drum-machine snare. So I was aware of that difference in what we were striving for."

"It was a really interesting time for technology," Gamson says. "*Cupid And Psyche* started before there was MIDI – we didn't use it on the stuff we did with Arif – and then it came out about halfway through the recording of the album. So there were all these new ways of working, and it opened up a whole other way of being able to work. We used to talk about it being like a Swiss watch." Among those taken with *Cupid*'s slick precision was Miles Davis, who opted to cover its American Top 20 hit 'Perfect Way' on *Tutu*. Gartside says he was "shell-shocked" by the news. Some time later, with Scritti at work on follow-up album *Provision*, he rang Davis and asked him to play on its first single, 'Oh Patti'. "He turned up, just came to the studio on his own," Gartside remembers. "Gamson and I later went to his apartment at the Essex House, and he was very courteous and generous. And then he would call at odd times of the day and night to see if something could be written for him. He was coherent and cogent, though he definitely had an elliptical relationship with the world as we construct it. He was kind of bonkers, but you could sit and talk to him." Not a lot less bonkers was Roger Troutman, the Zapp frontman who added his inimitable voice-box keyboard interpolations to *Provision*'s 'Boom! There She Was'. (Troutman was recently killed by his own brother in a bizarre shooting/suicide.) "If one allows oneself to use the word 'genius' just for want of a better term, then I wouldn't deny Roger that status," says Gartside. "He just was an extraordinary man, and very influential not just in terms of the voice-box thing but in terms of his arrangements and his way of dealing with funk and articulating rhythm. Although it's not the business of *Anomie And Bonhomie* to display rhythmic sophistication as an end in itself, I do now have a much more profound understanding of rhythm from having spent time with people like Roger."

Davis and Troutman aside, the experience of making *Provision* was not a happy one for Scritti. "It was a bit of a mis-step," says David Gamson. "People were encouraging us to do the same sort of thing – 'Now you've broken through, it'll really blow up' – but the second one should have been something completely different. I don't know, the life just got squeezed out of it completely. The record took a really long time to make, and it was recorded in London during the coldest winter in years." Even worse was the year of promoting it: 12 months of Gartside's "touring the world talking bullshit" while Gamson and Maher moped in the shadows because nobody wanted to speak to them. Though *Provision* reached No. 8 in Britain, its standout tracks were let down by weak filler like 'Best Thing Ever' and 'First Boy In This Town'. Scritti were trapped in a formula and Gartside knew it. Thus began the half-decade retreat. Much of his Nineties were spent hiding away in South Wales, doing little besides ambling through the local fields or playing darts in the pubs of the Usk Valley. "I guess I had a vague idea that maybe I'd chill out there for a year," he says. "I think at least five went by with me only half-noticing. I'm not being disingenuous when I say I have an extraordinary lack of a sense of time. I guess there would have been a fair amount of disaffection with the business of making music, and there would have been moments of anger and sadness… but there was also a lot of fun, mainly with old friends who were able to drag me from the cottage to go out drinking. You could argue it was something I needed to do. It certainly wasn't particularly useful or conducive to building a career."

In a pop world growing increasingly used to "sabbaticals", Green's disappearance was less striking than it might once have been. Perhaps this had something to do with the fact that our last proper sighting of him involved his singing a rather crap version of the Beatles' 'She's A Woman' in the company of dancehall ruffneck Shabba Ranks. Yet Scritti had made some of the more graceful and intelligent electro-pop music of the reviled Eighties, and they were missed. "I really didn't speak to anybody in that period," Gartside says. "I'd split up with my manager. I'd split up with my girlfriend. I lived alone and severed all ties. I can be a terribly lazy man, so I was quite happy to do nothing for a long time. But somewhere in the back of my mind was always the idea that I would make another record – even through the times when I felt terribly unhappy with my history in the industry." Eventually the day came when he mastered his fear of entering the music room he'd set up in his whitewashed cottage. And when he did, he knew it was time to incorporate the influence of the hip hop he'd steeped himself in for the better part of two decades. Far from writing songs that reflected his bucolic environment (*a la* Robert Wyatt, for instance), he instinctively returned to the sounds of the American streets which had so intoxicated him on his first visits to New York. "I'm mistrustful of the idea that music easily or naturally expresses environment or place or even disposition," he says. "I'd wake up and wander round the churchyard and then I'd come home and rock EPMD, and that was perfectly appropriate

213

– or maybe the incongruity was perfectly appropriate. I admit there's an enormous unresolvedness at the centre of this – well, it doesn't *have* a centre. A sense of identity and place have successfully eluded me to date, so it doesn't feel that odd." The reawakened zest coincided with his sister's suggesting in 1997 that he move back to London and take over her flat in Dalston: "I really couldn't think of a good reason not to. I mean, I'd made these trips up to London to buy hip hop and dancehall records, and blasting them out in my little cottage was an essential part of staying alive." He was less than enthralled by what was happening in Britain. "Acid house was a culture I was neither in a position to enjoy nor particularly interested in. It was too four-on-the-floor for me. It wasn't funky. So I stuck with hip hop, and subsequently with what followed grunge, which was more interesting to me. I'd become pretty interested in skate culture by that time, and actually did skateboard myself, despite my advancing years. It was another taste of stuff from America." As his recruitment of Lee Majors and Mos Def attests – the latter is one half of the highly regarded Black Star – Gartside is passionately evangelistic about hip hop. "The scant level of approval of, or interest in, hip hop amongst a lot of people continues to surprise and disappoint me," he says. "I just feel like saying, 'Wake up, get with the fucking programme!' I think it's important to recognise that hip hop has a historical and cultural status that's undeniable, unavoidable, and as big and as strong as any other genre of music. The Beatnuts are as important an influence on my life as the Beach Boys."

"Green is a very astute observer of what's going on in pop culture," says Gamson. "He's very good at picking out talent. We'd gotten a record from a rap band that didn't do that well, and there was a guest thing by Mos Def on one track. Green was like, 'Who's *this* guy?' Mos Def sort of blew up after we'd connected with him." If Gartside has any regret about working hip hop into the Scritti sound, it's simply that he didn't do it earlier. He blames his failure of nerve on a certain uneasiness about tackling this paramount Black art form – an uneasiness dispelled by the time he began writing the songs for *Anomie And Bonhomie*. "Obviously as outsiders, if you can put it that way in the relationship to any kind of music – I think it was Beefheart who said music was 'free where I get it' – we were very concerned with the politics of dealing with all of that," he explains. "Finally I resolved any problems about political correctness. It was just time to do it. And provided one is continually reflective about hip hop and one's relationship with it – and provided you're not entering into exploitative relationships with rappers – then it's cool to do."

Which rather begs the question: how does a tall, vaguely posh-sounding Welshman enter into *any* kind of relationship with an African-American rapper? And how, for that matter, did Gartside manage to earn the trust of such Black performers as Shabba Ranks and Roger Troutman – not to mention Miles Davis? "It's the telephone, it's that simple," he says with a shrug. "You just, you know, ring people up. Or you find intermediaries, people who might know somebody in their world – it's chains of communication of various lengths and links. You get in touch and you make enquiries and you extend feelers and you send tapes of backing tracks... and if you and the music pass the evaluative standards that are in place, and if people's heads are nodding and you're not obviously an asshole... I'm surprised people don't do it more often. I won't pretend it isn't fraught with a certain awkwardness for everybody. I mean, they haven't met people like me before, and when they roll in with their posses, they're people from a different culture and you have to find a common way of talking about either the subject matter of the song or whatever, and you have to hang and you have to make it work... there's definitely that tentativeness between us all. From their point of view, it's totally bugged: 'Jeez, why would he ring? What's the deal here?'"

What *is* the deal here? And how well does *Anomie And Bonhomie* stand up as a synthesis of Nineties ghetto wordsmithery and compressed Eighties funk? Do tracks like 'Tinseltown To The Boogiedown', 'Smith'n'Slappy' and 'Die Alone' even come close to bridging the cultural gulf between Harlem and Cardiff? 'Tinseltown' itself, it must be said, is a gem, the play between Gartside's Garfunkelish purr and the raw rhymes of Mos Def and friends creating a scintillating pop-hop hybrid. But the album's other high spots tend to be those that most recall the Scritti of the last decade: the tingling 'First Goodbye', up there with such spun-sugar ballads as 'Overnite' and 'A Little Knowledge'; 'Mystic Handyman', a jollied-up Jamaican number recalling the wondrous 'Word Girl' ; and the closing 'Brushed With Oil, Dusted With Powder' a leaf from the book of Paddy McAloon, one of Gartside's few real Eighties peers. Conspicuous by their absence are the hyper-syncopated keyboards that graced the songs on *Cupid And Psyche* and *Provision*: thanks to a strict "no-keyboards" policy that reflected an allergic reaction to the Eighties, *Anomie And Bonhomie* is surprisingly heavy on guitars, many played by Green himself. "Being on my own forced me back on my own resources in terms of learning technology and thinking about arrangements and how to get away from the Eighties thing," he says. "You know, how was I going to make all this sound euphonious to *me*? At the end of it, I decided I didn't want any keyboards. I mean, there weren't really any keyboards on any of the music I'd been listening to since *Provision*. Hip hop doesn't feature keyboards per se. Nor did whatever guitar music I'd finally got back into." *Anomie*'s no-keyboards/sequencers mindset is ironic considering the involvement in the album of Gamson, whose intricate Synclavier programming had been such a defining signature of Scritti masterworks like 'Small Talk' and 'Absolute'. As it turns out, Gamson and Gartside had fallen out after *Provision* and not talked for several years. With Gartside in hibernation, and drummer Fred Maher producing the likes of Lou Reed in New York, Gamson had taken an A&R job with Warner Bros. in LA. (Among the artists he produced there was the formidable Me'Shell NdegéOcello, whose bass playing features prominently on *Anomie*.) "I wrote Gamson a letter, and he flew over to London to see me," Gartside says. "And now we're much stronger and deeper friends than we've ever been before. This time the division of labour was much more clear: 'I'm staying this side of the glass, you're staying that side of the glass. If you say I've sung the vocals enough times, then that's fine.' Gamson was pretty insistent that Me'Shell would be good. I wasn't sure she would get with it. There was a panicky moment where I could easily have left the dinner table and jumped on a plane, but we got into the rehearsal rooms and battled it out. When we needed a third guitar, Wendy Melvoin came in. Me'Shell and I had our clashes, both being fairly headstrong people, but Wendy and [drummer] Abe Laboriel Jr. were very calm and civilising influences."

"It was a much more enjoyable experience than even *Cupid And Psyche*, because there was no big drama," says Gamson. "There was no pressure to follow anything, whereas even *Cupid And Psyche* was coming off the indie thing. Now it's like, 'What's he even doing making a record?!' So it could be anything it wanted to be. Working with Green is always challenging, because he'll always come up with some idea that's like, 'You just can't *do* that...' And then the thrill is figuring out *how* to do it. I do feel like this record, more than the other two, is really his vision. I also have to say there's absolutely no consensus on the album: ten different people have ten different opinions about it. Personally I think it's totally weird, and I have no idea where it fits in. But I don't think Green cares about that."

So does another year of "touring the world talking bullshit" loom for Gartside? And can we expect another long sabbatical in the first decade of the new millennium? "I pray not," he says. "I hope enough problems were

sorted out by either directly addressing them, avoiding them, or whatever…
and that enough resolutions were come to, and scores settled, and feelings
overcome. I'd really like to continue to make music. I'm not quite sure what
opportunities will come my way to do that, or whether they'll be denied me,
but I'll certainly make a far greater effort to stay with it rather than buckle
and disappear."

MOJO, 1999

18 Lonely Kind
Luther Vandross

Album bought in London in 1985

EVER SINCE David Bowie first overheard him improvising a line from 'Young Americans' and asked him to work on the 1975 album of the same name, Luther Vandross has been in great demand as an artist, session singer and producer. From singing Kentucky Fried Chicken jingles to producing his long-time idol Aretha Franklin (on 1982's electrifying 'Jump To It') may seem a giant leap, but it's one he's taken in his stride. He knows he is doing something altogether subtler than his obvious rivals in the Sophisticated Soul category. "I'm not singing ditties", he tells me. "These are not little lightweight songs. These are songs which call upon things that have happened to you… or more important, that *haven't* happened to you."

He isn't about sex or sweat or seduction; he's not a Love Man, with a brass bed onstage. This is music about control, restraint and grace, the loneliness of the soul – sumptuous chords and grooves to make your heart fall through your stomach. It's about a polished, glossy voice finding its way, taking its time, exploring, paring away words, exulting in itself in a manner that perhaps only Al Green has rivalled. He has worked with the best and demands the best. "He knows exactly what works and he leaves nothing to chance," says backing singer Lisa Fischer. In bass player Marcus Miller, he's found a co-writer/producer of near genius, and together they've fashioned a contemporary soul sound that combines the best of the old and the new, the raw and the cooked – technical perfection that serves rather than detracts from the refined, contained emotion of Vandross' voice. Real-time bass and drums play alongside programmes, grand pianos climb around sequencers. On *Any Love*, his latest and best collection so far, both the playing and programming are nothing short of sublime, whether on dance tracks like 'Come Back' or on the bravura seven-minute balladry of 'Love Won't Let Me Wait'.

There are moments on the album, especially the title song, where one hears an anguish coming through that has to be real and personal. He himself has no qualms about admitting that his ongoing weight problem is only the manifestation of a deeper pain and loneliness. The furtive rumours about his sexual orientation present added problems for a Soul Man making Love Music for "laydeez", even if that is not the way he himself sees his art. (His actual relationship with women bears a curious similarity to Michael Jackson's, though for him they are less mother figures than idolised divas. Both have a passion for Diana Ross.) When he slimmed dramatically from 23 stone to 14 for the *Give Me The Reason* album and tour, a British magazine started a vicious rumour that he had AIDS. His subsequent ballooning back up to 20 stone must have dispelled all doubt. "All that was implicit in those rumours, I always dismissed as nobody's business," he says. "To this *day* it's nobody's business. You'll find out when the door is locked!"

At the Circle Star theatre in San Carlos, California, Vandross takes the stage looking for all the world like an improbable cross between Solomon Burke, the portly bishop of soul, and Sylvester, the late, lovable disco queen. With him on the small circular platform are his exotic and immaculate backing singer-dancers Lisa Fischer, Ava Cherry and Kevin Owens, figures who offset and choreograph emotions the rather uncoordinated Vandross cannot himself enact. The Circle Star is one of the smaller, more intimate venues he is playing on the tour, a pleasant change from the arenas and coliseums which have taken up most of it. He pads about like some camp banana republic dictator, an awkward figure amidst the swirling forms of

Fischer, Cherry and Owens. But then, all his energy and concentration are dedicated to one thing, which is lifting those notes into the audience and filling the theatre with the ache of their sound. And inevitably the Black matrons with their plastic roses cry out softly "Sing it, baby" and "Take your time", urging him to hold back on the epic reading of Burt Bacharach's 'A House Is Not A Home' as though he were making passionate love to each of them. And it doesn't matter that he's not some burly stud like Teddy Pendergrass, because – like Eddie Murphy once said – "all you got to do is sing and the ladies go crazy."

What does he think about when he's onstage? "Oh, usually I'm thinking that the stage is revolving the wrong way, or that one of the guys just played something fabulous, or that Lisa is looking gorgeous or ... or I look down and see this shadow on the stage and I think, 'Oh God, isn't my stomach big!' And sometimes I think about being lonely. Sometimes I get so, so, so, so fuckin' depressed in the middle of those songs that I just close my eyes and almost dissociate myself from the planet... because those songs can sometimes be too much of a reminder of things I can't always address. It catches me from the blind side, and I just close my eyes. See, my favourite time is in the studio, four o'clock in the morning, no lights at all and no one around except the engineer, and Marcus asleep in the other room. The escape is unreal. I'm impenetrable and vulnerable to nothing at that point, and it's the best. And sometimes I go back there when I'm onstage."

VANDROSS was born 38 years ago on the Lower East Side of New York City. His father was an upholsterer; an older sister sang in doo wop group the Crests. At Taft High School, Vandross quickly fell in with the friends who became his closest colleagues through the Seventies – guitarist Carlos Alomar, piano player Nat Adderley Jr., singers Fonzi Thornton, Robin Clark and Diane Sumler – and found a dreamer's escape into the music of Aretha Franklin, Diana Ross and Dionne Warwick. "Music insulated me," he says. "I grew up with tunnel vision." With Clark, Thornton and Alomar, he became part of Listen My Brother, a workshop group that rehearsed in the basement of Harlem's legendary Apollo Theatre.

Five years later all three of them were working with Bowie – "at that time to me, he was just a weird man who dressed like a dog on an album cover" – and overnight Vandross became one of the most in-demand session singers in New York City. Bowie told him he'd be a star within a year. With three other singers from the Listen My Brother days, he formed the group Luther. Two albums for Atlantic's Cotillion label later, it was clear Bowie had been a bit optimistic. Disco was big and Vandross' music didn't fit into it. "Singers were almost frowned upon," he laughs. "A singer was simply a vehicle for the producer's vision." Retreating into the lucrative discipline of jingles, he waited till the end of the decade, gracing the occasional dance record – Change's 'Searching', for example – with his increasingly distinctive voice. Other artists he sang with include Bette Midler, Carly Simon, Roberta Flack and Quincy Jones.

His time finally came in 1981, when Epic signed him on the strength of three self-produced demo songs. The resulting 'Never Too Much' was a hit and the beginning of a career that's grown steadily from album to album. Along the way it has taken in such masterworks of modern soul as 'Till My Baby Comes Home', 'The Night I Fell In Love', 'The Other Side Of The World', 'See Me', 'Anyone Who Had A Heart', 'For You To Love' and 'The Second Time Around', the latter a splendid reworking of a song from one of his early Cotillion albums. Only the conspicuous lack of hit singles from his six platinum-selling LPs rankles him. "It's my job to get the product from A to M," he says. "So if the truck breaks down between N and Z, don't blame it on me. My product is flawless. 'Any Love' is a perfect record both emotionally and commercially, but it peaked in America at No. 44. That is inexcusable." It's a career, too, which has seen more than its fair share of tragedy. In 1985, a Mercedes that Vandross was driving in his adopted home of Los Angeles crashed, killing his friend Larry Salvemini. Then, in June 1987, his long-time drummer Yogi Horton jumped to his death from a 17th floor hotel window in New York. He had been drinking and complaining to his wife that he wasn't being properly credited for his contributions to Vandross' music. These aren't things you get over easily. It's testimony to the power of the family Vandross has built up around him that he's survived them so well. Guitarist Doc Powell says Vandross is a leader, friend and big brother all in one, adding that they've shared many of their most difficult times together. "I was always a group person", Vandross says. "Even now, you see I'm the lead figure in a group of excellent people. I like ensemble participation."

Happiness for Vandross is lying in bed in Beverly Hills, watching wrestling on TV with one eye while admiring his growing art collection with the other. When he speaks of recent acquisitions, it is with a little boy's pride and excitement: "I have a major Hockney, a major Matisse, a Picasso drawing, and a Leger. I'm learning and I'm loving it." Besides, he says, it's good business sense. He doesn't want to get to 60 and find, like Chuck Berry, that he doesn't have any money.

The tragedies and disappointments notwithstanding, he is grateful to be doing what he does. "What if I was trapped in a style of music that everyone else loved but I hated?" he says. "That would be a special kind of nightmare."

The Times, 1989

19 The Spangle Makers
Cocteau Twins

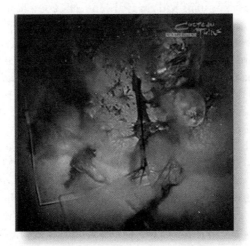

EP sent by 4AD Records, 1983

"FUCKING *HELL*," the tiny, tortured woman says as she shakes her birdlike head. "I just wish I knew what the fucking hell *happened*. 'Cause everyone's moved on and I'm just sat here now going... going..." Gone? Not for the first time in this conversation on a balmy afternoon in Bristol, Elizabeth Fraser cuts off in mid-flow, places her head in her palms, and looks deeply pained. She's not the young waif anymore, the gothling runaway who came to London from Scotland nearly 20 years ago and entranced the indie-pop community with her fluttering, faerie-child vocal lines. She's a mother of two, knocking on 40, a trip hop diva. But you can still make out the faint blue-grey outlines of old tattoos on her upper arms – marks that date from her Grangemouth youth. They almost look like fading numbers on the forearm of an Auschwitz survivor.

Fraser desperately wants to make sense of what happened in the final days of the Cocteau Twins, the two-boys-and-a-girl trio whose vaporous, rapturous dream-pop was one of the defining – and most influential – sound signatures of the Eighties. For Fraser there's so much that's unresolved, so much left unsaid. And as she struggles now to complete her first, eagerly anticipated solo album, she seems to be asking herself whether that lack of resolution is causing some kind of blockage. "I'm actually going to have to go back and think about everything and look at things again," she says with as much calmness as she can muster, in a voice that's lost most of its Scottish inflection. "In the Cocteaus, our relationships had always been really complicated, but we could always overcome that if we were into the music. And I stopped being into it altogether, so I started to remove myself from the unit and… I don't know, I think it was hard for the other two to think about giving it up and not… oh, fucking hell, man, *this is really shit!* I'm sorry… I've just not figured it out… it's really hard… I don't know what I'm talking about, and there's nothing I can do about that… nothing I can do…" The anguished face disappears again behind a lattice-work of fingers. Am I going to lose her?

"Liz wears her pain on her sleeve, and on her every facial expression," says Ivo Watts-Russell, who signed the Cocteaus to his 4AD label in 1982. "You can tell she's going through the kind of hell most of us actually go through but learn to disguise. She just never learned to disguise it. You're looking at this person who's displaying this vulnerability that you yourself feel, and you've got to love her for it. You just want to say, 'There's nothing for you to worry about, because you have this incredible talent'. You want to protect her."

WHEN ROBIN Guthrie first encountered Fraser in the grim petrochemical town of Grangemouth, it was her dancing that caught his eye. Something about this miniature whirling dervish suggested she might be able to sing. And he needed a singer, someone to give voice to the sounds in his head. Sounds that might just get him out of Grangemouth. "It was a small town, and I wanted out of there," Guthrie says. "I didn't realise that doing music was difficult or anything. It just was a means to an end. In a town like that, unless you have a lot of energy when you're young, you tend to just stay there. And I didn't know exactly what I wanted to do with my life, but I knew what I *didn't* want to do."

"It was always obvious Robin was a person that could make things happen," Fraser remembers. "He could focus the energy, whereas me, I'm all over the place. It's just great floodings of stuff – feelings, mostly. I had a lot of problems with… well, it's to do with confidence, isn't it? Robin's very controlled, and he's got a direction and he channels it all into that. And that was great for us, and the Cocteau Twins was much more coherent because of that. It was just perfect timing, and I can't imagine what else I would have been doing with myself. And that's partly the problem: I've always been so indebted to Robin for getting me out of Grangemouth!"

Seventeen years after the pair of them left Scotland, Guthrie remains an oddly compelling blend of rage and cuddliness. Sitting in a café in Richmond, a short scooter ride from where he lived with Fraser till their break-up in 1993, he's an indie-rock John Goodman, a chuckling bear with fierce, piercing eyes. (Perhaps it's more than coincidence that, three double espressos into the conversation, he quotes Goodman's line about "entering a whole new world of pain" from *The Big Lebowski*.) In contrast to his former partner, his Scottish accent is undiminished by his years of residence in London. "Robin definitely had chips on his shoulders, and we can only guess at what made him so angry," says Watts-Russell on the phone from LA, where he now lives after Beggars Banquet's Martin Mills bought him out. "But at the same time, he was so open and warm. He became friends with most people who were on 4AD at that point, and he was always incredibly generous with his time."

Guthrie now runs a label called Bella Union with Simon Raymonde, the third member of the Cocteaus troika. He also has a new band, Violet Indiana, a duo comprising himself and ex-Mono chanteuse Siobhan de Maré. The only reason he's talking about the Cocteau Twins at all is that 4AD – the group's home for most of their career – is about to release *Stars And Topsail*, a compilation of their peak moments from *Garlands* to *Heaven Or Las Vegas*. It's a selection he made himself, though the title came from Fraser, and it's one version of the story of Guthrie and Fraser – the godparents of shoegazing, the bridge between the Banshees and My Bloody Valentine, Curve, Dead Can Dance, Sinead O'Connor, and even the dreaded Cranberries, who cleverly mated Cocteaus dream-pop to anthemic U2 rock and briefly went mega-platinum Stateside. The album charts the journey of two innocents – Start-Rite foundlings who came to London with a dream and a drum machine – from sub-Siouxsie bedsit Gotherama to quasi-ambient conflations of guitar effects and sequenced rhythms alchemised by Fraser's supernatural vocal lines. It boasts at least a dozen of the most shimmeringly beautiful pieces of music ever recorded, and would have had more if 4AD had been able to agree terms with Mercury, the Cocteaus' label for their last two, criminally underrated albums.

From the blissed-out raptures of *Head Over Heels* to the deep dark sorrows of *Four-Calendar Café*, Guthrie and Fraser touched the musical firmament, then fell to earth. Along the way came profound emotional damage, chronic drug abuse, three-way codependency, children… and finally recovery.

A MENTAL Polaroid from the halcyon days of early Eighties indiedom: the Cocteaus about to take the stage at the Venue in London, supporting their 4AD idols the Birthday Party. A trio of misfits with wild indie-goth hair and unkempt charity shop togs: a lurchingly tall bassist, a doughboy guitarist, an elfin girl with stark staring eyes. All three crapping themselves with fear. "I was just fucking wigging out all over the place that night," Fraser remembers. "I was totally, completely imploded. I thought, 'I can't take any more of this, I've got to get off this stage because I really shouldn't be up here'. So I found myself in a fucking alcove that I hoped would be some exit doors, but it was just an alcove with some curtains over it! I was stuck there, at the side of the stage, for what felt like an eternity but in reality was probably only a minute or so. And I had to talk myself out of that alcove. And then it was over, and everything was okay again."

"Supporting the Birthday Party at the Venue was the pinnacle of our career at that point," chuckles Guthrie. "We couldn't imagine topping that at the time." He adds that Fraser's Venue "wigout" was but the first of many. "The worst was in the Hague when the band was just the two of us, and she just freaks out and fucks off after two songs, and who's left standing there like a prick? I think that's why shoegazing was invented, 'cause I couldn't look anywhere else! It was, like, *'Come back, bitch!'* Everyone got their money back, and the promoter tried to beat us up."

Guthrie, Fraser and bassist Will Heggie had come to London after recording a demo tape in Guthrie's mum's living room. They took copies of the tape to John Peel and to 4AD, the label with which they felt the most affinity. Founded by Watts-Russell and Pete Kent under the umbrella of Beggar's Banquet, 4AD had made its name with Bauhaus and blossomed into a stable of acts that included Modern English and the Birthday Party. "I remember when the Cocteaus came down, because they were the weirdest looking bunch," says Simon Raymonde, then working behind the counter in the Beggar's record shop. "Liz had chicken bones round her neck, and Robin had this wild hair. And you could hardly hear anything they said because they were so quietly spoken. They got to the shop really early in the morning to give the tape to Ivo, so I said I'd take it from them."

"From the tape I'd had no idea that Liz had the voice that she had," says Watts-Russell. "I would still say that she's my favourite female voice that's ever existed. When I started to work with the Cocteaus, I just had the feeling of finding purpose, I suppose. Whatever anybody else felt about them was really unimportant, because I knew I could move forward with extreme pride." Recorded for the princely sum of £900 at London's Blackwing Studios, *Garlands* was a decent first stab at snaring the early Cocteaus' sound, at that point a kind of DIY take on mid-period Banshees. Guthrie set up hypnotic guitar loops, Heggie played globular post-punk bass lines, and Fraser warbled and ululated over them like a highland Kate Bush over a micro Joy Division. The record doesn't exactly stand time's test, although the great 'Blind Dumb Deaf' merits its place as the first track on *Stars And Topsoil*. "I can't honestly say I loved it," says Raymonde. "I liked parts of what Liz was doing, and I was into the sound a little bit, but I kind of liked the Banshees more at that point. But I think the way it was put out was clever, and the imagery was really good. And you shouldn't underestimate Peel's championing of it, of course, because whatever he said did catch on." As anyone who listened to Peel's Radio 1 show back then will recall, *les Cocs* were a *sine qua non* of his mid-Eighties playlists. Live shows, it must be said, were a different matter. "One review in *NME* described us as 'Two fat blokes and a dumpy, screeching girl'," recalls Guthrie. "Which stuck with me, 'cause that was secretly how *I* felt about us!"

"There's this myth about how they sent a tape to Peel and everything just sort of floated along naturally thereafter," says Watts-Russell. "That was so far from the truth. I was convinced that he would love them, but it took a long, long time to get him to listen to the tape." *Garlands* took up long-term residency in the Indie album chart and the Cocteaus recorded the *Peppermint Pig* EP with the Associates' Alan Rankine producing (not a happy match, by all accounts). Next thing they knew, the trio were supporting Orchestral Manoeuvres In The Dark on a European tour. "The OMD tour was the end of them playing the game in the music industry," says Ivo Watts-Russell. "They learned that from the hard experience of going out and playing 50 dates. I think it forced the issue of Robin and Liz's love for each other, because I always thought Liz felt threatened by Robin's friendship with Will." By tour's end, Heggie had quit, opting to stay in Grangemouth. Guthrie and Fraser went on as a duo, playing a string of shows in 1983 before retreating to the little Palladium studio in Stirlingshire to make their second album.

"With *Head Over Heels* I became a producer," says Guthrie. "I decided I was gonna fucking do everything. I didn't know how to engineer, but I got a few pointers from the guy who owned the studio. I was just smoking loads of dope and finding out what you can do, and of course nobody told me the rules for making records. I was a hands-on, pragmatic kinda guy, so that's how it came about. That was the birth of my sonic sensibility. It was my way of hiding behind a lack of musicianship. It wasn't really a low self-worth thing, it was me recognising the fact that I couldn't copy Jimi Hendrix solos. What I could do was build little fuzz-boxes and echo units from everyday electronics, so I sort of hid behind that. And I've pretty much done that for the last fuckin' 20 years."

From the first crashing beat of 'When Mama Was Moth', *Head Over Heels* was all about cascading sound, ecstatic massiveness – a swooning electro-psychedelia that made the sceptics (this writer included) doff their caps. It took the Banshees of *A Kiss In The Dreamhouse* to peaks of flanged, flooding beauty: the sound of crazed love and tumbling joy, consciousness dissolving in a druggy blur. "I think I just liked being spaced out, and that's how a lot of it was born," admits Guthrie. "*Head Over Heels* was a big stoner record, because it was about smoking far too much dope." Brian Eno was impressed enough to entertain requests from 4AD to produce the next Cocteaus album. Says Watts-Russell, "I remember him telling Robin, 'I wouldn't have had the courage to do what you did on *Head Over Heels*'."

For all the fey, Goth-goes-pre-Raphaelite stuff going on in the early Eighties, *Head Over Heels* towered over the competition. If Soho soulboys scoffed at Fraser's pressed-flowers stream-of-consciousness lyrics, those who fell for her voice understood that her words were a kind of private language, equal parts lullaby and babyspeak. "Fraser plays both infant and mother," noted Simon Reynolds and Joy Press in their book *The Sex Revolts*, "duetting with herself in an endless serenade." (The "Gothic" issue, incidentally, is one that rankled strongly with anyone – including this writer – who loved the Cocteaus but detested the Cure and all those awful "positive punk" bands of 1983. "I had an understanding of what Goth was, but I honestly didn't realise we were participating in it," says Ivo Watts-Russell. "For me, it was like having an ugly child and not being able to see the ugliness. I still don't see that there was anything Gothic about what we were doing. 4AD was just a handful of people who really did have the same common purpose and were really emotionally involved in what they were doing.")

One convert to the Cocteaus cause was Raymonde, who accompanied 4AD's Ivo Watts-Russell on several of the *Head Over Heels* tour dates. "I thought that album was a real step up from *Garlands*," he says. "You have to say that Ivo had an incredible ear for talent, because he obviously heard something in that first album." When the tour ended, Raymonde offered Guthrie and Fraser free time in a Camden studio where he worked. The three wound up recording a track that later appeared on an *NME* flexidisc. "About a month later," Raymonde remembers, "Robin called me up and asked if I wanted to come and do some writing with them in Scotland. And I said, 'Yeah, alright'. Words have always been fairly economical amongst the three of us."

The son of legendary Sixties arranger Ivor (Dusty Springfield, Scott Walker *et al.*), Raymonde brought a new melodic sensibility to the group that was instantly discernible in 'Pearly Dewdrops' Drops' and 'The Spangle Maker'. "Simon introduced a bit of balance into the whole thing, and so much more musically," says Guthrie. "His great strength was just taking my framework and embellishing it. Quite often I would put together this basic guitar thing, and the drums and bass, and he would come in and play keyboards or play my bass line, but better." Adds Watts-Russell: "Musically, I think Simon brought a sense of bottom-end melody that hadn't been there. His bass lines were more sort of interweaving than Will's had been." 'Pearly Dewdrops' even snuck into the Top 30 singles chart, prompting an invitation – declined, naturally – to appear on *Top Of The Pops*. "Robin and Liz were always quite reticent about how things were perceived," Raymonde says with a wry smile. "*Top Of The Pops* was too many balloons and dancing girls, and we would have looked stupid." Instead the trio went back to Palladium to start work on *Treasure*, a cleaner, more layered album than *Head Over Heels*. "We went into the studio for one month with nothing and came out with a finished album," Raymonde recalls. "So this was the first time we were actually living in a studio and being with each other 24 hours a day. And I look at that album as a record of brilliant ideas that weren't totally realised, because we were all still a little uncomfortable about saying what we wanted." Guthrie is more blunt: "My feelings about *Treasure* at that time were that it didn't quite gel. Musically, we were pulled in a different way and it sounded a bit forced. And I think it sounds very dated, compared to anything from *Victorialand* onwards."

This time the song titles consisted simply of desperately precious names like 'Persephone' and 'Aloysius', sitting targets for critics of twee Victoriana. Not that this unduly bothered the Cocteaus. "Liz was never interested in what people might think, and we thought the titles were quite cute," says Raymonde. "We just let her get on with that side of things." Guthrie and

Fraser had already had their fair share of unhappy experiences at the hands of the music press, whose Cocteaus features generally consisted of passages of jejune rhapsody interspersed with sullen, blood-from-a-stone Q&As. *NME*'s Danny Kelly spent eight hours grilling the hapless trio in a desperate attempt to pry the "truth" out of them – and got no closer than anyone else had done. The real truth was that they had very little to say. "We were very insecure about the press," says Raymonde. "There would immediately be this thing, like, 'What do they *want*? What are they trying to find *out*?' And perhaps not being particularly articulate ourselves at that point, it was almost like a battle before the tape machine went on. We're thinking, they want to know something and we don't know the answer, and they're going to *find us out*. So we'd best just shut up. We just used to close ranks, I think, and not look at how we made our art… at all. We actually used to say to each other, 'Let's just not fucking talk about this'. We never used to even sit in the same room and go, 'What are we gonna do now?' We would just *do* it."

Journalistic musing generally centred on Fraser and the supposed mystery of where her extraordinary voice and all-but-indecipherable lyrics *came from*. Inevitably such musing backfired, turning Fraser even further in on herself. "These days you can get to the source a lot quicker," says Raymonde. "A lot of people are more willing to talk about their past or their background, but in those days there was no way Liz would have talked about her background or how she'd come to reach down and bring up this stuff." The conjecture impacted indirectly on the way Fraser wrote. "People started commenting on her words and she got really paranoid," recalls Guthrie. "So she started trying to cover up what she was saying. If you write down the lyrics to *Treasure*, they're all English, but she'd twist them so it sounded different. And then it got to the point where she started to make words up and was just picking them out of a foreign dictionary: 'I don't have to articulate my feelings, it all comes out through the music.' And it did."

The image of Fraser singing onstage, bashing herself on the chest as these miraculous sounds poured from her throat, is an indelible one from the period. She visibly cringes at the mention of it. "Well, you see, I didn't like me very much," she manages to say. "And I probably still don't, and that… explains that. I underestimated singing, I underestimated the whole… I've taken it for granted. Singing's not a lukewarm experience for me, it's really not." She once described her singing as trying to make sense of "a confusing situation going on in my head". Four years ago, she told me music had "kept me out of prisons and mental institutions, probably". Asked now if she likes being revered as one of pop's great vocalists, she pauses for several awkward seconds. "Um, I've never really been able to enjoy the perks, and that's one of them. I don't even know whether I should be trying to enjoy them or not. I'm not sure it matters, or that it should matter to me. But I know some people enjoy it. They've got their heads round the concept, and they can get on and enjoy it and that's brilliant. I think it's all part of wanting to protect myself, and I don't want to be taking on other people's ideas. I'm too vulnerable, and I need to sort myself out and get some ideas of my own, really."

For Fraser, it's more important that people hear the original Tim Buckley version of 'Song To The Siren' than that they hear the 1983 hit version she sang as part of 4AD project This Mortal Coil. Yet even Buckley only occasionally came close to her sublime vocal lines on 1998's *Blue Bell Knoll*. These lines follow paths – trails begun by Joni Mitchell, extended by Kate Bush – that no singer had ever fully explored before. Arguably the only real reference point for her singing is the sound of the female choirs on *Les Mystère des Voixs Bulgares*, an album (released in the UK on 4AD, no less) that Fraser herself describes as "like music from outer space" and cites as a major inspiration. "I think it was with *Blue Bell Knoll*," says Simon Raymonde, "that I truly appreciated that here was a genius, someone who was totally natural and had no inhibitions about singing, even though her own head was often her own worst enemy. She'd do something, and I'd feel it was the greatest thing anyone could have done, and she'd come in and go, 'Fuckin' shite!'"

What made Fraser's performances on *Blue Bell Knoll* still more remarkable – and so much richer than 1996's rather restrained *Victorialand*, recorded as an "acoustic" album by Guthrie and Fraser without Raymonde – was the scant space Guthrie and Raymonde had left her. Recorded in a new 24-track studio in Acton, built by the Cocteaus themselves, the instrumental tracks made full use of an array of new toys the boys had acquired. "Rob and I sat there for weeks on end enjoying all these new tracks we had," says Raymonde. "We were double-tracking acoustic guitars and putting pianos on everything – doing stuff we'd never really been able to do before, and with no clock ticking. And then Liz came in and said, 'Where am I supposed to *sing?*' So we had to bounce everything to 24-track and leave a few tracks for her. And the fact that she didn't have very much room, plus the fact that the record was fairly full up in the arrangement sense, made her think, 'Well, I'm just going to go off and do *more* melodies'. And it was fucking amazing what she did on that record, a total joy to listen to. And those are the moments that you never forget. She went through slightly different periods of coming in, working out melodies, and then putting words to melodies.

Or she would come in with lyrics already written out and just fit them to the songs. It was quite a cut-and-paste way she was working, but I suppose that got her into this style that she developed. She had a habit of taking one word and spreading it over several notes. She was never concerned with the sense of the words as much as with the poetry of sound."

"In a way we just made the same record over and over again," says Guthrie. "We just did it with a different level of confidence. Me and Simon would be sitting in the studio with a track we thought was brilliant, and Liz would come in and just fucking blow us away by taking it somewhere that we never thought it would go. And that happened more often than not." Concludes Fraser: "I think you can tell when we've been at our most rich, and when being creative's been dead easy. *Blue Bell Knoll* was dead easy."

BLUE BELL KNOLL may have been easy, but life as a Cocteau Twin was becoming harder by the day. After manager Raymond Coffer secured the group a deal in America, Robin Guthrie could finally afford the drug habit he'd always aspired to. "We were just sort of hitting the realisation that we were quite popular," remembers Raymonde. "And that's probably when the coke kicked in, because there was more money coming in. From a financial point of view, the group was actually on a surer footing. But from that period on, things started to get more problematic. Publicly we were doing fairly well, but inside the group, things were a bit messy. Robin had a lot of issues he hadn't dealt with, plus that whole thing of coming from a very working-class dysfunctional family in Grangemouth. He was a bit of a cynic and pretty much hated everybody in the music business. He distrusted everybody, because he always thought, 'What do they *want?*'"

"I have a very vivid memory of having a gold disc with a big pile of cocaine on it during the making of *Blue Bell Knoll*," Guthrie says. "And after a few hours, Simon said, 'This is making me feel really weird, I'm gonna go home now'. And I didn't go home for the next ten years. I loved it. I mean, I hated it, but… well, I couldn't stand me. I loathed myself so much, but it was everybody else's fault, coz *they were all fucking wrong.*"

"I don't think Robin knew cocaine could get that bad," says Watts-Russell. "With heroin, you kind of knew you were going to be in trouble, but cocaine was always somehow more acceptable. I should have known, because it had always been clear he was an addictive personality." Guthrie says he was "very lucky not to have been killed many times" in the course of his addiction. Not even the birth of his daughter, Lucy Belle, stopped him.

"Robin was taking more and more coke and was fairly uncontrollable," says Raymonde. "Liz was hoping fatherhood would smarten him up a bit, but it took him a little bit longer than she'd hoped."

"It was partly due to Simon, and my manager and Liz to some extent, that I continued taking drugs for so long," says Guthrie. "Because I was so enabled by everyone, and with the best intentions, because they just wanted to make everything better for me. Simon would go out on Tuesday at nine in the morning and buy me wine." For a while the music only got better. Partly-inspired by Lucy Belle's arrival and recorded at the group's new September Sound studio in Twickenham, *Heaven Or Las Vegas* was the Cocteaus' best yet – an album of ambient ear candy driven by bright, dancey rhythms and boasting almost intelligible words. Ivo Watts-Russell claims it is not just his favourite Cocteau Twins album but his favourite of all the albums ever released on 4AD. "*Heaven Or Las Vegas* is quite uplifting, isn't it?" muses Fraser. "I wonder how that happened. Probably not telling the truth enough." Guthrie slowly spiralled out of control: "I spent the first two years of Lucy's life off me face. When you've got a little two-year-old coming down the stairs and all the curtains are drawn in the middle of the day, it sort of has a profound effect on you." At least as decisive as his impending rock bottom was the slow awakening to reality of both Fraser and Raymonde. "I started going to Families Anonymous meetings," says Fraser. "And that's what changed things, because I did something where there was no turning back. And then Robin started to look at his stuff."

"We all went out to Arizona and checked into this place," says Raymonde. "Liz and I were like Robin's family members, and we had to sit there in these very emotional groups and deal with all this stuff. I thought I was just going out there to find out why my best mate was a druggie, and I actually found out a lot of other things about me. When you're living with a drug addict, you take on the enabling role... and I started to realise I was as fucked up as *they* were! I'd actually been their parent for ten years! I was just this sponge for all their crap. I thought it was normal, but when I had the opportunity to talk about it, suddenly it just came out in this massive gush." In the desert, Guthrie had an epiphany that led eventually to his recovery: "One afternoon I jumped the fence, walked out to a dried-up riverbed, and sat crying on this log for a couple of hours. And it got dark and the stars came out – there was nothing man-made anywhere – and all of a sudden the size of me and all my fucking problems was put into perspective. And that's stuck with me. When I get in a bit of a state, I think back to that moment."

The huge changes the group were going through screamed from every track on 1993's *Four-Calendar Café*, the first Cocteaus album released by their new label Mercury. Indeed, it remains one of the great pop tragedies that the trio's defection from the sacred indie homestead of 4AD all but cost them their fan base. As a result, what is perhaps their greatest – and certainly their most cathartic – album fell on deaf ears. "There was a frustration with 4AD," says Raymonde. "It's hard to recall exactly what the problem was, but really it was distrust and being let down on a certain number of things. You know, thinking that for a band that's really keeping this label afloat, why are we on such a ludicrously low royalty? All those resentments built up, and they never got discussed. They improved things just a little bit, but never enough for us to feel like we couldn't do better somewhere else." The fact that Watts-Russell was reinventing 4AD as a hotbed of American indie bands such as the Pixies and Throwing Muses drove a wedge of sorts between him and the Cocteaus. "I remember standing in the Town & Country in London, and they were just about to come onstage," he remembers. "I suddenly found myself surrounded by about three or four people who'd been part of the Cocteaus' circle, and they were asking me all sorts of questions. And I just realised I had no answers to any of them, and the reality of our lack of relationship was hitting me. Then the Cocteaus walked onstage and I burst into tears. And I realised I couldn't continue going home every night and going to sleep cursing Robin Guthrie for the rest of my life. I didn't know what to do, and the only thing I could do was stop it. So I called a meeting with their horrible manager and told him we were going to let them go."

Raymonde claims the group wanted the "anonymity" of a major-label deal but "didn't look at all the tiny intricacies" that make up such deals. "We ended up on this merry-go-round that we just couldn't get off," he says. "Labels and money and contracts… everything was just totally mad at that point. From 1990 onwards, the whole business side of things was out of control. We definitely lost the plot there for a while." For his part, Guthrie says that "after being on Mercury for one month I would have thrown my grandmother out of an aeroplane to make up with Ivo." Yet both men believe *Four-Calendar Café* to be their unsung masterpiece. "I thought people would understand," says Raymonde. "I was in the very fortunate position with that album of recording all Liz's vocal lines and just being reduced to tears most days. She'd give me a piece of paper with all the words of the songs so I could follow, and here, typed out, were some of the most beautiful lyrics you could ever have read, about something I was totally aware of. And then hearing her sing those words with such emotion. She was dealing with so much shit that she'd just stuffed down inside for so many years. She'd had a very traumatic childhood, but I didn't know until we all went into rehab."

Most startling was the new clarity of Fraser's phrasing, and the economy and transparency of her grieving lyrics. (*"I'm not real and I've been lying,"* she trilled on the opening 'Know Who You Are At Every Age'; on 'Evangeline' she sang *"There is no going back/I can't stop feeling now".*) "Of course, for a lot of people it was like, 'Good grief, she's actually singing words! What the hell's going on?!'" recalls Raymonde. "But when you look back to her singing styles, I would say it was a very important thing for her to go through, because it made her realise she can sing any way she likes. In the early days she had that kind of warble, but inside she had a certain kind of aggression that only popped up occasionally. So for years people wondered why Liz never said anything, and then when she did they wished that she'd kept quiet!"

"I seem to remember that it felt easy to be honest at that point," Fraser says. "And it was a relief, and I felt the benefits of releasing something. Plus I like it, I think it was done well, so I'm not embarrassed by that show of emotions or whatever it was. It wasn't a bad product at the end of the day, and that makes me feel better."

"For half of *Four-Calendar Café* I was in the darkest hell ever," remembers Guthrie. "And then I went into rehab and finished the record. Now the strange thing is that all the fuckin' happy songs were done when I was fucked-up, whereas all the dark, miserable ones were done when I got clean." A month before the Cocteaus went on tour to promote the album, Guthrie and Fraser split up. "It's not a good idea to go out on tour with your ex-boyfriend," she laughs. "We had moments where we were all up at the same time and in the same great space, and that was fun, but that didn't happen very often." The tour took its toll, too, on Raymonde: "I remember we were somewhere in America and they had a massive row, and I thought, 'I can't sort this out anymore'. So I just flipped and got on a bus to the airport. But we worked it out, and they got on quite well for about a year."

After the tour, Fraser met and fell in love with Jeff Buckley, a relationship that lasted 18 months. When she mentions his name, she bursts into tears. "He was so natural, my God! God, I really miss him! What a talent he was. He was just adorable." She talks of the evening when, on an impulse, she and Buckley decided to record together. "It was really only one little session, through the night. We just got an engineer to come in for a few hours. He was very free, so it was very easy for him to do those things. It was nothing for him to do that stuff, it was like breathing. He just had to do it. It was just something you did. And I wasn't like that. I'm *not* like that, so... you can imagine what it sounded like! But it was the makings of something fun if I'd been more chilled out." Observes Raymonde, "when Liz went out with Jeff, I think that must have been really difficult for Robin. He didn't talk about it much, but I think he found it hard. I think he still loved Liz, even though he knew he couldn't have a relationship with her anymore."

Milk And Kisses, the final Cocteaus album, was cut at September Sound in 1995. "It was quite an easy experience," says Raymonde. "Things were fairly stable at that point. Musically we were branching out a little bit. Liz was getting more into kind of dance things, more beat-oriented music. I had more energy, because I'd stopped assuming the role of carer. I felt more confident as a human being in my own right, and I worked out a way of being in the Cocteau Twins without it taking over my whole life." Yet despite a sprinkling of gems – 'Serpentskirt', 'Seekers Who Are Lovers', the magnificent 'Calfskin Smack' – it was clear the fire had all but gone out. "When I got clean, I just lost it," laughs Guthrie. "The Cocteau Twins was a fully functioning band that had a positive way forward, and that was because I just fucking led it, really. I instigated everything, and pretty much in a total control-freak junkie sort of way. And everybody was fucking scared of me. When I got clean I got into this sort of place where you've got to let everyone do their thing. Well, that was the end of the band, 'cause I just lost interest. It wasn't going the way I wanted and it lost focus, and I was going, 'Yeah, whatever'." Guthrie's passivity made the sessions amicable, but Fraser too was losing interest. After another tour – remembered by Guthrie as the best they'd ever done, with Fraser "singing like an angel" – the trio regrouped to begin work on a third Mercury album. Guthrie: "My heart wasn't in it, Liz's wasn't in it, and Simon's I don't think was in it because he was just too confused by the situation and expending so much of his energy trying to keep the peace between us. I'd have been happy to finish it if I'd felt anybody else had been, but it was just one hand clapping."

One day Fraser called up from Bristol, where she was now living with Damon Reece (then of Spiritualized, now of Lupine Howl). She told Guthrie and Raymonde she was leaving the Cocteau Twins. "I just knew it was over," she says. "I was pregnant again, and commuting from Bristol. The strain was enormous. And I just didn't like what we were doing. I tried to fake my way through the thing, but I knew this wasn't a temporary feeling. To me, this was it."

"YOU'VE CAUGHT me at a time in my life where I've really got some issues to fucking get my teeth into," Fraser tells me as our lunch comes to an end. "It's unfortunate that I'm trying to sound as if I know what I'm talking about when the whole thing's just blown my mind. I suppose I'm a bit paranoid about… I know the others have been *very, very angry*, and I've had to stay *very, very cool* so I didn't do anything stupid." She pauses to reflect. "Maybe I'm not sounding grateful. I appreciate that the Cocteau Twins was very special, very special. And that's why I thought it had gone on too long. I thought it was getting really shitty and turning into something that was rubbish, and I really didn't think I should be encouraging anyone to keep it going."

The liberation of quitting the Cocteaus notwithstanding, Fraser is struggling to get a grip on her solo career. Working with Reece on her first album for Geoff Travis' Blanco y Negro label, she is drawing on the confidence gained from her feted appearances on Massive Attack's *Mezzanine* and Peter Gabriel's recent *Ovo*, but for the moment has put recording on hold. "I really don't find it the easiest thing in the world to be creative," she says. "It's taking me a long time to do this project of mine. There seem to be a lot of things taking me away from it, and I don't know whether that's a good thing or not. There's quite a lot of music. I think about half the music's got vocals on, and half the vocals are now lyrics or sounds. So they're all at different stages. I suppose what I'd really like is for people to hear my changes 'cause I feel them so dramatically. It seems a really honest and truthful thing for me to do to document these moments and for people to experience them in that way. I've mostly really, really liked what I've been singing. I still love working with sound and everything, but it's a real challenge for me to talk and write and be making sense. It's really hard for me to do that. But it's a challenge I'm gonna go with, because I think I've got a lot to gain by getting my head round that stuff and just taking it on."

Meanwhile, back in Twickenham, Robin Guthrie talks of his own life beyond the Cocteaus. With the humility of the addict who's thrown in the towel – he's now been clean for nine years – he knows it's not going to be easy to get his new group off the ground. "Nobody wants to know about some old guy who was in a band," he smiles. "The media will be interested in Liz because she was the singer and the focal point, but I'll be sort of struggling a little. But I also know that I love what I do just now, and I know it's very, very pure. Since I got clean, it's been one of the joys of my life to come back and find I don't need drugs to make music."

Let's leave the last words to Guthrie's partner in Bella Union, the enabler and peacemaker of the peculiar troika. "Being in the Cocteau Twins," Simon Raymonde grins, "was always odd. It was never normal."

MOJO, 2000

20 I Want to Take You Higher
Spiritualized

CD bought in London in 1995

WITH AS MUCH *double entendre* as can be wrung from the phrase, Jason Pierce has billed tonight's *soirée* as "The Highest Show on Earth", the event in question being a concert performed at an altitude greater than any in previous musical history. "High" is certainly how you feel 114 stories above Toronto, scoping the city from the central viewing deck of the CN Tower. And that's before Spiritualized have even struck the first note of a laser-strafed set that will guarantee them immediate entrance to the next *Guinness Book Of Records*. The group are a little more than halfway through a six-week tour of North America, their second visit to the continent in 1997. The 27-date trawl has already taken in such landmark venues as San Francisco's Fillmore and Minneapolis' First Avenue; it will continue on to the East Coast and to the South, with shows at New Orleans' House of Blues and Austin's Liberty Lunch.

On the back of a transcendental and widely hosanna'd performance at London's Albert Hall last October, Pierce and colleagues are in a buoyant mood. For a band who've turned the studio into an almost Spectoresque lab for their symphonic storms, the tour is a reminder that Spiritualized were originally launched as a purely live entity. As they break into the opening cosmic-gospel medley of 'Oh Happy Day' and 'Shine A Light', it makes perfect sense that they should be performing halfway up the Canadian sky, dazzling a select gaggle of Torontonians with their huge, hypnotic sound. (Their acclaimed light show has been trimmed in order not to confuse low-flying aircraft.) Pierce's music has always been about reaching for the stars, soaring heavenwards to leave behind the mundane world we inhabit. "Mr. Spaceman", as he's dubbed himself since his days in Rugby's brave and seminal Spacemen 3, aims for nothing less than exaltation, a kind of euphoric disembodiedness that's reflected in the title of the band's third album, *Ladies And Gentlemen We Are Floating In Space*. (The very name Spiritualized suggests some strange process of discorporealisation.) In this sense, getting "high" is about so much more than the narcotic stupor to which Pierce refers in so many of his songs. It's about being swept away by dense, shimmering waves of sound that weld Stereolab and Steve Reich to the Doors and *Dark Side Of The Moon* – and carry you, ecstatic, into the firmament. No matter that Jason Pierce remains statue-still for the entire CN Tower set, or that his eyes and lips barely open as he sings: close your own eyes and you're instantly rushing with him through the star-flecked cosmos. How far the band have come from the blissful enervation of their debut *Lazer-Guided Melodies* (1992). As they burst joltingly into 'Electricity' – a song no less thrilling than the classic of the same name by Captain Beefheart, himself a cited influence on *Ladies And Gentlemen* – it's like hearing Spacemen 3's 'Take Me To The Other Side' yoked to Spector's 'River Deep, Mountain High'. "I think you have to be honest to make this kind of music," Pierce will tell me a week later. "But it also has to be a lot larger than life. It has to deal with the extremities, it can't deal with mediocrity. It's not about the day-to-day stuff – it's the big picture." Perhaps God isn't in the details after all.

Watching Pierce on stage – a surprisingly strapping fellow for a man assumed to be a far-gone drug fiend – you can still make out the taciturn boy who skulked behind Pete "Sonic Boom" Kember in Spacemen 3. Thinking back to those fuzz-toned days, you realise how alone and adrift they must have felt in the relentlessly bouncy mid-Eighties. Self-raised on a small-town diet of the music they learned about in fanzines such as Lindsay Hutton's *Next Big Thing* – from the Cramps and Roky Erickson to the Stooges and

Esquerita – they wanted no truck with Little England, dreaming instead of Vox amplifiers and demented Americans in sunglasses and polo-necks. "I liked the fact that the Cramps let people know about their influences, rather than just saying, 'We landed and came up with this sound'," Pierce says in his soft, patient voice. "It was through the Cramps that I learned about things like the Red Krayola." Pierce and Kember hit on a fanatical psych-punk sound that drew from the twin streams of the Stooges and the Velvets, throwing in explicit references to mind-altering medication. "The idea of space just seemed to fit in with what we were doing," Pierce explains. "It seemed like we *were* spacemen, like we weren't doing the things that made it easy to slot into normal life in Rugby."

A small coterie of acolytes took notice. Almost everyone else ignored them. Nor was the Spacemen cause helped by invidious comparisons to the similarly drone-friendly Jesus and Mary Chain. "I couldn't see any similarities to what we were doing," Pierce says. "I've since come to love *Darklands*, but I still don't get the first one, and I still don't think it mirrored what we were doing at all." Revisiting the Spacemen albums *The Perfect Prescription* (1987) and *Recurring* (1991), it's extraordinary how many of the elements that make up Spiritualized were already in place at the time. The Velvets influence may be a little more to the fore (e.g. on 'Transparent Radiation'), and the general prostration before the Stooges, Suicide *et al.* a little too confining, but the interlinked themes of intoxication, space travel and religious rapture (e.g. on 'Walkin' With Jesus') are no less overt than they are on *Ladies And Gentlemen*. What's most obviously missing is the epic quality of Spiritualized on the latter and on *Pure Phase* (1995) – the careering intensity of 'Medication' and 'These Blues'. It was only after a bitter parting with Kember – to whom he hasn't spoken in eight years – that Pierce began working towards what he called "the ultimate sound", one that combined exultation with Lou Reed vocals, fusing spacey guitars and keyboards with "soulful" horns and strings. Taking the remains of Spacemen 3 with him and adding his then-girlfriend Kate Radley on keyboards, he created the 13-minute symphony – and Spiritualized blueprint – that was 1991's 'Feel So Sad'. A year later, at the height of the shoegazing vogue, *Lazer Guided Melodies* took its place alongside Primal Scream's 'Higher Than The Sun' and My Bloody Valentine's *Loveless* as a pinnacle of the new drug pop.

Next to its successors, it must be said, *Lazer Guided Melodies* now sounds listless to the point of torpor. "It was an incredibly frustrating way of working," Pierce confesses. "The musicians at that point were just people who played parts for me. Since then, I've tended to work a lot more *with*

241

musicians. Now it's not such a strain, in the sense of having to get the sound I hear in my head. And that's not just the core of the band, but people who've played on the records like Dr. John and Alexander Balanescu." More exciting, and more beautiful, was *Pure Phase*, suspended between the crazed rush of 'Medication' and (unforgettably graced by the Balanescu Quartet) the gossamer loveliness of 'All Of My Tears'. Not that you'd have known it from a pop press which had shifted its allegiance from dream-pop to Britpop. "It just showed what a transitory thing hipness is," remarks Pierce of the album's fate. Fortunately, by the time Spiritualized had finished work on *Ladies And Gentlemen*, Pierce was back in favour. He says he started the album with a view to eliminating the most obvious ingredients in the band's sound. "Before, I was doing stuff like putting glockenspiels against tubas and bass harmonicas, trying to get different sounds. Now we've actually got the basic horns/strings/backing singers line-up that's all over every record from Memphis to Philadelphia. Of course, some of the old stuff went back in – the tremolos and the drones. Those are things you can't change anyway, like my voice. What tends to stay is the stuff that doesn't sound familiar – it's a strange editing process. 'Cop Shoot Cop' [the long closing track on *Ladies* featuring the aforementioned Dr. John] has elements of everything from the Red Krayola to Miles Davis, but not in an obvious way. The closest things we could talk about when we were making it were *Clear Spot* and *There's A Riot Goin' On*. Not that they sound like this record, just that they used the familiar line-up and came up with something so *odd*!"

The result is a record that takes *Pure Phase* as a departure point, but dispenses with its long electronic interludes. *Ladies And Gentlemen We Are Floating In Space* brings together late Brian Wilson and *Screamadelica*, 'Heroin' and *The Sun, Moon & Herbs* in a huge river of sound that courses through the chords and riffs. Here are surging peaks that rival 'Bittersweet Symphony' and *OK Computer*, troughs of despair and druggy blankness that rival the Velvets at their most nihilistic. "*Ladies And Gentlemen* was probably the best two years of my life," Pierce says. "It was an *ecstatic* time." Yet for all the horns and gospel choirs and Dr. John piano licks, it's a fundamentally classical, funk-free sound: one need only compare Spiritualized's 'Stay With Me' to the Lorraine Ellison classic on which it's loosely based to gauge the difference between Pierce's white light/white heat "spiritualization" and the choked agony of Black soul.

Critics have made much of his obsessiveness on the album – linked to his break-up with Radley, now married to the Verve's Richard Ashcroft – but the voice of 'Broken Heart' and 'All Of My Thoughts' is so sweetly defeated, it's the very opposite of "soul". (Sometimes Pierce's lyrics verge on the maddeningly vacant: 'Cop Shoot Cop''s *"Jesus Christ died for nothing, I suppose"* is a priceless example of his impenetrable cool.) I ask to what degree his music expresses the yearning for religious bliss. "There is that kind of feeling," he says, "but I know enough about how consciousness works to know that music isn't tapping into some cosmic spirit. Somebody wrote in a live review that there were five of us in the band and God on feedback, but I don't believe that. I mean, it's powerful, but then music is *physical* – you *do* feel it in your spine."

Spines are certainly reverberating as Spiritualized tear into 'No God, Only Religion' high over Toronto. With keyboard player/Radley-stand-in Jim Lewis playing the song's horn riff, and the gaunt, pipecleaner-thin Sean Cook forsaking his bass to blow an ear-bleedingly loud harp solo, the band enters the abandoned terrain of the best jazz-rock, bouncing off each other as the number builds to a frenzied climax. Damon Reece is an admirably untamed and intuitive drummer, driving the song to a point of furious intensity. Locked together in a trance are Pierce, second guitarist Mike Mooney, and saxophonist Ray Dickarty. Sometimes Spiritualized cross the fine line between trance and boredom the wrong way. Tonight, more often than not, they reach the peaks. "The CN Tower was probably the best show we've ever done," Pierce tells me in New York, 38 floors over Times Square. (We must stop meeting like this.) "There's no point in doing places like that or the Albert Hall and not really excelling. There's no point in going to the top of the CN Tower and just being a kind of bar band in the corner. It had to be amazing, and it was. After *Lazer-Guided Melodies*, I went more for how I thought jazz was created – people feeding off each other and inspiring each other – and I think it shows live." A major inspiration in this department was the experience last year of supporting Neil Young, whose long-time manager Elliot Roberts also looks after Spiritualized. Pierce even spent the night on Young's ranch after the band's San Francisco show in November. "I love the way Neil and Crazy Horse work off each other musically," he says. "When we were touring with them, 'Like a Hurricane' became a more screaming, psychedelic thing, and I think that affected the way we were playing."

How did Spiritualized come to be managed by Roberts? "Erm, I just rang him up. I don't think people in England had been getting what we were doing, and I thought someone like Elliot would. The fact that Neil's been with him since Buffalo Springfield was as good a recommendation as anyone could get." Like Young himself, Pierce is famously averse to compromise, a trait that's seen Spiritualized incur hefty debts over the years. "I've over-borrowed to do certain things," he admits. "I don't like the way bands would do a special show for the press in London with a horn section or whatever, and then drop the horns for the rest of the country. So when we did *Lazer-Guided Melodies*, we toured with a full horn section everywhere." The elaborate packaging of *Pure Phase* and *Ladies And Gentlemen* also came directly out of the band's pocket. "So much music is about compromising with commerce," he says. "And there are so many different levels of that. The boy groups are the industry at its purest, but even the supposedly cooler, more independent bands have the same kind of business behind them. They're just not so blatant about it. I don't know whether my attitude toward things like MTV has been tainted by the fact that we *haven't* had those opportunities. But even if we *had* had them, I'm not so naive that I don't understand the way they work."

One of the more insidious marketing techniques of recent years has been the use of behind-the-music "stories" to beef up inadequate music. Pierce is particularly bored with the press trying to get the scoop on his drug use, and on the demise of his relationship with Radley. "I don't think anyone genuinely listens to lyrics in that way, but it comes with the marketing of records. With the Righteous Brothers' 'You've Lost That Lovin' Feelin'' or Ray Charles' 'I Can't Stop Loving You', you don't listen to them and think, 'This is about a moment in the author's life that he's set to music'. You relate it to your life – it doesn't have anything to do with the author anymore. But often today the music isn't strong enough, so they have to market a story instead. And I'm involved in it, obviously: if I hadn't been doing interviews, I wouldn't even have come to that conclusion." Given that Spiritualized portray drug use in a remarkably matter-of-fact, demystified way, it's strange that people seem so intent on portraying him as an irreparably wasted junkie. "I love the Hunter S. Thompson line – that if he'd really done all that, he'd be dead," he says. "I think it all comes down to the counter-culture: it's still seen as rebellious behaviour, and it still works. I've never tried to use drugs as a selling point, and I've always thought that if you *have* to take drugs to enjoy a band, there's something wrong with the music." Regarding his former paramour, who pulled out of the American tour because of poor health, he confirms that Radley "is still a member of the band [and] will be playing again next year". Asked whether the tabloid fascination with their separation and its effect on songs like 'Broken Heart' was annoying, he claims he didn't read the stories. "One of the first *NME* pieces took this line, and no matter what I said after that, it didn't seem to change the story.

It happened once before with Spacemen 3, when they already had the story that Pete was a wealthy ex-public schoolboy who lived in luxury while I lived in the slums."

Pierce seems happy to be on the road in America. As we speak, he is looking forward to the Avalon in Philadelphia – "one of the best-sounding halls in the world" – and to playing Austin, where his friends the Butthole Surfers live. (The Buttholes' Paul Leary was one of several prospective candidates to mix *Ladies And Gentlemen*.) "I really like America, and not just the East and West coasts. I think Americans *get* Spiritualized, in that they appear to be in it for the music. They want to know about Gil Evans and Miles Davis. I meet very few fans of the group who are just contemporary music fans – like, into British music of the Nineties. They're not into us and any four given British bands; they're more into the history of music and finding out what they've missed. I'm the same, basically. I'm not into being hip to what's contemporary. I think there's so much stuff out there that's been done better before. See, I don't think what we do is radical at all. It's only radical by contrast to other things. I don't think it's that difficult to be ambitious and stay true to what you want to do."

MOJO, 1998

21 Darker Days
PJ Harvey

CD bought in London in 1993

POLLY JEAN Harvey sits in almost regal splendour at the end of the very long and pompous Promenade Room of London's Dorchester Hotel. Buffed Eurotrash couples wander past without a flicker of recognition or interest. "Oooh, this is the comfiest thing I've ever sat in," she purrs in the charming Dorset burr that is her speaking voice.

Two and a half years ago, on September 9, 2001, Harvey learned she had won Britain's prestigious Mercury Music Prize for *Stories From The City, Stories From The Sea*. Unfortunately, when the news came in she was staring in disbelief from her Washington D.C. hotel room at smoke pouring from the nearby Pentagon. Her achievement had been rendered meaningless by the apocalyptic trauma that was 9/11. "I woke up to people hammering on the door, saying the Pentagon was on fire," she remembers. "Sadly, I didn't feel at all present in terms of winning the prize. And it was an honour for me to receive it." For fans of Harvey, perhaps the best singer-songwriter of her generation, *Stories* had been her most satisfying album to date – not least because it was her happiest yet. Trebly and sparkling, full of the euphoria of love and the mad energy of her part-adopted Manhattan, the album followed the fuzzy techno-murk of the equally great *Is This Desire?* – a record implicitly haunted by her break-up with her sometime hero Nick Cave – like sunshine bursting through black clouds.

It's typical, then, that she has turned around and marched off in precisely the opposite direction on her sixth album (seventh if one includes her 1995 *4-Track Demos* set). Ever contrary and never pandering to expectation, she elected to make *Uh Huh Her* everything that *Stories* wasn't. "With *Stories* I wanted to explore a highly produced melodic sound, and with this record I wanted it to be kind of ugly," she says. "I was looking for distressed, debased sounds. So all of the guitars are either guitars tuned so low, it's hard to detect what notes they're playing, or they're baritone guitars or they're played through the shittiest amps I could find."

Sold? Or at least intrigued? You should be. Part of a pantheon of Nineties rock artists that includes Beck, Björk and Radiohead, Harvey has made the most sensual, rapturous, courageous music of the last decade – songs of dark intensity and dense funkiness that ride on granite-hard riffs worthy of Keith Richards. Any artist with 'Sheela-Na-Gig', 'Rid Of Me', 'Working For The Man', 'The Garden' and 'Big Exit' in her catalogue must be considered an elemental force. "She's got a house-big heart," Nick Cave sang of her in 1997, "where we all live and plead and counsel and forgive." Harvey's former paramour could have been speaking for her many fans. "I think of myself probably as an artist in terms of it being my life's work," she avers. "I want to explore and challenge myself. I'm not doing this for any other reason than to see what I can produce – and can that be of worth and help to people? And I think people like Thom Yorke and Will Oldham are the same. They challenge themselves."

Pop-culture commentary being what it is, Harvey is now having to field endless questions about her emotional well-being. Listening to *Uh Huh Her*, it's not altogether surprising. 'The Life And Death of Mr. Badmouth' is the album's vitriolic opening track, and also its worst. (If it's not about her sometime beau, actor/director/singer Vincent Gallo, it probably should be.) 'Who The Fuck?' is wilfully vicious. 'Cat On The Wall' is grindingly, obtusely unmelodic. Lead radio track 'The Letter' is hardly Top 40 fodder. What gives, Pol? "Almost across the board, people take this as an autobiographical record," she states patiently. "I spend my entire time trying to explain to people that I'm a creative writer. People jump to conclusions and I can understand it, because if I'm very interested in an artist – whether it's Neil Young, Bob Dylan, whoever – I want to imagine that those stories are true. But I think also that when I listen to those writers, I project my own stories into their songs. And I'd like people to be able to do that with mine."

It's part and parcel of our diseased celebrity culture that we assume artists *want* to air their dirty laundry in public. The clear boundary Harvey sets up between her life and her art demands our respect – and certainly gets mine, however frustrating it makes my job. When I ask whether love-sickened songs such as 'The Slow Drug', 'It's You' and 'The Darker Days of Me & Him' reflect a view of romance as addiction, she politely slams the door in my face. "I'm not someone that would divulge my view on anything like that in an interview," she responds with a calm smile. "I'm a very open-minded person, and I don't have one particular shadowy view of love. I think of myself as a very hopeful person. I was painting a particular desperate atmosphere in ['The Darker Days'] and wanted it to be so. I choose to paint other atmospheres in different songs."

In that gravely beautiful song, which closes the album, Harvey longs for a land with "no neurosis, and no psychosis/No psychoanalysis… and no sadness." Is she ever likely to reach such a place? "One can wish for it and long for it and sing it out loud. Wouldn't it be great? I was particularly pleased with those words. At that part of the song, the music disappears and you've just got the voice, just there, and I sang those words in a particularly sibilant voice. Plus I always wanted to get the word 'psychoanalysis' into a song – it's not the easiest one to slip in there!" The truth is that she appears to be a centred, grounded person – not the artsy snob and anorexic control freak some might imagine. If one fears for the emotional health of a woman who's stepped out with not just Nick Cave but Vincent Gallo, perhaps one should turn it around and be happy for those testing gentlemen that they got to spend quality time with her.

It says plenty about her that she spent much of 2002/3 in the Dorset bosom of her bohemian but very stable family, helping to nurse her dying grandmother. "I didn't even do any writing or anything then," she says. "She was my last grandparent, so I wanted to absorb as much of being with her as I could at that time." Recorded mostly on four- and eight-track machines, the lo-fi *Uh Huh Her* marks the first time she has produced herself without help, playing most of the instruments too. Working with drummer Rob Ellis and engineer Head – West Country lads both – almost brings her career full circle, back to her bare-bones 1992 debut *Dry*. "I chose them in the first place because they were two people I knew I would not be inhibited in front of," she says. "They know me so well that I can be completely myself with them. That felt very important to me, because it was the first time I'd felt confident enough to produce myself and I knew they would support me in that."

The album's release kick-starts a year at least of touring and promotion. A US trek this summer takes in two and a half weeks of the Lollapalooza festival. Headlining the days on which she plays will be Morrissey – now a near-neighbour in Los Angeles, where for the past year she has rented a place on the Sunset Strip. "I'm constantly driving past his place and waving hello to him," she says. "LA's an unlikely place for him, but I would have said the same about me."

Partway into the making of *Is This Desire?* – maybe her most compelling album – she had a crisis of self-belief and almost fled the music business to become a nurse in Africa. Does she ever doubt herself these days? "I don't anymore," she says. "I think in the last five years or so I've felt, more than ever, that I'm doing what I'm supposed to be doing. And I feel very lucky to have found my life's work. I've found something where I can try and give something back to other people. I think that's quite a big thing that a lot of people want to find – some way of giving. I'm able to do that with music."

Tracks, 2004

22 Long Player
Ron Sexsmith

CD bought in Woodstock, N.Y., in 1997

THE FIRST THING you might say about Ronald Eldon Sexsmith is that any other aspiring singer-songwriter with a name like that would have changed it years ago to, say, Jim Tunesmith or Woody Blacksmith. *Ron Sexsmith?!* How is a man gonna make it through this world with a moniker like *that?!* Especially when sex is hardly the first thing that comes to mind when you hear Ron's sweetly droopy songs. Yet the fact that Ron Sexsmith is called Ron Sexsmith is one of the many things I love about a man I regard as one of the most unjustly unappreciated talents of the past 20 years. I love the name because it's real if faintly strange: no one could possibly have made it up as a cool-sounding show biz ID. And for me that's all of a piece with what he represents, which is a profound honesty, a purity of expression in a world of insufferable musical disingenuousness – the kind that prompted Jonathan Franzen to write recently of the tiresome Conor Oberst that "he was performing sincerity, and when the performance threatened to give sincerity the lie, he performed his sincere anguish over the difficulty of sincerity".

From several angles, Sexsmith really isn't remarkable at all. He doesn't very obviously stand out from the crowd of journeyman troubadours who write conventional soft-rock songs about feelings and everyday emotional crises, generally in 4/4 time using acoustic and/or electric guitars and usually easy or pleasantly melodic on the ear. There are a lot of North American guys out there – Sexsmith is Canadian – who do approximately what he does and who, like him, protract their unglamorous careers one modest album deal at a time. Many come to Britain twice a year to play the Borderline or (if they're luckier) the Barbican. Eighteen months ago, I saw Sexsmith play to a sparse gathering of the faithful at London's Scala and was left wondering if maybe he *was* just another workaday North American singer-songwriter – an 'Average Joe', to cite a song from his almost flawless second album *Other Songs*. Any fully subscribing member of the Sexsmith church – which includes the many famous peers (Costello, Elton, Feist, Steve Earle, Daniel Lanois, Chris Martin... almost *ad nauseam*) who've lined up over the years to protest his lack of global renown – must occasionally wonder the same thing, as each slow-growingly lovely album creeps quietly out on each minor indie label to further deafening silence. Before you know it, you're just a poor man's Nick Hornby banging the drum for a Ben Folds or a Boo Hewerdine. But then you go home and play one of his albums and remind yourself you were right all along.

It wasn't always this way. Against the odds – not *all* the odds but most of them – Sexsmith's debut came out on the major Interscope label and gave the shy 30-year-old from St. Catharines, Ontario, a brief taste of the expensive-studio rock high-life. "I was just amazed that I even got in the door," he says. "It just seemed so unrealistic, coming from where I came from, and just how I looked and the kind of music I was doing. And I think for some reason in the early Nineties there was this opening where a guy like me could come through." *Ron Sexsmith* was produced by Mitchell Froom, who "got" him and framed such sensitive, delicate songs as 'Secret Heart' and 'Wastin' Time' in appropriately subtle arrangements that didn't scream for attention. Six months after the record was hailed by Froom client Elvis Costello as 1995's best album, I met Froom to discuss various of his productions (from Crowded House's *Woodface* to Costello's own stunning 'Couldn't Call It Unexpected No. 4'), and he spoke about working with the Canadian: "Ron had maybe 50, 60 songs, many of which just weren't for me at all. But then when he got signed, I met him and really liked him, and he was talking about people like Nilsson and Tim Hardin and Charlie Rich – names you just don't hear very often. He could have made a record like Christopher Cross or something, and I think that's what the record company was hoping for. But I said he had a very sweet voice and soft style and that we should do the record very intimately. It seems to be a record that singer-songwriters respond to: John Hiatt, Nick Lowe and several other singer-songwriters must have called me about it. I felt somewhat vindicated, because there were certain people at his company who felt we'd gone in the wrong direction. There are two songs on it which to me are the real heart of the record, 'Wastin' Time' and 'Secret Heart'."

I liked 'Secret Heart' and its companions, but wasn't wholly convinced by a guy who seemed on first hearing/viewing to be a kind of non-pinup version of Jackson Browne. It took *Other Songs* (1997) to make a lifelong fan of me. Again produced by Froom but even more intimately (with less studio echo and more brushes from drummers Pete Thomas and Jerry Marotta), songs like 'So Young' and 'Strawberry Blonde' showed Sexsmith to be a singer of miniatures – of fragments and snatches, what the late Elliott Smith (his only real peer in that era) called "passing feelings". He was the polar opposite of a bombastic anthemist. Naturally you could have pointed to forebears, antecedents: certainly there was something of heyday-Costello in there (how Declan-esque is the title 'Clown In Broad Daylight'?!) and the ghost of Harry Nilsson (to whom *Ron Sexsmith* had been dedicated) was invoked by melodies that also pulled from the wellsprings of McCartney and Ray Davies. But the package as a whole was quite distinctive and singular: like Elliott Smith (or for that matter like a dozen under-appreciated singer-songwriter greats from Marshall Crenshaw to Aimee Mann), he has fashioned a sonic-poetic space that's his alone. Who else could have written 'Child Star', a disarmingly simple, almost spookily empathic ballad about the archetypal prodigy cast aside by the fame machine? Who else would have been capable of the unmannered compassion invested in *Retriever*'s 'For The Driver' or *Cobblestone Runway*'s non-denominational 'God Loves Everyone'?

It may be the concision and stillness of Sexsmith's songs – coupled with the effortless beauty of his melodies and a voice whose timbre verges on a kind of *angelic plumminess* – that makes him so special. Frequently he will take an everyday phrase – e.g. 'Honest Mistake', 'Hard Bargain', 'Former Glory', 'Disappearing Act', 'Thinking Out Loud' – and wrap an exquisite fragment or micro-narrative around it. And if the grain of that voice speaks to you, then he becomes a kind of companion, a maker of songs that synch completely with one's own experience of life. "I guess what it's about is following through with an idea," he says. "You get this idea, and it may be very small, and you kind of walk around and think about it. That's kind of my stock-in-trade, really: people see me walking all over town and I'm usually singing to myself like a crazy person or something. Or I'm doing the dishes or something. Because I hear other people's songs sometimes where I'm like, 'Okay, you got started with something good but then you kind of... let it slip or something.' If I'm listening to somebody's song and I don't understand what they're going on about, I sort of lose interest, you know? A song like Leonard Cohen's 'Hey, That's No Way To Say Goodbye', for example, profoundly influenced me, because in three verses he says everything that two people would need to say about going their separate ways. It was so concise that I wanted to try to do that. I've made a lot of records where the production wasn't quite right or where I wasn't singing very well, but the songs have survived. And that's what I set out to do, because I'm not good at anything else. It's just this one thing that I'm supposed to be good at, and I don't take that lightly."

I've followed Sexsmith right through his subsequent six albums proper, from 1999's *Whereabouts* to 2008's *Exit Strategy Of The Soul*, knowing there will always be at least five or six songs I'll end up holding close, harbouring like the vulnerable children they are – like, in a sense, Sexsmith himself is. More often than not, they're the songs of sorrowful acceptance, of humble fatalism: a lot of his most moving ballads were written about the slow death of his first marriage and the break-up of a family that included a son and daughter. I particularly treasure the haunting 'So Young', tucked almost inconspicuously towards the end of *Other Songs*, and a clutch of deeply sad songs ('Still Time', 'Doomed') on the gorgeous *Whereabouts*, which also featured 'In A Flash', an extraordinary, almost Elizabethan-style song about death – or at least the evanescence of almost everything, "there one moment and then gone in a flash" – arranged starkly for picked acoustic guitar (Sexsmith) and wheezy pump organ (Froom).

"*Other Songs* was when my career was just getting off the ground," he says. "But it was also towards the end of my relationship with my first wife. So I think I got painted early on as being kind of melancholy, and that's something that's kind of stuck with me for some reason, even though for the most part I've tried to write songs that were hopeful and funny. Back then, even when I was writing something like 'Thinking Out Loud', I always felt I had to tiptoe around stuff because I knew my wife was going to hear it and I hated being in that situation. But I didn't want to candy-coat anything either. There was that opening when a guy like me could come through with an acoustic guitar and sing without irony about stuff. Because the Eighties was all obviously about fashion and hair and all that kind of stuff, and I couldn't get arrested. So here I was just trying to raise the flag of the singer-songwriter in the mid-Nineties."

I also adore faster-paced tracks like the drolly Kinksy son-of-God parable 'Idiot Boy' (with its Beatle-esque middle eight; Sexsmith is nothing if not a master of the middle eight), the jauntily Costello-ish 'Disappearing Act' and *Retriever*'s driving 'Wishing Wells', a rare Sexsmith venting of frustrated rage at "all the smug and smirking juveniles" and "bloodthirsty thugs". The disappointments of his career have become almost a *leitmotif* of his music. After what felt like the inevitable failure of *Exit Strategy…* – released on Ironworks, a label formed by Kiefer Sutherland, yet *another* celebrity admirer – he was so down in the dumps that he contemplated giving up altogether. Despite the support of his second wife Colleen Hixenbaugh, herself a musician, he sank into a depression only alleviated by a vacation that produced a batch of new songs. "At the end of 2008 I'd just done this awful tour," he says. "I really just wanted to give up. I didn't want to make any more records or do anything. And after Christmas my wife said, 'Why don't we go to New Mexico?' We have these friends there who let us stay in their guesthouse. So we went down, and when we got there Colleen had rented me this guitar. And I'd hardly played the guitar around the house for a while, because I was mostly into the piano, so it was kind of like rediscovering an old friend and I just started writing all these songs. I'd get up and walk to this café, which was about half an hour away, and by the time I got back I would have a song almost completely finished in my mind. So I went down there with nothing, and when I got back I had about seven songs. But still I was gun-shy, because I didn't really see the point anymore."

The new songs in turn galvanised him into seeking a new producer to scatter some commercial dust over them – and thus maybe give our melancholy hero his first real shot at the ephemeral phenomenon known as Success. However, everyone including Colleen was astonished when the producer turned out to be Bob Rock, the man who'd masterminded Metallica's eponymous, none-more-heavy "black album" (1991) and who more recently had sat behind the console for perennial stadium-fillers Bon Jovi. Was this, then, going to be the Bon Jovification of Ronald Eldon Sexsmith? "I thought originally that Bob mostly just did hard rock music," he says. "I love hard rock, and that's where we really connected, because we're both big fans of, like, Deep Purple and the Kinks and Bowie – but

I was at this Juno Awards party and I was asking everyone for suggestions for producers. Bob said that he was a fan, but people say that all the time and you're always tempted to go, 'Okay, so name a song, then...' I didn't say that, but I did send him the demos for the songs a little while later, and he got right back to me. So then the problem was, 'Great, he wants to do it, but how do we pull the money together?' And at that point I was just so excited and I had a feeling that I hadn't had in a while, so I just said to my manager, 'I don't care how you do it but we have to do this and make it happen'. And Bob was great in the studio: I felt I was in real good hands and I never questioned his taste. It's not a shy record, it just sort of comes crashing through the door. I've made these albums that were quite slick before, like *Retriever* was quite slick, but with this one I was just trying to rise to the occasion. Because producers are like movie directors. If I'd made this record with [Daniel] Lanois, it would have been very different. They all come with their own bags of tricks. Part of this, too, was a response to... I mean, Toronto, where I live, is a very hipster town, and I'm constantly out at the bars surrounded by a lot of indie-scene alt-country types, and it drives me up the wall. I mean, they're all really nice people, but I just don't feel like I belong in that scene. My friend Kevin from Broken Social Scene said, 'Oh, you don't wanna work with Bob Rock, you should work with the guy that did Radiohead or something'. And I said, 'Well, first of all he wouldn't be interested in working with me, and second, I don't sculpt my records in the studio, you know, I go in with finished songs.' And you know, my heroes are like Elton John: there's a guy who made great albums but also had hits on the radio. Joni Mitchell had hits on the radio. I've always wanted to be an album artist first, but with a song or two that would be the sort of calling card. And Bob's in that league – he makes successful albums – and I was hoping maybe some of that would rub off on me. I'm sure there'll be purists out there who'll hate the record because they want you to be one thing. Even Bob asked me if I was afraid people will think I've sold out, but I said, 'Well, how can you sell out on something that you never bought into in the first place?'"

The resulting *Long Player Late Bloomer* may come as a shock to those who worship *Whereabouts* or *Other Songs* (or, for that matter, the Steve-Earle-produced *Blue Boy* and the marginally poppier albums recorded with Swedish producer Martin Terefe), but if you can suspend disbelief for long enough, you will more than likely come to love the album's glistening AOR/pop-rock sheen, which is aimed like a golden arrow at traditional rock radio – to the extent that such a thing exists anymore. With his blond highlights, mutton-dressed-as-lamb ear studs and general LA demeanour, Rock may be the anti-Mitchell-Froom par excellence, but he has done exactly what he was supposed to do, which was bring out Sexsmith's melodicism in its full, rich glory. Though the songs reflect the singer's morose mindset after *Exit Strategy…*, Rock's sound leaps out at you, the album's rippling tunes crying out to be heard on daytime radio. (Lo and behold, 'Believe It When I See It' has actually slipped on to the playlist at Britain's BBC Radio 2. Furthermore, Rock had already given Sexsmith his biggest commercial success to date by convincing Canadian superstar Michael Bublé to cut *Retriever*'s 'Whatever It Takes' – the bonus track on the man's chart-topping *Crazy Love*.)

Not that *Long Player* is all streamlined pop-rock, you dig: in among the "big" songs are the softly swaying Latin groove of 'Miracles', the dobro-flecked 'Nowadays', and the twangy Nashville opener 'Get In Line', whose frisky beat belies a lyric of mordant self-loathing: "It was just sort of a funny song I wrote because I had this awful co-writing experience where these people made me feel like I was worthless or something. And that's the great thing about songwriting, this stuff will just come out in a song and you can get your revenge! Though they may never know. So I think this album is coming with a dark cloud over it, but in general – and it sounds like a cliché – it was very cathartic for me to try to put down all the hopeful songs for a few records. The president of Warner Canada was listening to it and he said, 'Wow, this is probably the happiest record you've ever made'. And I was like, 'Hmm, get this man a lyric sheet!' I always liked songs anyway where the music was kind of coming from a different place to the lyrics. There's a lot of disillusion on this record, but humorously so, I think. On the last bunch of records I think I've been trying to write these more hopeful songs – just for my own head – and they didn't really get me anywhere. And with this record, I think, there's a creeping pessimism coming in that wasn't there before. Or maybe it was, I don't know."

Accompanying the album's release is a moving documentary about Sexsmith by director Douglas Arrowsmith. Interspersing footage from the Rock sessions in late 2009 with chronological biography and talking heads (most of the above-mentioned Famous Fans), *Love Shines* blows the trumpet for a very special man – a natural melancholic who's always striven to do the right thing despite crippling self-doubt. One comes away from the film with a genuine sense that he doesn't know how great he is: there's something almost Asperger's-ish about this manchild *savant* who doesn't own an iPod and still takes his clothes to the local Laundromat on the streetcar. Or has Arrowsmith overplayed this?

"I actually *like* going to the Laundromat," Sexsmith says. "I've written a lot of songs there and it's just down the street and I don't drive so I'm always on the streetcar. It's not an issue for me. Sometimes, as you get older, you hope you'll have more of a nest egg or something, because financial stress can be a drag. But I've been really fortunate, you know. Another thing that I don't think the movie really addresses is that there seems to be this desperation to have a hit or something, and it's not about that at all, you know. I mean, I've always tried to write hit records – all my heroes had hit records – but it's more about trying to improve my situation. I have a great band, for example, that I can almost never afford to take on the road with me. I've seen how other people tour, and they have their crew and all that, and you kind of want to get to that place. And it may never happen, but I'm always shooting for that, you know. I didn't set out to be a cult artist."

The divine irony is that, while Sexsmith longs for the confidence of a Bruce Springsteen, if he ever came out onstage with all guns blazing he would no longer be the Sexsmith that his fans want – the bashful poet of introversion and subtle observation whose unsung journey we've followed for 16-plus years. "On my last tour," he says, "if I saw a person whispering into someone's ear from the stage I would start to get all paranoid that they were talking about me and saying I was fat or something, and it would totally destroy my whole mood for the whole show – even though they could have been saying something really nice. It's funny, because all last year while I was waiting for my record to come out, I'd gotten this live Neil Diamond DVD and I couldn't stop watching it. And that was kind of where I wanted to be – not be Neil Diamond, but when he comes out onstage he completely owns it... he's Neil Diamond and he's not embarrassed by that, and people love him. And I thought, 'Well, that's where I want to be. I want to come out and be comfortable in my own skin'. I'm trying to get to a place where I have a shield around me or something."

Isn't it enough just to know how deeply he connects with the people who "get" him? "I get a lot of nice emails and people coming up to me on the street, all that kind of stuff. But from time to time, I do forget, you know? The film catches me in a down period where I think I'd lost all my confidence, and it's hard to see all the good things when you're depressed. It's kind of amazing how the ego works, and how fragile a person can be. And then all of a sudden you get an email from a person in Australia and it can lift your whole mood. I am confident in terms of the work I'm doing, and I know that when I have an idea for a song I can see it through. But every now and then I guess I need to be reminded that it hasn't all fallen on deaf ears – that I exist."

Ladies and gentlemen, Ron Sexsmith exists.

Rock's Backpages, 2011

23 A Passing Feeling
Elliott Smith

CD bought in New York in 1997

A YEAR AGO, I sat in the living room of Roger Steffens, curator of a Bob Marley archive that was then in the process of being sold to the Marley estate. Elliott Smith had died in Steffens' Echo Park neighbourhood two days earlier, so I asked Roger if he'd ever met the singer. "Take a look out the window," he replied. Below us on a sloping hill was a modest, single-storey box surrounded by trees and bushes. In the hazy half-light caused by the brush fires then surrounding LA, I could just about discern the glow of a lamp in one of the windows. "That's the house he died in," Steffens said. "Looks like his girlfriend must be home."

I felt vaguely sick looking down at the bungalow. I imagined Jennifer Chiba alone in the kitchen where Smith had lain bleeding to death with a knife in his chest. For my sins I couldn't resist snapping a picture of the house. I thought of how he had been on my mind for the three weeks I'd been in Los Angeles – right up to the moment I got the shocking news that he was dead. His music had affected me from the moment the first of his songs came on the soundtrack of Gus Van Sant's *Good Will Hunting*. The instant I heard the soft double-tracked voice and plucked nylon strings of 'Angeles' and 'Miss Misery', I knew this was the real thing – a singer-songwriter with a style, a musical "grain", completely his own. A dreamlike melancholia that was utterly modern and unmawkish… a folk music for junkies… a ghostly intimacy. "I just sort of do my thing, whatever it is," he would tell me a few months after that. "I don't really even know what it is. I know that if you're not in a band and you play acoustic guitar, there's an inclination to box you into a corner. Playing an acoustic definitely makes it more possible to be more sensitive as far as what you're saying goes, but it doesn't mean that it's any more sentimental than a band."

Jeez, there were so many formulaic singer-songwriters out there, so many sensitive boys and girls with acoustic guitars and fuck all to say. And so few who bucked the clichés: Beck, Aimee Mann, Ron Sexsmith, Polly Harvey, Rufus Wainwright… and now this unassuming dude from Portland, Oregon. Sure, there were faint traces of Paul Simon's *Graduate* soundtrack in his songs for Van Sant's film. Big deal. There was also something so un-smarmy – so un-Simon-like – about them, and this was what I took away from it. "Elliott's music is literally the most important thing in *Good Will Hunting*," Minnie Driver, the movie's love interest, told me. "He's like a character you can't see."

Catching up on what I'd missed – his first two solo albums and the songs he'd recorded as a member of Portland's Heatmiser – I arranged to interview him in New York in the spring of 1998. He was already a lo-fi star by this point. He'd sung 'Miss Misery' to 200 million people live at the Oscars. His great *Either/Or* album had come out on Kill Rock Stars the previous year and was soon to appear in the UK on Laurence Bell's Domino label. He'd just finished recording his first album for the big-money DreamWorks label. We met on a warm afternoon at NYU, where he was due to perform that night. By a maddening coincidence, Alex Chilton – one of his heroes – was gigging at the same time in a nearby club. "I love the way Chilton sang," he would say to me on another occasion. "It was just really cool to hear Americans singing that way, because at the time it was all gravelly voiced guys." In his set that night, he performed Chilton's Big Star classic 'Thirteen', template for so many of his own tremulous ballads. (Chilton was across town performing 'Tee Ni Nee Ni Noo' and 'The Oogum Boogum Song'. Go figure.) In conversation, he was gentle, intelligent and bullshit-free. There was a plainness about the way he expressed himself. He didn't say a lot, but what he said was thoughtful, humble, and at moments dryly funny. Gleaning from his lyrics that he was, at the very least, familiar with the milieux of addiction, I asked how many of his drug songs were based on firsthand experience of chemical dependents. "I don't really know," he replied. "I mean, I'm definitely in them, but on the other hand it's not like a diary or anything. But yeah, it's good to call them dependents, 'cause that was the point... as opposed to them being songs strictly about drugs. There's all sorts of ways people can be dependent."

When *XO* (1998) and then *Figure Eight* (2000) came out on DreamWorks, it was thrilling to hear Smith flesh out his sound with all manner of new toys – stray exotic accoutrements that happened to be lying around Sunset Sound studios in LA. "It was the first time I'd recorded by myself in a real studio," he said of the *XO* sessions. "There was a lot of stuff there, so there's a lot more instruments on the record. There's strings and there's piano on a lot of things. There's one song with a suspended orchestral bass drum that you hit with a mallet. There's some Chamberlin and some Mellotron type of things. It's always good to try as many things as you can, and then just not keep the things that aren't adding anything."

The influences of Smith's beloved Beatles, as well as of *Big Star Third*, *Imperial Bedroom* and other favourite albums, were brilliantly woven into songs like 'Waltz #2' and 'Baby Britain'. Whether they were loud ('Amity', 'Junk Bond Trader', 'LA') or quiet ('Tomorrow Tomorrow', 'Everything Reminds Me of Her', 'Pretty Mary K'), both albums were full of bittersweet, ambiguous mood-songs – songs as redolent of McCartney as they were of Lennon. "My songs don't feel sorrowful to me," he said. "I'm happy some of the time, and some of the time I'm not. But, like, when I see a movie that moves me or whatever, it's usually happy and sad at the same time. Same with *Anna Karenina* or something." And to think that in England we were drooling over Badly Drawn Boy.

THEN EVERYTHING seemed to go wrong. Disturbing rumours of heroin addiction filtered out from his adopted Los Angeles, along with stories of squabbles with his record company. If Smith was fighting with DreamWorks' sainted Lenny Waronker – who'd nurtured countless gifted singer-songwriters from Randy Newman to Rickie Lee Jones to Rufus Wainwright – that could only be a bad sign.

He was said to be working on the follow-up to *Figure 8*, but the release date kept being deferred. Fans were shocked when he appeared, wasted and frail, at the Sunset Junction Street Festival in August 2001. Sessions with Jon Brion, retro-friendly producer of albums by Aimee Mann and Fiona Apple, ground to a premature halt – "scrapped", Smith said, "because of a blown friendship… that made me so depressed I didn't want to hear any of those songs." At a meeting with Waronker and DreamWorks A&R man Luke Wood, he said he wanted out of his contract. He'd now added crack to his daily intake of heroin and prescription pills, the resulting paranoia causing him to believe that DreamWorks employees were tailing him – and even breaking into his house to steal music files from his Apple Mac. This didn't seem like the Smith I'd met, though he did admit to me that *Either/Or* originally bore the title *Grand Mal*, not because he was epileptic but simply because "a lot of the songs were made up during a part of last year that was kind of a drag". (We now know that he was drinking heavily when he lived in Brooklyn between 1997 and 1998.)

In California, things got much, much worse. On November 25, 2002, in the company of his musician girlfriend Jennifer Chiba, he got into a fracas with the LAPD at a Beck/Flaming Lips show and spent the night in a jail cell. But the following year, Smith and Chiba both cleaned up, Smith detoxing himself from several heavy-duty tranquilisers. At the Neurotransmitter Restoration Center in Beverly Hills, a man with the unfortunate name Dr Hit weaned him off the drugs he was addicted to, though the treatment wiped him out in the process. When the singer emerged from the darkness in January 2003, he came clean. In an interview with the LA magazine *Under The Radar*, he was keen to demystify his drug use. "There's such a taboo of even talking about [it]," he said, "and then there is the added problem if you play music. Then there's this sort of melodrama that surrounds it, which wouldn't necessarily surround someone who doesn't play music. Actually, I thought I would just try to avoid it, but I'm not different from other people with drug problems." In the same interview, he mentioned a charity he had founded. He didn't explain *why* he'd set up the Elliott Smith Foundation For Abused Children, but in retrospect it made perfect sense when you scrutinised some of his lyrics. Consider the magnificent 'Waltz #2', a Costello-esque song in 3/4 time born of Smith's guilt at abandoning his adored mother, Bunny. In reference to "the man she's married to now", Smith sings *"Here it is, the revenge to the tune/'You're no good, you're no good, you're no good'."* Later in the song he adds: *"Tell Mr Man with impossible plans to just leave me alone/In a place where I make no mistakes."* Going back earlier still, the title song on Smith's 1994 debut *Roman Candle* talked of revenge against a man who *"could be cool and cruel to you and me/Knew we'd put up with anything."*

Domestic violence permeated 'No Name #2' and 'No Name #3' from the same album. 'Southern Belle' on *Elliott Smith* (1995) was an indictment of a man who was emotionally murdering his wife. *"How come you're not ashamed of what you are?"* Smith sang. *"And sorry that you're the one she got?"* A number of songs intended for *From A Basement On A Hill* – including one called 'Abused' – have, unsurprisingly, been dropped for the version of the album assembled by *XO/Figure 8* co-producer Rob Schnapf but approved by Smith's estate (made up of his divorced parents and their respective spouses). What we are nonetheless left with is a collection of harrowing tracks that leave little doubt as to his frame of mind in the years leading up to his death.

Shot through with intimations of death – self-inflicted or otherwise – *Basement* does not make for cheery listening: there are no pop experiments, no quaint Chamberlins and Mellotrons, in this angry, mangled soundscape. 'Let's Get Lost', the album's prettiest tune, is merely its most blithely escapist. 'Don't Go Down', 'Strung Out Again', 'King's Crossing', 'A Fond Farewell', 'A Passing Feeling' and 'Little One' all bespeak despair in its blackest form. The title of the final song, released earlier as a single, is a virtual slogan for drug addiction: 'A Distorted Reality Is Now A Necessity To Be Free'. One song, 'Last Hour', seems to touch on the abuse Smith had written about earlier. *"Your opinion was the law of the land,"* he sings; *"a single thing that I couldn't always understand."* Could the abuse Smith suffered as a child in Dallas explain the shame and self-loathing that drove him to kill himself at the age of 34? If so, it would hardly be strange. Clean and stone-cold sober when he stabbed himself twice in the heart, this was a man who'd reached the limits of bearable pain – whose self-hatred exceeded even that of Kurt Cobain.

THE RELEASE of *From A Basement On A Hill* provides a field day for media vultures more fascinated by death and destruction than life and artistic creation. The column inches expended on Smith's death – some of them irresponsible conjectures that, *a la* Cobain *et al.*, he was murdered by Jennifer Chiba – will probably outweigh the words written about him while he lived. Such is the cultural necrophilia of our time. If all this ghoulishness introduces a few more people to the delicate, intelligent, haunting music he made in his short lifetime, some good may yet come of it.

The more I listen to *From A Basement*, the more extraordinary it sounds. As beautiful as it is disturbed, its best tracks ('Coast To Coast', 'Let's Get Lost',

'A Passing Feeling', 'Shooting Star', 'Last Hour', 'Little One', the intense and almost hallucinatory 'King's Crossing') rank with the peaks of Smith's earlier albums. In all of them, he desperately seeks to make sense of his relentless existential agony. "People do battle with themselves every day," he'd told me in 1998. "People seem so chaotic internally, but being filtered through something like a record or a book… filters it down into something that can be understood. It seems like if people didn't communicate, they wouldn't understand anything about themselves at all." Smith communicates a great deal in the body of songs he left behind – and he understood more than a few things about himself as a result. But as with Nick Drake, Ian Curtis, Kurt Cobain and so many other misfit visionaries, his articulations of pain and shame weren't enough to heal him.

A passing remark from my 1998 encounter sticks hauntingly in my mind. It was his response to a question about why he so often double-tracked his singing voice, and it struck me as deeply sad. "I like how double-tracking sounds," he said. "I like that it makes me sound less like *me*."

Uncut, 2004

24 The Revelator
Jack White

Album sent by XL Recordings and signed for my son Fred in 2006

WE'RE NEARING the end of a punishingly intense set by the Dead Weather, a second side-project created by the White Stripes' Jack White. For 90-odd minutes the focus – or at least the spotlight – has been on singer Alison Mosshart, who for much of 2009 has been moonlighting from her regular gig in UK-based band the Kills. Directly behind her, White has been playing drums while intermittently contributing vocals – on the ecstatically exciting 'Cut Like A Buffalo', on a searing reading of Them's 'You Just Can't Win' – from his drum stool. He is not simply a very good drummer; he drums like he never played another instrument in his life.

Mosshart is a fine frontwoman if you like that sort of junkie-vamp thing, but the air is thick with anticipation of the Dead Weather's drummer emerging to remind us of what made him great in the first place: his singing, his guitar playing, his sheer presence on record and stage. We want to refresh our memories of the Motor City stripling who seized the rock world's attention in 2001 and instantly established the White Stripes as, in John Peel's words, the most exciting thing since the Jimi Hendrix Experience. "There's a lot of things I can't do with drums to connect with people," he will tell me later. "And for some reason the guitar does. Why? Who in the hell knows, but it does. Because I go out and play a couple of songs on guitar with the Dead Weather every night, and all of a sudden it's different."

Rewind a few hours to the subterranean bowels of the Depot in Salt Lake City, where White lurches into the venue's green room in sunglasses, lean and weary from an overnight drive through the Rocky Mountains. The previous night's show in Denver was suffocatingly hot: White looks as though he could have shed half a stone behind his kit. Seated on the edge of a small sofa, he ponders a remark of The Edge's in Davis Guggenheim's new documentary *It Might Get Loud*, wherein the U2 guitarist refers to White as "the brassy showman... the snake-oil trader", weighing that up against his recent and rather novel experience of not being the frontman in the Dead Weather. "It's a battle I don't really know how to resolve," he says, his voice slightly pained. "I have people right now saying, 'Why are you playing the drums? What's your point?' I don't know. I fight it back and forth, I have guilt about it, and I have okay feelings about it, but the main thing is that nobody around me seems to want to grab hold of it." He pauses to look back over the last extraordinary decade of his life, taking stock of what got him *out front* in the first place. "For a long time," he says, "I worked with a lot of different people, none of whom – because of a sort of *garage-rock guilt* – wanted to be too ambitious. Some people might think you're egotistical or think you're bold and brassy, but then it turns out all their idols are Iggy Pop or Dylan or the Stones. These are all people who grabbed the mic and walked to the front of the stage. So I could never understand that. You can do it without hubris, and you can do it without spitting into somebody's face."

White *did* grab the mic and *did* walk to the front of the stage. Moreover, he *has* managed to do it without hubris or spitting in anyone's face, for all the envious poison that flowed the White Stripes' way after *White Blood Cells* catapulted them out of Detroit's incestuous garage-rock scene in 2001. He's been the single most radical, dynamic, unpredictable and intense musician to emerge from the retro-roots boom of the Nineties, a charismatic lo-fi figurehead for mutant Americana whose body of work – with the Stripes, with the Raconteurs, and now with the Dead Weather – is already a startling testimony to his talent. He has taken the key folk strains of American music and imprinted himself on them in a way that only a handful of his peers

– from Brits such as the Stones and Zeppelin, to fellow yanks like Dylan and Beck – managed before. Furthermore, he's done it in a way that's been conceptually interesting from the start. A decade's worth of mutation and reinvention have made him philosophical about his mission to keep tradition alive. "The intent to push forward in the era after Warhol, Dylan and the Beatles is a tricky one," he says. "I'm not too sure what 'forward' is anymore. I think *inward* is a better direction, getting more soulful and getting away from plastic computer production." At the base of everything, the blues remains a constant. "The blues is still number one for me," he says. "It *is* the truth. Even when I'm producing other acts, my first question is, 'What version of the blues is this person – and how do we get to the *rawest part* of it?'"

THE STORY of how John Anthony Gillis, born in 1975 in southwest Detroit, found his way to the blues and became Jack White is the tale of a kid hopelessly at odds with his peers and taking heroic punk revenge on them. "There's a battle with social anxiety that I have yet to really resolve," he confesses. "I know there's a spot where my voice and presence don't cloud the intention of what I'm saying." The youngest of ten children born to a Catholic couple in the rundown working-class neighbourhood of Mexicantown, Gillis found music as a calling in his juvenile quest for "something deeper" as he deflected the jibes of the playground Eminems who blighted his schooldays. "Someone asked me whether they should send their kids to the high school I went to in Detroit," he reflects. "I said, 'It's great to have all this diversity and go through these struggles in these rough neighbourhoods, but I look back and I can't really decide whether it was good or bad. It's like saying I was in the Bataan death march in World War II and it made me a better person. I mean, it's still a horrible experience, you know?'"

Music for the young Gillis was "about these little tiny accomplishments, like learning how to play a drum fill or play along with one of the records I liked... I don't think I ever thought of it as different from anything else, like going outside to play army men or something." But with the friendship of his pal Dominic Suchyta, he travelled deeper into the roots of the Hendrix and Who and Stevie Ray Vaughan albums they'd borrowed from their older brothers. "This was the late Eighties, so it was a bad period in terms of what popular rock'n'roll bands were out there," White remembers. "By the time I was 15 I had bought Albert King's *Live Wire / Blues Power* and we were saying, 'Wow, these are all Stevie Ray's licks...'" A year later, Gillis and Suchyta were not only listening to Howlin' Wolf but playing the latter's version of 'Sittin' On Top Of The World' in a band with Jack's older brother Eddie. "Once we got to that level," White says, "I started moving left and right of Howlin' Wolf to see what else was cooking. There was no way you couldn't hop over from that to Robert Johnson and everything else." Hop over he duly did. At a Radiohead show in Detroit, he heard the primordial *a cappella* blues of Son House's 'John The Revelator' on a p.a. mixtape and found himself dragged deep into the pre-war Delta. House's 'Grinning In Your Face' remains his favourite record of all time. "So it was Howlin' Wolf to Robert Johnson to Son House," he says, "and then to Charley Patton after that."

It wasn't only blues that got his attention. While working in an upholstery shop run by musician Brian Muldoon, Gillis heard a North Carolina duo called Flat Duo Jets and fell hard for their frantic punkabilly minimalism (delivered, like the Cramps and the Jon Spencer Blues Explosion, *sans* bass guitar). The Jets' sound, moreover, perfectly complemented a burgeoning Detroit immersion in Sixties garage punk – the sound of rock returned to some raw and untamed state, exemplified by groups such as the Sonics and the Shadows of Knight. "I didn't really know about a lot of those bands," says White, "but most of the garage-rockers in Detroit were record collectors who'd worked at record stores and just knew what albums to get and what albums *not* to get." Drumming in Goober & the Peas, and then playing guitar in the Go – as well as pairing up with Brian Muldoon in Two Part Resin – Gillis was a teen fixture on the Detroit garage scene, a music community that took advantage of cheap overheads in a city left to rot. But it was only when he met Megan Martha White behind the bar at Memphis Smoke, in suburban Royal Oak, that he found his musical anchor – not to mention his first wife. Marrying on September 21, 1996 – with Gillis taking Meg's surname for his own – they were soon making music together.

Meg's drumming is probably the first thing anybody remembers about their initial exposure to the White Stripes: *Is it for real? Is it an ironic novelty? What does it mean?* To Jack White it didn't "mean" *anything*: it just *was* – a primitive cave-stomp of a rhythm that set him free from all musical and cultural constraints. "I thought, if we just left a lot of space and hit the notes here and there, we wouldn't really need to know how to play these instruments," White says. "I still wasn't that great of a guitar player, either. I was like, 'I'm really a drummer so I'm not really supposed to be doing this, but I'll do it because there's someone else that wants to make music for a second'. It actually felt way better than I expected. I'd been in other lo-fi bands and done recordings, but it wasn't powerful like that. It didn't make a point." Naming themselves after George Washington's quote that the white stripes in the American flag "shall go down to posterity representing liberty", the duo played their first show at the Gold Dollar on July 14, 1997, and soon became an entrenched part of Detroit's garage rock scene, playing on bills with rising luminaries the Dirtbombs, Bantam Rooster, and the Von Bondies. "We'd always go up to Detroit, and just right away it was such a great scene up there," says Jack Lawrence, now of the Dead Weather and the Raconteurs, then of Cincinnati's Greenhornes. "We'd stay at Jack's place. None of us thought we'd make it to this place. Especially like being a two-piece, you wouldn't say this band was going to play giant arenas and headline giant festivals. It was surprising just to witness that start to happen. No one thinks they're maybe going to be a star. And now Jack is the same person, but he fills that role very well."

Approached one night by Italy Records owner Dave Buick, the White Stripes were asked if they wanted to make a record. "Dave wanted to put out a 45," White says. "I asked how much it cost, to which he began to tell me about the expenses incurred for a single from the factory. I told him, 'We don't have that kind of money'. I didn't understand that he would of course be paying for it." The singles 'Let's Shake Hands' and 'Lafayette Blues', their sleeves hand-painted in trademark red and white in limited editions of 1000 each, appeared in 1998 and were riotous blasts of garage-rock madness, the first punkily bluesy, the second like some crazed Cajun surf record. Dirty guitars exploded out of the mix over Meg's minimalist pounding, while White's voice was a yelping hybrid of the young Robert Plant and a snarky Sky Saxon. "I think the guilt of garage rockdom brings a lot of people to irony," White says. "To pull off something like the White Stripes, a lot of bands would have tried to make it funny. And we never did that."

What got overlooked in all the subsequent storm-in-a-teacup furore about the Whites pretending to be siblings was how remarkable it was for them to end their marriage, yet keep working together. Separated as a couple by 1999 – and divorced in early 2000 – they were able to stay friendly enough to record their first album for Californian label Sympathy for the Record Industry. ("You wish that two people could really be happy with each other," read the first of many cryptic messages White snuck on to Stripes CD covers.) In many ways, indeed, the pair *seemed* more like brother and sister than estranged spouses, artfully exploiting the childlike quality of their relationship as White built up the mythos surrounding them. But it was the elemental simplicity and unpretentiousness of Meg's drumming – tracking rather than counterpointing Jack's riffs and vocal lines – that held the key to the loosing of his imagination. "I strive for Id only so I can accidentally run into Ego when creating," he emails me a few days after the Salt Lake City gig. "Meg is Id-ridden and that's why I like to play with her. The rest of us are just trying to be like that and get somewhere simple and beautiful. She's an enigma to me. She is, in a lot of ways, the best musician I'll ever play with. There's a naive genius to her. I don't really know *what* she takes from the Stripes. My ears prick up when she actually mentions something about what we've done. I'm so interested to hear what her take on it is. But it quickly dissolves into 'I don't know *what* she's taking from that… I'm just so happy that she knew we played that show!'"

Recorded on a 16-track board at Jim Diamond's Ghetto Recorders, *The White Stripes* (1999) ran the gamut of White's themes and obsessions, from grungey garage fuzz to mangled Delta blues to blazing punk rock that channelled Detroit legends the MC5 and the Stooges (and arguably even Iggy Pop's pre-Stooges gonzos the Iguanas). Versions of folk-blues staple 'St. James Infirmary', Robert Johnson's 'Stop Breaking Down' and Dylan's 'One More Cup Of Coffee' – along with the insertion into 'Cannon' of a chunk of 'John The Revelator' – make the parameters of White's influences plain. The sound of his guitar remains the single most savage thing to come out of the whole garage rock scene in the Michigan of the late Nineties. In 2003, he would call the album "the most raw, the most powerful, and the most Detroit-sounding record we've made". Which makes sense till you hear the duo's home-recorded second album *De Stijl*, whose title and design both reference the ultra-formal artistic movement of the same name that thrived in Holland between 1917 and 1931 (and whose blocks of red, black and white colour gelled perfectly with White's own emerging aesthetic of constraint and limitation).

De Stijl ("The Style") is where the White Stripes truly step out of the indie shadows and insist we take them seriously, not least because of a handful of tracks ('Little Bird', 'Why Can't You Be Nicer To Me?', 'I'm Bound To Pack It Up') that nod explicitly and unashamedly in the direction of Led Zeppelin. "We were sort of hitting a new wall there," White says of the album. "Songwriting-wise I was coming from the same places that Jimmy [Page] and Robert [Plant] were – Robert Johnson, Tommy Johnson, Blind Willie McTell. We were feeding from the same trough. Like, if you want this to be powerful *and* feed from these same influences, there are going to be moments where you sound like Led Zeppelin. So then it was, 'Oh well, maybe it does sound like that, but I know in my heart I didn't sit down and try and copy Led Zeppelin. So what do we do? Do we leave them off the record?' At the time we didn't have enough songs to do that. So we moved on in the knowledge that that was starting to get set up by us." A culmination of the whole Americana wave of the Nineties, *De Stijl* was the first alt-blues album not to pretend that Led Zeppelin didn't exist – particularly in the deployment of searing slide guitar. White had been paying close attention to the lo-fi explorations of blues and Appalachian bluegrass that synched with the launch of *No Depression* magazine and the 1997 reissue of Harry Smith's immortal Fifties *Anthology Of American Folk Music*. Like many an indie urban critter, he was seduced not just by Son House but the Caucasian mountain blues of the Carter Family and their kind. Hearing Beck's idiosyncratic take on Americana on *Mutations* (1998) was an inspiration. "He was a big deal to me in high school and I've told him that," White says. "I was staying at someone's house and they had videotapes of Beck playing outside and talking about Blind Willie McTell. And I thought, 'Oh my God, Beck likes Blind Willie McTell too!'"

But Beck also inspired White to move beyond the small-pond hipsterism of the Detroit scene. "There was something about him that made it possible for me to, say, go to the shopping mall with my mom and it wouldn't be uncool," White says. "You'd put a spin on it and say, 'Well, *hell* yeah, I'm going to the mall with my mom!'" With *De Stijl* provoking a minor backlash among local scenesters for whom the merest hint of success was inherently suspect, he began to tire of the snooty narrow-mindedness of his peers. "Those kids who grew up *just* liking punk rock and the attitude of it have to learn as adults that Gene Krupa is really good because he's really good at playing the drums," he says. "I came at it from the other side, that Krupa was an incredible drummer and if you couldn't play that well, then who the hell are *you*? A lot of this is about identity crisis and snobbery, but it starts to influence the way people perceive the music you're making *currently*. The problem was that a lot of people thought the Sonics were cool for *not* being popular, but they were missing the whole point that those guys were *trying* to be popular and chasing after hits."

Not that White – or Meg – imagined for a second that the White Stripes would ever have a hit record. Plying their trade in the hipster dives of Detroit, they freed themselves of foolish dreams and concentrated on ploughing their singular furrow. "It was a bad experience that was good for me," he says. "To have settled into the Stripes thinking, 'I don't care anymore, this is what I like... no one else is going to like the music I'm interested in, so I'm just going to do this and tour this, and if I can make enough money to play the shows' – which we figured out we could, because there were only two people in the band – 'then everything is going to be alright. I mean, I genuinely thought nobody was going to like this two-piece band dressed in red, white and black playing blues music. We made three albums before we got signed. So it was fulfilling and safe, because it didn't have any worries about fame or trying to get anywhere."

Imagine the duo's surprise, then, when a visit to England in the summer of 2001 suddenly put their name on everyone's lips. Paying their own fares to London to play the venerable 100 Club on July 26 – three weeks after the US release of the Memphis-recorded *White Blood Cells* – the Stripes were subsequently the beneficiaries of a John Peel session that got the indie community buzzing. "I still don't know what happened," White says of what was an insane month. "Even after Peel died I was still in the mode of, 'I don't know what the reason is, but I'm just gonna thank this guy!' There could be 15 reasons, but I'm just going to pick him because he played us first in front of a live audience at Maida Vale, and that was what first made us think, 'Oh my God, people actually *care* about this!'" After a packed-out show at the tiny Boston Arms, even the *Daily Mirror* was moved to ask if the Stripes were "the future of rock and roll". Hooking up with the management firm of LA lawyer Ian Montone, the Stripes struck smart licensing deals with XL in Britain and V2 in the States that retained ownership of their recordings.

Post-Britpop, Britain had fallen back in love with mutated American Retro, commencing with the Strokes but climaxing in a mass love affair with the Stripes. If the Strokes were about Bowery lapels and louche cool, the Stripes were a red-and-white/blood-and-milk serving of ür-Americana: industrial swamp-blues from a suburban garage. That hip Brits were responding to a "white blues" band with its roots in the Brit blues boom of the Sixties was a neat irony. At the Astoria later that year, *White Blood Cells'* opener 'Dead Leaves And The Dirty Ground' was thunderous, with Jack feeding off the impassive Meg's Mo-Tucker-meets-John-Bonham stomp and alternating between two mics in a voice that was equal parts Plant, Beastie Boys and – when he lost himself in a kind of hysterical falsetto hyperbabble – the Sweet's Steve Priest. A cover of Dolly Parton's 'Jolene' transcended camp through the sheer passion White invested in its lyric. Best of all was when he grabbed a battered, amped-up acoustic and slashed out bottleneck licks like some crazed Beck version of George Thorogood: *"It's so hard to love/Someone that don't love you!"* It was simply electrifying, though the jury was out on whether this was the takeoff-point for a long-term career or just another trading post on the alt-roots/blues/country trail.

White himself was freaked out. "It was nothing but questions, because I was just scared," he says. "I thought it was all over, and they weren't *really* going to get it. People like the Milkshakes and Holly Golightly would tell us how the *NME* would put you on the cover and then hate you next month. And not only that, but we'd been doing this for three years. So it was like, 'Oh, please don't do that to us!'" Partly out of a determination to mess with the media before it tried to "dissect" them [White's term], they concocted the story of being blood relations – a fabrication they would come to regret once it became a virtual national obsession.

The special relationship between the Stripes and the UK was enough to persuade the duo to make their next album in London. On Guy Fawkes' Day, 2001, they went into Liam Watson's lo-tech Toe Rag studio in Hackney with Golightly and recorded the hilarious three-way conversation 'Well, It's True That We Love One Another', just to see how the place felt. The following April, they returned to record the stunning *Elephant*, though it sat in the can for almost a year while *White Blood Cells* continued to sell. Much was made of the cheap analog recording of tracks such as the thundering 'Black Math' and the anthemic 'Seven Nation Army'. "I've never been anti-technology full stop," White says of his ethos. "That's like being Amish, whereas I'm more Mennonite. I see the beautiful uses for technology, but I try to be mature and realise there's a pinnacle that each technology reaches that oftentimes is followed by a sharp drop in quality. Namely the digital age. You can't tell me digital equipment sounds better. It doesn't. It's only easier to use."

By the time it came out, White's relationship to the Detroit scene had become still more fractious. Though he dated former Von Bondies guitarist Marcie Bolen for the best part of a year, the resentment he and Meg incurred from the garage rock community climaxed in a fight in a Detroit bar with that band's singer, Jason Stollsteimer. 2003 had in any case turned into the Stripes' own *annus horribilis* – the "Satan" they urged to get behind them on their next album. Jim Diamond threatened to sue after claiming he'd produced *De Stijl*. White dated actress Renée Zellweger after appearing as a wandering singer in Anthony Minghella's Appalachia-based *Cold Mountain*, then broke up with her after a car accident that damaged his index finger. The only real relief came from his producing the splendid *Van Lear Rose*, a comeback album by his Nashville heroine Loretta Lynn. "Those were very dark times," he says of the *annus* in question. "Things were coming to a head on all levels and I didn't really know if I wanted to do any more music or do anything anymore. Anything. It was very bad. *Get Behind Me* was desperate."

Recorded at home in Detroit, *Get Behind Me, Satan* immediately asserted its differences from the Stripes' blues template. 'Blue Orchid' blasted the gate open, but the marimba-and-piano instrumentation on second track 'The Nurse' – broken up by intermittent arrhythmic guitar-and-cymbal slashes – asked more of some fans than they were prepared to give. "I honestly didn't go into that record with any plans *not* to play guitar," White says. "I rented a Steinway piano and put it in my living room, and that was kind of a big deal to me. So I started feeding off of that, and then I bought a marimba. We recorded the whole thing on a staircase too, so that Meg was on the landing and I was upstairs doing the vocals and everything was on the stairs. The songs were sort of tripping over each other. I'd be writing 'The Denial Twist' or 'White Moon', and they were really painful, but then something like 'My Doorbell' was playing too, and that felt like a Jackson 5 kind of song. I just kept doing it and I didn't really care where it was coming from."

The fickleness of the fans who didn't buy *Satan* – an absurdly underrated album that sold half as well as *Elephant* – disappointed White, but only made him more determined to stick to his course. "I saw that our fans kept turning over and over," he says. "We'd never see the same people for two tours in a row." Consolation of a kind came when he met his soulmate, model Karen Elson, on the gothic video for 'Blue Orchid'. They were married by a shaman in Brazil in June 2005, with Meg as the bride's maid of honour. Karen has subsequently given birth to two children, Scarlet Teresa (born 2006) and Henry Lee (born 2007). "Career and family are at odds with each other at all times," White admits. "You can't have children and not want to spend all your time with them. But I already had children in my music and songwriting, and I can't abandon them either. There's time for everything. I pay attention to it all." By the time Henry was born, White had got out of Detroit and moved his family to the tiny Nashville satellite that is Leiper's Fork.

He was already talking about working with his fellow Motor citizen Brendan Benson in 2004, so when word came out of Detroit that they'd formed a new "supergroup" with Greenhornes rhythm section Jack Lawrence and Patrick Keeler, it wasn't a total surprise. "Jack's always done five things at once," Meg, apparently unthreatened, told *Rolling Stone*. "He was in two other bands when we started this one. This is not unusual." Benson had lived three blocks from White in Detroit, and White often stopped by to say hello. When *Broken Boy Soldiers*, the Raconteurs' debut, came out in 2005, he told me he "didn't have very many friends left in Detroit anyway". 'Steady, As She Goes' was an instant classic on 7" vinyl, while the (not quite) title track 'Broken Boy Soldier' was a brilliant dissertation on immature indie musicians, set to a galloping garage-psych groove and boasting an inflamed White vocal that recalled the Steve Marriott of 'Tin Soldier'. On 'Intimate Secretary' and 'Call It A Day', White and Benson came together perfectly in Beatlish harmonies that summoned the ghosts of *Revolver*. "I don't know what we wanted it to do as a band," White claims. "I didn't have any premeditated notion about, 'This'll be the power-pop band that I'm in at one point in my life… or the conventional rock'n'roll band or whatever people think of it as'. I just knew Brendan was a great songwriter and the only songwriter in Detroit I saw that had the ambition for craftsmanship. So I thought, 'That's someone I can write songs with, as a co-songwriter' – which was the first time I'd ever done it. And I didn't think anything more of it than making that record and then going back to the White Stripes. But we got another one out of it very quickly, so there was inspiration there."

When White did go back to the Stripes, it was under the auspices for the first time of a major label. "I try not to let pretense hinder a creative situation," he says of the decision to sign to Warner Bros. "I have views, but I also know that there are times to rub shoulders and have my back scratched. If the environment doesn't facilitate creativity, then it's time to change the environment." The recording environment changed, too: forsaking the mixed blessings of lo-fi recording, the Stripes went into Nashville's plush Blackbird studio, sonic home to Mariah Carey. Fortunately the resulting album was as raw, radical and eclectic as anything Jack White had overseen in the first decade of his recording career. *Icky Thump*'s title track and first single was an electrifyingly eccentric jab at American xenophobia, 'You Don't Know What Love Is' channelled Neil Young in Crazy Horse mode, and 'Catch Hell Blues' featured some of the most unbridled guitar playing of White's life. 'Bone Broke' was a gnarly stomper of the 'Black Math' variety, 'I'm Slowly Turning Into You' a redefinition of heavy metal, and there were bagpipes on 'Prickly Thorn, But Sweetly Worn' as White tapped his Celtic ancestry. "There has to be some kind of struggle going on," he told Ben Thompson. "It can be anything from time and money to lyrics, to the kind of mood we happen to be in at the time… but the mood that me and Meg are in lately has been extremely happy – really positive and easy-going."

When Meg had an anxiety attack prior to a planned Stripes US tour in September 2007, White returned to the Raconteurs just to stay busy. *Consolers Of The Lonely* was something of a damp squib after *Broken Boy Soldiers* – there was nothing on it as instantly arresting as 'Steady, As She

Goes' – but the reworking of Terry Reid's 'Rich Kid Blues' was a stunning homage to late Sixties Britrock. In the meantime, White bought a building in Nashville and began work on the Third Man complex that now houses a recording studio, a vinyl record store and other facilities. One of the first sessions at Third Man was intended to be a one-off collaboration. White being White, it turned into the Riot Grrrl-meets-Royal Trux combo that is the Dead Weather.

"IT'S GIVING me a very different experience," White says of the Dead Weather's fevered, PJ Harvey-ish grind. "I'm producing *as a drummer* and I'm *writing songs* as a drummer. I've also worked with a lot of females over the years, you know – Meg, Alicia Keys, Loretta Lynn, and now Alison – and I get a lot out of that. 'If it's there, don't get in the way' is the only rule I have about it."

"The Dead Weather has been very different from the Raconteurs," says Jack Lawrence. "Jack says you take a group of guys in a room and throw one woman in there and everyone's attitude changes. You can't help it. Plus I've always had Patrick as a drummer, so having someone else behind me is different but exciting for me." Already many acolytes are making predictable noises about White spreading himself too thin – maybe even burning himself out, *à la* Prince at Paisley Park. "There's a voice in me saying slow down, but I don't feel stressed at all," he says with a shrug. "I don't feel I'm half-assing anything. I just feel it needs to be done. If the songs aren't any good, then maybe there's too much going on, but I haven't felt that yet. It all feels inspiring so far, and they're all things I'm proud of."

What about hurt feelings? Neil Young has made a virtual career out of upsetting sidemen. "If you take chances, you risk hurting people's feelings," he concedes. "I don't think I know any better. Sometimes I think it would be smarter not to put out a record like *Get Behind Me* after a record like *Elephant*. But it's a tricky world when you're forced to mix art with business. Which is basically what I'm doing now with Third Man Records. It's coming into that snake-oil salesman thing, because we're in a different environment now where we have to sell ourselves. The days of just writing songs and playing them are like vanishing dreams. I'm forced to be a hustler in a lot of ways. Third Man is just an institution for me to come to terms with that hustle and turn it into something creative and beneficial to artists and the formats on which people hear them. I'm trying to find that balance where there's creativity and art to it, as well as keeping myself afloat."

"Jack's always pushing to go places he hasn't been," Lawrence attests. "The biggest influence – the greatest thing that I'll walk away with – is that you learn how to push yourself. Seeing him do it makes you want to do it too. You want to push yourself and not settle, just because *he* does. Just walking into the studio or the record store is really inspiring. I don't think a lot of people who have success take it to another level like that and bring it back around. People sometimes would rather just buy a big house and live on the beach. So to turn it all around and keep it going, you just don't see that very often."

WHITE STEPS forward to duet with Alison Mosshart on 'Will There Be Enough Water?', the simmering six-minute epic that closes the Dead Weather's *Horehound*. Immediately he dominates the room, building the slow-burn song into a launching pad for one of his frenzied solos. Nor is there anything macho or onanistic about the spectacle of this thirtysomething boy-soldier lost in music, giving himself up to the song's violent emotion. It's magnificent to watch.

"Maybe I can explain the power of music the way I'm seeing it now through my children's eyes," he said to me as he left for soundcheck. "Their interest in it is so natural, so unforced. With paintings, for instance, you sometimes have to be taught to understand the beauty of them. But with music, you don't really have to be taught: it either immediately speaks to you or it doesn't. And I see that in my kids. It's nice to go back and relive that approach to it."

Uncut, 2009

277

25 A Song For Her
Amy Winehouse

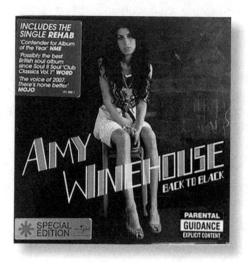

CD bought online in 2006

IN HER MOST infamous song, the defiant and splendidly stroppy 'Rehab', Amy Winehouse sang that she would "rather be home with Ray [Charles]" than do 70 days in a treatment centre – and that there was *nothing* she couldn't "learn from Mr Hathaway" that anyone might teach her in, say, the Priory. I noted the namecheck for the tragic American soul singer who'd taken his own life in 1979; I wanted to pitch a magazine feature about Donny Hathaway and figured a quote or three from Winehouse might further pique interest in him. To my lasting chagrin the interview never happened, unsurprising given what we all know now of the state she was in at the time. Still, I loved her for loving Donny, loved her even more than I already loved her for her own music. And even though I didn't think her version of [Hathaway's version of Leon Russell's] 'A Song For You' a patch on Donny's, I was pleased for his legacy that she covered it and talked of him on the posthumous *Lioness*, on which her impromptu words *("Donny Hathaway, like... he*

278

couldn't contain himself. He had something in *him, y'know?"*) were the last sounds the listener heard. She also performed spine-chilling live versions of his 'We're Still Friends' and 'I Love You More Than You'll Ever Know'.

The notion that Hathaway couldn't "contain himself" was a revealing one in the context of Winehouse's own life and eventual death. Perhaps she heard something of her own restless desperation in his plangent tenor voice; possibly she was haunted by his suicide, a jump from a 15th-floor hotel bedroom on New York's Central Park South. She too couldn't "contain" herself – couldn't contain her pain other than through medicating it or writing about it. As she told *Spin*'s Steve Kandell in April 2007: "I thought, 'Fuck, I'm going to die if I don't write down the way I feel. I'm going to fucking do myself in.'" In the song that defined her better than any other, 'You Know I'm No Good', she told us she was trouble. She also told us she was troubled.

ON THE DAY it came out in the UK, I sat in a car and listened to *Back To Black*. As the CD played, I was unable to move, startled by the greatness of what I was hearing: not just the raw power of the voice, not just the liberating shock of her lyrics, but the soul and sophistication of her new musical touchstones. These reference points had little to do with Motown and more to do with the Black pop of early Sixties New York, Chicago and Philadelphia. "I don't listen to a lot of new stuff," Winehouse told Steve Kandell. "I just like the old stuff. It's all quite dramatic and atmospheric. You'd have an entire story in a song." For those of a certain vintage and musical snobbery, she was channeling a sensibility that put her in the company of another great British soul siren, Dusty Springfield – and doing it not to fetishise the retro tropes of Sixties soul but to subvert them, to use them as canvases for language that was closer to hip hop than to Holland, Dozier & Holland.

I'd noted *Frank*, naturally, but not much more than that. Did the world really *require* a young jazz singer from North London? Wouldn't she simply disappear after a couple more albums and a couple more appearances on *Later With Jools Holland*? Truth is, I wasn't really paying attention. Had I listened properly to 'Take The Box' or 'In My Bed' or 'Stronger Than Me' – or what she did with Billie Holiday's 'There Is No Greater Love' – I'd have got the boldness of what she told interviewers was her "straight jazz/hip hop crossover". As if there was anything "straight" about *that*.

I happened to be in Los Angeles on March 19, 2007, the day after *Back To Black*'s US release – and the same day Winehouse played the Roxy on

Sunset. (It was the only show she ever did in LA.) Another Amy (Linden) had just interviewed her for *XXL* magazine and met me for coffee shortly afterwards. We talked of Winehouse, whose live American debut she had witnessed at Joe's Pub in New York. Though *Frank* hadn't even been released in the States, she – like Winehouse, a white Jewish girl – was paying close attention. So were a lot of hip hop and R&B artists she knew. Nas and Mos Def were early Amy adopters and champions. Wu Tang's Ghostface Killah released a mix of 'You Know I'm No Good'. Jay Z was at the Joe's Pub gig. Many African-Americans heard Winehouse on the radio and assumed she was Black. In July, *Spin* crowned her "the Dangerous New Queen of Soul".

The Roxy show was sold out, but I followed a lead of Linden's and hustled for a ticket to a gig the next night at Silver Lake's Spaceland. I still have the ticket and it's still intact: in one of her increasingly frequent no-shows, Winehouse cancelled the date. A spokesperson for the club "couldn't get a straight answer" as to why. I had to wait till late July to see her perform in her home town.

"DAD, WHAT ARE all those people doing there?" Winehouse apparently asked this of her father as she peeped out at the crowd assembling that night in the balmy open air of London's Somerset House. It's hard to believe she was unaware she was now the most notorious pop star on the planet, with *Back To Black* on its way to becoming the UK's biggest-selling album of the year. I expected a shambles. Instead I got a performance of astonishing self-assurance from a girl who simply *had it*: had what her idol Tony Bennett called "the complete gift". Here's what I excitedly scrawled the next morning:

From Silver Lake to Somerset House, via a Miami wedding and a Mercury Prize nomination: would Amy stand me up a second time? Well, she didn't, and she told us – more than once – how she'd looked forward to this for "months". I'm guessing she's caught a show or two here herself, experienced its summer-piazza feel for the pleasant change it makes from your average concert venue.

I was instantly smitten by Winehouse's sophomore opus Back To Black: *not by novelty item 'Rehab' per se (I'm bored to fuck by Priory Rock) but by the album's other treasures, which all did something I didn't think possible: take the basic Sixties soul template, tweak it just enough for a tattoo'd post-hip hop generation, and turn the whole ritual into something vitally personal and contemporary.*

Me? I was never convinced by Joss Stone and never will be. But this little slip of a Jewish street princess comes over 100% credible, customising her soul and ska influences to fit her fucked-up persona. Someone said Winehouse's lyrics read like pages from a drunken teenager's diary, but they're more than that: they're piercingly believable, achingly sharp, rid of cliché.

Great artists combine artfulness with something that's rawly their own: the key is that we can't separate the two from each other, to the point where it ultimately doesn't matter anyway. With Winehouse, we're drawn in by an uncanny mix of hip (hop) toughness and about-to-implode vulnerability (which might just be part of her "act" – how can we know and why, frankly, should we care?)

Here she is, this skinny slumming hip hop Ronnie Spector with her mascara mask and piled-high beehive, the sole female onstage with a besuited band that look like rude boy bodyguards: the two Black dancer-singers, the three white hornmen, the guitarists and drummer who resemble some late Sixties Kingston session band. Here she is, underplaying every vocal flourish and girlish provocation, and we can't tear our eyes from her dark elfin figure. We want to know more, to know how dangerous this really is. The remarkable thing is, she's not a brat at all. She lets her music do the talking. (Stop the press: she's a total pro!) She sings brilliantly, saving herself and placing every line just so, periodically letting herself go in a melismatic cry from the heart. The voice is essentially Lauryn Hill's, as the passage from 'Doo Wop (That Thing)' tacitly acknowledges, but you don't actually think Fugees or Miseducation *when you hear it.*

While the whole effect – the iconography and *the choreography – is a hair's breadth away from Stax-Motown pastiche, it never feels like that. In fact, the essential feel of* Back To Black *isn't Stax/Motown at all but the early Sixties girl-group soul that came out of New York's Brill Building, infused with the street-sharp mood of ska and bluebeat (and even 2-Tone, as the cover of the Specials' 'Hey Little Rich Girl' makes clear). 'Me And Mr Jones', perhaps her most startling song, almost feels pre-soul. 'Wake Up Alone' and the heartbreaking 'Love Is A Losing Game' are more Luther Dixon or Berns/Ragovoy than Berry Gordy or Booker T. & the MGs. The genius of* Back To Black *is that it recreates the ornate feel of that music while emphatically yanking it out of the museum.*

"What kind of fuckery is this?" I'm not sure I know, other than that Winehouse gets me deep in my gut. I dare say she'll crash and burn like every other codep dipso celeb in London, but even if she does she'll have left behind at least one remarkable record. As she winds up with the Zutons' 'Valerie', everyone is smiling and jumping with joy: live music doesn't get any better than this.

Winehouse's singing that summer night was effortless, as good as any I'd ever heard. Without straining for effect, she moved you with the pure contralto sound of her pain, the loose slurring of every phrase she sang. "I'm a fierce singer," she once declared; "it's not a tame thing." Even the sadness sounded sensual. Did booze assist the looseness? At that point, did it matter? You were in her hands. You trusted her with every song, this tiny white bird surrounded by burly Black musicians in *Blues Brothers* suits.

If I'm rigorously honest, I have to hold my hands up and say: Yes, I was already in thrall to the spectacle of the emaciated Amy and her drag queen beehive – the "Ronette-from-Hell", as Amy Linden dubbed her after that Joe's Pub show. I was mesmerised by her transformation from bolshy BRIT School girl to cartoon freak on stick-thin pins. Given the tales from the tabs – already at their fiendish work of hounding and demonising her – it was impossible not to register her constant scurrying to the wings of the stage to snuggle with her pork-pie-hatted rogue of a husband, the ignominious Blake Fielder-Civil. Was this not Sid and Nancy *redux*? Not quite, as it happened. Yet it was the most obviously toxic pop relationship I'd observed in a long while: two very damaged young souls playing at being grown-up outlaws, trapped in a feedback loop of chaotic codependency. Not to mention trapped in the weirdness of her constantly performing the songs she'd written about this most undeserving of male muses. "I'm still singing about [him] every night on my knees," she said to *Spin*. "But when I'm with him, I feel like nothing bad can happen."

"I write songs 'cause I'm fucked up in the head," Winehouse is heard saying in Asif Kapadia's lauded 2015 documentary *Amy*. "[It's getting] something good out of something bad." And there we have it: the age-old alchemy of transmuting pain into great art. But here's the finest irony: throughout the process of writing and recording the first batch of *Back To Black* songs in Miami, Winehouse was entirely sober. You can write about alcoholic implosion and shattering heartbreak. You just can't do it drunk.

BEFORE *BLACK*, there was *Frank*. And before *Frank* there was a bolshy teenage girl with black hair and a big mouth from which issued a still bigger voice. It's the voice you can already hear in the grainy home movie of a slumber party at the start of Kapadia's *Amy*, serenading her friend Lauren on her birthday like she's a louche American diva of 45.

Classic American music seeped into Winehouse's young soul from her earliest days. *Frank* was "frank" about teenage female sexuality, but it was also named after Sinatra, whose records Mitch played throughout the first nine years of his daughter's life. At the family home in the unlovely suburb of Southgate, little Amy also heard the big Black voices of Sarah Vaughan, Dinah Washington, Mahalia Jackson. Music came as naturally to her as breathing; it was never anything she had to study or think much about. One hears all this in the version of 'Moon River' she sang with the National Youth Jazz Orchestra in 2000. No one so much as recalls her warming up her voice before going onstage. Actual study came less naturally to her. At school she was, by turns, bored, precocious, hyperactive, attention-seeking and unhappy. She was a heavy weed-smoker. She may have had ADHD. Possibly she was just acting out the pain she felt at home, where Daddy was often absent and Mum often sad. At least one of Amy's teachers wondered what her lippy disruptiveness concealed. Music aside, the only thing that interested her at school was language and literature – extending to the poetics of hip hop artists, as it did to the elegant lyrics of the great Broadway and Tin Pan Alley songsmiths.

Much has been made of her lack of vanity and venal pop ambition, yet the fact remains that she went to three London stage schools: Susi Earnshaw's, Sylvia Young's and the BRIT school that's produced so many fledgling aspirants. Asked in 2006 for five words to describe how she was feeling, she offered as the first two "driven" and "motivated". (Somewhat paradoxically, the last three were "easy-going", "maternal"… and "alcoholic".) Winehouse's talent was too glaring for people not to notice it and try to harness it. But was she someone who'd have betrayed her gut musical instincts to achieve stardom, fleeting or otherwise? Regardless of her signing to the management stable of super-Svengali Simon Fuller, I doubt it. It's also true that the jazz on *Frank* did not emerge in a commercial vacuum – that Norah Jones, Jamie Cullum *et al.* had brought "jazz" out of its marginalised shadows and given it a pop imprimatur it had never enjoyed before. And yet, again, the album's songs were hardly what the average 19-year-old would have offered up as a fast track to fame. They sounded like extensions of Winehouse's diary entries, conversations with herself about what it meant to be a North London teenager breaking free in the East London milieu of hipsters and hedonists. Whether singing about cheating on an older boyfriend ('I Heard Love Is Blind') or about the older women she saw making plays for men who might be millionaires ('Fuck Me Pumps'), Winehouse told it like it was. She was snarky, irreverent, confrontational, and unsparingly honest with herself. In 'What Is It About Men?', she sang of Mitch's history repeating itself through her – the "Freudian fate" that condemned her to emulating "all the shit my mother hate". In behaving like her father had behaved, it was as if she were trying to get closer to him. "We're good friends," she remarked blithely in 2007. "He doesn't know what he's talking about, and neither do I."

A 2002 clip of Winehouse singing 'There Is No Greater Love' to a throng of Island staffers was an early sign of her sheer *chutzpah*. It's not as if this young girl isn't nervous, seated awkwardly in a leather armchair; it's that the moment she starts singing she simply *is* her voice, without any self-consciousness or concern for what others might think. Island sent her off to Miami to work with Salaam "the Chameleon" Remi, who – among his other credits – had worked with Nas and co-written the Fugees' 1996 hit 'Fu-Gee-la'. She also worked on *Frank* with engineer "Commissioner Gordon" Williams, who'd been instrumental in the recording of Winehouse's beloved *Miseducation Of Lauryn Hill*. These men were the perfect facilitators for *Frank*'s inspired jumble of "jazz/hip hop crossover" tracks, Remi producing and co-writing the album's signature statements – 'Stronger Than Me', 'In My Bed', 'Fuck Me Pumps', 'You Sent Me Flying' – while Williams, in New Jersey, worked on less strident pieces like 'Know You Now', 'October Song' and the self-lacerating 'What Is It About Men?' Other accomplices – Luke Smith, Jony Rockstar, Jimmy Hogarth – assisted on standouts such as 'Help Yourself' and the immaculate 'Take The Box'.

But the entire feel of the album was shaped by Amy herself: the swagger, the sexy shamelessness, the mortification. When she sang of Moschino bras and Marlboro Reds, she put you smack-dab in the middle of her Camden life of promiscuity and pool halls. The music on *Frank* might have been American, but the attitude and aesthetic were pure Noughties London.

ONE OF THE sadnesses of looking at the photographs in Charles Moriarty's *Back To Amy* – the images that led to the cover of *Frank* – is seeing an Amy who still looks healthy, even a little heavy: "plump and kind of sassy", in the words of her former manager Nick Godwyn, albeit a little blotchy from booze. (Blake Fielder-Civil remembered his first impressions of his future wife as "juicy".) This Amy is still a very young and apparently happy kid with, yes, her whole life ahead of her. Crying out from Moriarty's nocturnal and interior images is the humour and vivacity of the girl, as well as her style and sexiness. The first sight of the Ronnie Spector beehive is here, captured at the Ritz Tower on New York's Park Avenue. A world away from Camden and Spitalfields, Winehouse could be a ballsy Brooklyn moll heading out for a night in Manhattan. She doesn't look like a packaged pop starlet here. Nor does she look like the tragic musical heroines she will be compared to: she's not Edith Piaf or Judy Garland, not Billie Holiday or Janis Joplin, even if she already shares with the latter a proclivity for Jack Daniel's and general laddishness. With no ethnic stereotyping intended, Moriarty's Amy looks – in the words of her former Island MD Nick Gatfield – like "a classic North London Jewish girl". There's a touch of Alma Cogan, a hint of Helen Shapiro, a little Laura Nyro, even a bit of Bette Midler. But classic North London Jewish girls don't generally end up sucking on crack pipes. Jews aren't supposed to booze, but Winehouse did from the earliest teen age imaginable.

Why *was* she so "fucked up in the head"? And if she hadn't become so (in)famous so rapidly, might she be alive today? There are so many pointless questions to ask about Winehouse's short life and times. It doesn't seem to matter how many brilliant musicians die young: the lessons are almost never learned by the subsequent generations of fame-seekers. Perhaps they *can't* be. Another fine irony of her story is that the very man to whom she owed her musical tastes – would she have been a singer at all without her dad's (very Jewish) love of Tony Bennett and co.? – was also the dad who went missing for much of her childhood before re-emerging to enable and facilitate the worst of her addictions. Just as anyone with a jot of genuine self-worth would have seen through the talentless charmer that was Blake Fielder-Civil, so any daughter with a sure sense of herself would have seen Mitchell Winehouse for the boor and opportunist he was: a mix of pub crooner and ex-footballer in a *shvitz* at Porchester Baths. 'Stronger Than Me', the emasculating song Amy wrote about her first serious boyfriend, should have been directed instead at the parents who gave their girl almost no useful boundaries – and looked the other way when it became clear she was bulimic.

The difficulty is that, without damage, we seem to get little authentic art. The pain, ache and shame we hear in 'You Know I'm No Good', 'Back To Black', 'Wake Up Alone' and 'Love Is A Losing Game' are what we demand of our suffering stars, as if we're being made privy to their most intimate confessions. Though Winehouse often cited Carole King and James Taylor as influences – favourites of her mum Janis (yes, Janis) – to my knowledge she never in any interview mentioned Joni Mitchell. Yet *Back To Black* is as much of a confessional masterpiece as Joni's sacred *Blue*. For Joni's *"acid, booze and ass/needles, guns and grass"* ('Blue'), read "[he] *sniffed me out like Tanqueray"* ('You Know I'm No Good'), *"nowadays you don't mean dick to me"* ('Me And Mr. Jones') and *"his face in my dreams, seizing my guts/he floods me with dread"* ('Wake Up Alone').

WINEHOUSE ONCE described her teenage self as "the rebel Jew". In a cultural sense – almost a *London* sense, one might say – she made herself over as non-white, as the "White Negro" beloved of Jewish writers like Mailer and Ginsberg. Whether it derived from Sarah Vaughan or from Toots & the

Maytals, her musical sensibility was almost entirely Black. Unlike most white singers who attempt to pass as Black, she embodied two things we associate with the greatest Black musicians: freedom and danger. Her "danger" extended to dissing not only her pop rivals – with a special disdain reserved for poor bland Dido – but people who actively worked on her behalf at Island and were doing their best to advance her career. (Not forgetting her Island labelmate Bono. "Shut up!" she burst out drunkenly at the BRITS show as U2's frontman held forth; "I don't give a fuck!")

While there was something refreshing about an artist who simply didn't give a damn – who didn't (appear to) care about tact – you had to wonder about Winehouse's anti-careerist "authenticity". Was it really necessary to be so cruel about manifestly lesser talents to prove how real she was? And after all, what *was* this "realness" of which we in the media spoke so confidently? Was it the same thing fellow self-harmer Richey Edwards meant when he bloodily carved "4 Real" into his forearm? Was it, in fact, just another mask designed to obscure the truth of the pain Winehouse carried and acted out through addiction – not only to chemicals (legal or otherwise) but to bingeing and purging, to tattoos and hair extensions? "The more insecure I feel," she once revealingly admitted, "the bigger [my] hair has to be."

"Do you want us to just sit here while you drink yourself to death?" comedian Simon Amstell asked of Winehouse on an infamous episode of pop-quiz TV show *Never Mind The Buzzcocks*. Much has been said of the hazardous rock'n'roll age that is 27 years; most of it's been discounted by hard data that proves pop stars are no more likely to do die at that than at any other age. Yet I'm not sure there *isn't* something significant in the fact that Joplin, Morrison, Hendrix and Cobain – like Winehouse – died at that midway point between 25 and 30. At 27, you can't pass any longer as a kidult, yet you know your twenties are drawing to a close, and that 30 will mark a major symbolic change in your status, potency and desirability. Adult responsibility looms heavily, and all the drugs in the world won't change that. "Life teaches you how to live it," Tony Bennett told Winehouse during her last recording session, "if you can live long enough." It was an exquisitely Zen-like formulation from a kind and decent man who'd have made a decent father-figure if Winehouse had only been listening – and hadn't spent her twenties to that point trying to rewrite the abandonment of her adolescence by idealising bad boys like Fielder-Civil. "I'll take the wrong man as naturally as I sing," she'd sung on *Frank*'s 'What Is It About Men?' As it was, she left the field clear for the significantly less damaged Adele – an obvious heir and disciple – to claim her neo-soul crown.

For all the grotesqueries on display in Kapadia's *Amy*, perhaps the most revealingly pitiful moments in the film were saved for the bitter end, when Winehouse was supposedly recuperating – though actually just drinking – on St Lucia. To see a young woman so deficient in self-worth that she'd allowed her father to bring a film crew to the Caribbean to film a documentary about their relationship was almost more painful than the paparazzi horror-show of her and Fielder-Civil's blood-bath binge at London's Sanderson Hotel in the summer of 2007. It spoke volumes about the self-loathing and confusion at the close of Amy's life. With an enabling and exploiting father like Mitch, who needed predatory crack dealers? Let me repeat an earlier question: if she hadn't been so (in)famous, might she still be alive? Could she have come to her senses and found the courage to attempt sobriety, to live her life without instant chemical fixes? The terrible and unavoidable truth is that great talent enables you to get away with murder – or, at least, with your agonisingly slow suicide.

The music remains: a small body of work that nonetheless contains several of pop's most majestic peaks. As Nick Coleman wrote of 'Love Is A Losing Game' in *Voices* – his study of "How A Great Singer Can Change Your Life" – "her impulse control may have been lousy, but her ability to represent its emotional consequences was peerlessly subtle and dignified." In the end, love *was* a losing game for her – but only because she had no real love for herself. By turning herself into a born-to-lose Brill Building version of Johnny Thunders, she gave us the most authentic reports of emotional torture – of frantic need and darkest despair – but abandoned the Amy who needed to heal and face herself. *"I should just be my own best friend,"* she'd sung on 'Tears Dry On Their Own'. *"And not fuck myself in the head with stupid men."* The real overdose was on attention: she was an attention-seeker destroyed by more attention than any sane person could possibly have borne. It was her misfortune, too, to rise in the era when Stardom had mutated into Celebrity, the enemy of authentic identity. And yet had she not been such a reckless addict – if she'd turned out to be, indeed, a "classic North London Jewish girl" – would she have stood out like the startling sore thumb she was?

We're all complicit in the vicarious fixation with what Winehouse herself called "walking car crashes". Damaged stars enact the excess and abandon most of us can't risk in our lives. They are the ones who go too far, fighting some unholy internal war so that we don't have to.

From Charles Moriarty's Back To Amy, 2018